Charles Edward Lewis

Reveries of an old Smoker

Interspersed with Reminiscences of Travel and Adventure

Charles Edward Lewis

Reveries of an old Smoker

Interspersed with Reminiscences of Travel and Adventure

ISBN/EAN: 9783337177225

Printed in Europe, USA, Canada, Australia, Japan

Cover: Foto ©ninafisch / pixelio.de

More available books at **www.hansebooks.com**

REVERIES

OF

AN OLD SMOKER,

INTERSPERSED WITH

REMINISCENCES OF TRAVEL AND ADVENTURE.

BY

CHARLES EDWARD LEWIS.

Toronto:
HUNTER, ROSE & COMPANY.
1881.

Dedication

ALL that is most kindly and pleasing in the following pages, I proffer most heartily to my friends; and those portions which may not be acceptable to them, I bequeath most cheerfully to my critics. I trust both parts may be received—the former, as an earnest tribute of reciprocal affection; the latter, as an inoffensive and easy exercise whose manifest errors may offer them the congenial task of correcting.

The volume as a whole, irrespective of its merits or demerits, but simply as a memoir of odd hours of thoughtful reverie, is dedicated to one who, regardless of its literary value, will prize it as the fragment of a life's history in which she has always evinced a loving interest; and if, on its perusal, she, too, would condemn much that may not meet her approval, then will she grant me her indulgence, as of yore, on being reminded that *she is the mother of*

THE AUTHOR.

MONTREAL, CANADA,
    May, 1880.

CONTENTS.

	PAGE
DEDICATION	v
BYGONES OF HISTORY—Introductory	3
A SEE-SAW AT SEA—Concerning the Pains and Penalties of Ocean Travel	31
THE SHADOW OF THE END	51
NORWOOD TO BRECKENHAM—A Pensketch of English Landscape	69
OUR CHARITIES—AND CHARITY MONUMENTS	83
FIRST EXPERIENCE UNDER FIRE—A Reminiscence of the American Civil War	113
GRANITE AND ASHES—Or Gleanings from the Sepulchres of Great English Story-Tellers	135
IMAGINATION; OR, IDEAL vs. REAL	171
CHISELHURST	249
AMNESTY	277

Bygones of History.

REVERIES
OF
AN OLD SMOKER.

BYGONES OF HISTORY.

I.

IN voluntarily assuming the somewhat onerous task which the consideration and writing of these reveries present, not the least of the many difficulties involved is, that I seem to set myself up, not only to supplant the brilliant efforts of many of the world's great advisers, but to impugn the integrity of their motives—to assail the sacred origin and utility of their doctrines, and worst of all to deny the hallowed exclusiveness of their right to preach. Here let me add (and it will be rather in exaggeration than extenuation) that notwithstanding all the orthodox odium attaching to the term, I must avow myself a "free-thinker" on all subjects pertaining to common sense. This, of itself, were provocation enough to send any man "to Coventry," but seemingly not satisfied with such an obnoxious and heretical attitude, I must needs go farther and show, if not maliciously, at least intentionally, something less than the minimum amount of reverence for our splendid heritage of Evangelical learning—not excepting even those theological puzzles presumed to underlie salvation, and the making out of which, unlike the pest of an unprogressive Tantalus, is regarded not as a penance but rather as a lucrative and highly popular profession, wherein each of the infinite variety of opposite conclusions are regarded as such an exclusive triumph of ecclesiastical erudition and scholarly ability, as raises the precocious adept out of the groping darkness of mean apprenticeship, out of the apathetic mysticism of mere professorship to that higher earthly Elysium of prodigious talent set up in opposition to the Limbo of idiots. There, although only dead to his novitiate, he undergoes amongst the initiated a kind of apotheosis, and becomes thenceforward, in the estimation of a substrata of comparative stupidity, that human prodigy of the class dubbed "Doctors of Divinity."

In raising my weak voice, and breaking the spell of hush and awe, that characterize the unthinking credulity of other men, it is not that I need to be admonished of the acquiescence becoming one of my humble attainments; on the contrary, my motive in thus relieving my mind gets both its impulse and inspiration in the mournful consciousness that to justify even the pretence of understanding, it is necessary to have mastered the preliminary and occult science of Schismatics; and, when we consider the chaos of perplexity in which our learned professors have involved, not simply the arts of peace, but the conditions of eternal bliss, it must be admitted for anyone, in the exercise of ordinary time and intelligence, to attempt to comprehend all the subtleties and sophisms pertaining thereto, were about as hopeless and fruitless a task as for a novice, like me, to attempt to demonstrate the fallacy of, or to budge in the slightest degree, those mammoth tomes and cumbrous systems which a learned dictatorial orthodoxy has grafted on the race ; and which, while they stand as firm, are also as opaque as the granite hills of New England.

Although without the excuse for my seeming presumption which comes of being, as all at least assume to be, "unbiassed," nevertheless, I may claim, instead, that my opinions are ventured in the outgush of natural impulse —that my ideas, however faulty and crude, present the virtue at least of "raw material," and have not been made up and warped and perverted by scholastic nursing or other sectarian training—that however strongly I may incline to certain views, my mind is neither pledged nor subsidized—and whatever my prejudices, I have no professional nor party interest in catering, with a view to profit or aggrandizement, to the claims of rival clique or clan or cause. This last consideration is my greatest encouragement—my best apology for intruding my sentiments in the frowning, cynical face of such an imposing array of "cultured" talent as we find enjoying in official capacity both a sacred and profane monopoly of all situations of vantage and emolument—not in the exercise of a calling simply, but employed in the routine business of inculcating ideas rather more ancient than modern, and in the cabalistic interpretation and promulgation of the laws of God and man. I may say that while I would confine myself as closely as possible to my own thoughts and language, I make no claim to originality; at least, none save that which bears in mind that all are original just in proportion as all are ignorant, and that for me or anyone else to expect to think exclusively of things that have escaped the observation of the watchful hosts who are moving by or that have gone past, would be as palpably unjust to them, and, indeed, as erroneous and absurd an assumption of pristine right as for a lost tribe of interior Africa to send a deputation thence across the boundaries into civilization, and following the example of more enlightened nations, lay claim to desirable localities by right of discovery. Ah, we don't know that they may not in course of time, when all we have thought and done shall have degenerated into apathy and forgetfulness, and need brushing up and renovating by some ingenious people at present fasting in ignorance and barbaric seclusion. Even now, it must be admitted, in the jungle of mental darkness which they inhabit, these latter would be discoverers, and in the open-mouthed, stupid amazement of their dusky brethren and of their "Ferdinand and Isabella," enjoy, as explorers, the same enviable distinction as do our own immortal Columbus and Jacques Cartier. But the reason is they live in intellectual as well as physical nakedness, and know no more about the world beyond their horizon than is evolved in the native progress of eating, drinking and sleeping as observed in their peculiar manner of living—only paying that attention to what is transpiring abroad, as is suggested by their own eccentric style of hospitality, made popular and interesting in the excitement occasioned by the reception and entertainment of a stray professor or a migratory missionary, whom we cannot deny they welcome, about Christmas time, with the same hearty relish we would a well-stuffed goose or an appetizing gobbler—and with an impulse and propensity very like our own, "kill 'em and eat 'em!"

Apropos of those systems to which I have referred, they may be excellent in their way, and actually represent the well-meaning fruits of centuries of pious scheming and scholarly toil to inaugurate a general social and ecclesiastical polity; thus viewed, they may stand out before the world splendid achievements in the line of intellectual and evangelical progress, and at the same time involve so much erudition and critical analysis in their application as to present, of themselves, more difficulties than the obstacles they are intended to overcome, and necessitate in their operation an ability even greater than that by which they were conceived. Jomini divined the Art of War in its highest excellence; but his rules, although surprisingly clever, required in their application what he lacked, viz., Genius; and in applying them personally he was worse than a novice, he was a failure. So, wanting that indispensable prerequisite, his systems were a clog and a hindrance, and instead of being the medium of his exaltation and triumph were the chief cause of his degradation and ruin. Great minds, however, do not require systems, and they originate those masterly plans which win fame, as the emergency calls for them, paying only sufficient attention to the study of general rules as to enable them to anticipate the tactics of adversaries who, while they may be men of ability, their tuition has made them martinets, and their devotion to the formalities of their profession lays them open to the designs of artifice; so as, in the case of knowing huntsmen who calculate to a dead certainty the invariable habits of the craftiest animals, while the former usually triumph in the breach, the latter fall miserable victims to the observance. This is as true of politics as of war, and applies wherever persuasion meets opposition or progress resistance. Indeed, a policy that would succeed in one case would, if observed to the letter in another, bring disaster; and an expedient that would suggest itself to a common sense mind, untrammelled with theories, would, by exemplarians, be tabooed as plausible but irregular.

II.

In the war of opinions, we find, all through history, the conflict of partisan zeal waging fiercely round certain standards, raised in the diverse views of men who, for some reason or other, have acquired a reputation for superior intelligence, and whose other virtues are presumed to be in the same laudable proportion. Many of these, with no more learning than is sufficient to propound perplexing problems, and no higher intellectual endowment than the mere "nack" of making a "noise in the world," come to be regarded as of prodigious importance and are severally assigned by the less intelligent masses the much coveted distinction of party or sectional leadership. These men, with a few honorable exceptions, represent the *tit-bits* Fate casts into the scale in order to adjust the equilibrium in social and political affairs, and at certain critical junctures, are thus enabled to count as the celebrated "straw" that breaks the camel's back, or as the fraction of a grain over that sunders the most ponderous cables of steel, and in a heroic worship that ignores minor and extraneous causes they get the exclusive credit for marvellous potency and even superhuman ability. Some of these have attained distinction, but failed as "Reformers," and it may not be altogether an absurd conceit to regard such as human prodigies who, coming into the world seemingly centuries before their allotted time, meander about the earth in intellectual abstraction and ideal isolation. They are remarkable cases of prolepsis and their principal difficulty seems to be to bridge over the, to them, unnatural space intervening between the time when they were and when they ought to have been born.

In the conflict of opinion to which reference has been made, it is observable that our highest authorities and most venerable counsellors exhibit the largest share of uncompromising hostility and unyielding intolerance. The struggle never ceases, although it is variable, and presents the more remarkable phases we term peace and war—nevertheless, the strife goes on, the only material change being in the weapons used—the "pike and broadsword" being, from time to time laid aside for the less deadly "tooth and nail." Thus, with the same bitterness of spirit, in either case, the conflict dwindles from the more chivalrous appeal to arms to the no less mischievous resource to abuse—in the first instance life is assailed, in the last character, and often those whom war does not give us the quasi right to kill in this world we avail ourselves of the blessings of peace to destroy in the next.

A goodly share of the bitterness and opposition that destroys the natural tranquillity of communities and peoples, and denominations and sects, comes down to us in the name and support of opinions and doctrines and schisms which were propagated centuries ago, and which, under a variety of forms and circumstances, have been debated and wrangled, and quibbled over ever since. In the chameleon-like category of *pros* and *cons* that have heaped alternate eulogy and obloquy on dicta coming down to us from extinct ages, and that have run the gantlet of so many hard knocks, and undergone so much mutilating, patching, and restoring, it is not surprising they should present themselves blackened, begrimed, distorted. If, then, we would try to think of them as they were in the fresh vitality of their living day, it is of the first importance to consider the characteristics of the times that gave rise to them; but in the effort to familiarize ourselves with the nature of exigencies in the past, that had so much to do with the moulding of thought, expression and expedient, we are met by an insuperable obstacle. I mean the difficulty of transposing our existence by those wretched routes and gilded vehicles through countless decades back into remote times, and trying to feel the influences that controlled, not only nations, but communities and sects, and individuals, whose language and sentiments it is absolutely necessary to understand, to correctly interpret the true meaning of their words and actions. This stupendous undertaking is universally shirked or adroitly smoothed over to suit the purposes of partisan writers and relic-mongers who go back and prepare the way for pleasure parties of marvel-loving excursionists—and these, we may add, not requiring to be transported bodily, are spirited about through the medium of a species of "half hour series" in which the hungry student, in the dreamy ecstasy of an appetizing imagination, is enabled to compass the events of centuries in a space the size of a refined sandwich and to swallow the tempting repast of an exhumed dynasty at a gulp. The literary gastronomers who dress and serve these bits of mummydom to suit the fastidious taste of modern epicures, are men who glory in the mission of reclaiming the hidden treasures of bygone days ; and this superhuman task, notwithstanding it is in direct violation of the laws of nature, they not only profess to have achieved, but with a generosity, sanctified by their own mental destitution, have bequeathed the invaluable store to posterity. So it is, like thieves in the night, we sneak in by stealth and gorging ourselves with all they can carry, strut abroad with the memory loaded down with obsolete wealth which only passes current till the more sceptical, whose want of credulity renders them unpopular, revenge themselves by exposing the fraud and proving it counterfeit. Of course, many who have a large amount of this sort of trash in stock are not especially anxious to have their authorities impeached, and tacitly consent to believe what it might be extremely embarrassing to discredit. Here we may note that the difficulty referred to, of feeling the live pulse of past events, is most frequently overcome by a convenient, and, in fact, necessary twist about. That is, by turning the back on an immense amount of fruitless research, we hit upon the easy expedient of inverting the order of time,—making the earlier action take its character from the subsequent impression, and dovetail with still later periods. Then, virtually, the stint of divining any sentiment or motive pertaining to the antique, resolves itself not into an ancient but a modern inquiry, and is no longer a matter of how *they* felt, but what *we* think. Contemporaries and eye-witnesses are repudiated as incompetent evidence, and to get a proper knowledge of what transpired in the times past we must read what is written in times present. The consequence of such a chronological atrocity is to make all generations and epochs assimilate and amenable to our own, and in this manner we virtually ignore the equitable principle that times as well as circumstances alter cases.

III.

I do not pick these flaws for the purpose of mere idle cavilling, but as suggestive of material discrepancies regarding many of those representations which our expounders hold up for our benefit and guidance concerning the teaching of opinions and events which, despite the alienations of time, are grubbed up, resuscitated, and rehabilitated, and set to modern use. Sickly deformities of truth some of them are too, with pedigrees sacredly remote, and many with physiognomies *à la Tousseau*, are only waxen images of atrocious notables, modelled in the bilious hallucination of art dreamers, and set up for adoration in a sanctuary of horrors. But, presuming, and that very rationally, that to divine the future we must know the past, we leave the musty record of the latter to be studied up by "book worms," who profess, after a short application to the subject, to give us a full explanation of all that has transpired. Aye, and some have even had the audacity to write over their puny memoranda, "History of the World!" History of the world! yes, History of the world. Far be it from my purpose to disparage their efforts, I need not; ignorance or policy may commend their egotism, but they are sufficiently reproved by the very knowledge of which they plume themselves,—the medium by which they seek to enlighten their age only going to show, simply, how little they know. Meanwhile these identical people themselves, who have enjoyed the rare privilege of glimpses over that boundless expanse of fallow mystery open to literary exploration, and those especially who have skimmed over and even so imperfectly surveyed the prodigious subject, ought, of all men, to feel the most humble and ignorant, and be admonished in their own estimation, how miserably inadequate, how mean their puny scrapings, and how infinite the great mass of forbidden knowledge beyond their reach! Again, were I disposed to disparage these so-called "learned men," from whom it is customary for great multitudes and unthinking masses to take their interpretations of law and gospel, it would be wholly unnecessary when it is considered how much more vigorously and effectively they disparage each other. It were a thankless task, indeed, to show that ever since the dawn of their enlightenment, the world has been plunged into even greater obscurity by the flood of their elucidation; but however this may be, there is one feature in their cultured physiognomy prolific in ugliness, which no amount of frescoing and patching, and *rouge-ing* will ever effectually screen—it is that most regrettable drawback that instead of harmonizing the elements of discord, they have continued sowing the seeds of that prolific growth—Dissension—the ploughing, and hoeing, and harrowing of which, under the direction of these "overseers," have cost mankind more sweat, and tears, and blood, than all the other "ills that flesh is heir to." Could we live in fraternal accord with the decisions of any one generation, we might be, all of us, unanimous and happy; but, as in the grab and greed of money-making, so in our instruction and enterprise generally, things are come to such a pass that one generation is thought a failure if it does not outstrip a preceding, and so all, or very much, that one proves the other attempts, and, not altogether unsuccessfully, to disprove. Taking History as an example, we may ask, how much are we indebted to our "scribes" for their evidence against their predecessors, and for their accumulation, or rather substitution, of authoritative record. Are we adjured not to read fiction? Where shall we find a more pretentious one than is comprised in the myriads of volumes of so-called historical fact showered down upon the poor, credulous, unsuspecting class who read and believe everything and anything that comes through certain scholastic channels, and purports to be a *bonâ fide* chronicle. Among other flaws in History, we may notice here, it records its "mountain" of prejudice with the same solemn, unimpeachable air that it ekes out its "molehill" of truth; and its only redeeming feature, if indeed we may call it such, is that later "historians," it may be with no higher object than to establish their own individuality, prove, or attempt to prove, it a lie; and thereupon set about clearing up reputations and events, that, according to them, have long been misunderstood, and either basked in the sunshine of unmerited esteem, or been draggled along under an ever increasing burden of undeserved obloquy. In the latter case they deserve our highest commendation, our heartiest support; we could even forgive them for exploding many pet theories, and for disqualifying many favorite authorities, but how can we suffer these ruthless spell-breakers to swoop down upon those beautiful creations of fancy whose reality and authenticity have always been zealously and religiously vouched for, and which believing them to be true has enhanced our interest and made our hearts throb with reverential awe and adoration. Some of these have been narratives of thrilling events, and anecdotes of great and good men set before us and impressed on our memories, as truthful examples and genuine specimens of actual life. With what a pang, then, of long dormant but not quite extinct boyish love and regret, do we surrender our faith in those delicious deceptions to dispel which, though they be all fancy, were a madness, perhaps, as unpardonable as that which shattered the famous Portland Vase. Aye, and why should not they be sacred too? Is it because the anniversary of their birth is not sufficiently mythical? None has the temerity to question or disturb the importance and gravity of those even more miraculous episodes in the lives of saints and other instructive items of hallowed origin submitted to modern credulity as a test of faith, then why question those precious examples of profane heroism that embellish the early record of our individual and national life? We leave David and his tiny "sling" alone, and Samson and his "jaw-bone," together with the "fox-tails and fire-brands." We do not interfere with the domestic accounts of Adam and Eve, nor contradict the wondrous narrative of the erratic tribe of Israel, then, why disturb the poems of Homer and Ossian, and Chatterton—why discredit the story of Crœsus, of Cincinnatus, of Regulus? Nay, I fain they had left us "Diogenes and his tub," "Arthur and his Round Table,"

"Tell and his apple," and last, but not least, "Washington and his little hatchet." In this connection too, we are reminded of a late publication by a distinguished writer and contemporary,* and again we see the hand of the exultant iconoclast raised, as thumbs once were in the Coliseum at Rome; now, it is not the miserable existence of some doughty gladiator that is in jeopardy, but the story of two precious lives in our nation's history—there is a flourish of that magic quill—a subterranean rumble is heard,—the foundations of our National archives tremble and quake—and, presto, that page whereon the posterity of Columbia were wont to portray the love and devotion and sacrifice of a heathen girl, yawns a blank, empty chasm; and the sublime tableau of Pocahontas, saving the life of Capt. John Smith, is no longer a matter of fact, but a thing of fancy.

We shall not stop here to estimate the delicious waste of tears that have been shed over what up to a recent period we never doubted were the "Last Words" of dying notables, recorded by men whose joyless mission it has been to haunt death-bed scenes; and, following the spirit of departing greatness into the vestibule of the other world, have listened, with their ear glued to the key-hole of eternity for the last intelligible utterances of expiring mortality.

Suffice it to say the examples above cited, and hosts of others belonging to the same category, are all that composed

---

* William Cullen Bryant, in his new History of the United States, produces evidence to disprove the story of Pocahontas.

B

the desert, the sparkling wines, the frosted confectionery, the floral exotics of that sweet, sumptuous historical banquet that regaled our hungry, credulous, boyish days; and yet, like all else we loved, they must needs be wiped out like fox and geese marks on a slate, and vanish away as have the pops and candied sweets of dear old Santa Claus. Nay, they do not perish for good, but will reappear in other forms of so-called truth to enchant and deceive and delight successive generations of juveniles, who will laugh and cry and applaud the marvellous *coup d'œil* as in pantomime, while the older ones, as they get sufficiently knowing to detect the pleasant deception are prevented from making a disturbance by being quietly removed from the audience. We talk of History, forsooth—it is not History at all in the sense we take it as being all unbiassed and reliable, but rather romance written by men who plume themselves on being something more genuine than novelists, and claim as an excuse for being prosy, that they are truthful. Here, too, we may observe how wonderful it is the little some of these are enabled to build upon, that is, I mean when they have cleared away all the rubbish accumulated by rival authors. Here and there a dead leaf, a dried twig, an irrefragable knot, and on these they base their interesting modern styled fabric, and grow those gorgeous avenues of arboreal magnificence that do not only represent the lordly manor of biographical story, and the stately boulevard of matter of fact events, but open up an ever green and blooming arch leading from the present back through the rut and slough of exhumed generations to the Renaissance. So it is from the tiny attic of this or that favorite author, we are enabled to look out, and at a glance behold the wondrous fascination of the past down through an illuminated vista wherein plays that mystic fount of literary lore, whose pyrotechnic splendors, dwindling away into the remoter gloaming, are confounded in the grotesque shadows of the antique, or eclipsed in the more refulgent lunacy of a traditional age. Notwithstanding, however, the little value we may be disposed to set on History as Fact, *taken as the commonly accepted standard of truth*, it is unimpeachable, and hence the libraries of the world always have been, and always will be, esteemed an invaluable acquisition to the intellectual wealth of mankind. But while, as we have intimated, it is impossible for a reflective mind not to feel a certain contempt for even such prodigious granaries of knowledge as these, nevertheless, in the popular disposition to believe and not to think, we find the ungracious task of arraigning history opposed by such potent, not to say, salutary influences as are dictated by public policy and social conservatism. So it is, that nursed and cradled on the bosom of a slumbrous faith, we glide tranquilly along, lulled, rather than disturbed, by the rippling wavelets; and hence the fretful sceptic, who obtrudes his unwelcome visage in opposition to the general current, is looked upon by sects and institutions somewhat as the festive occupants of a Mississippi steamer regard the protruding muzzle of some ugly " snag."

IV.

It is so much more congenial to favor than condemn, and feeling that the treasure of the dead is the birthright of the living, we would not see it ruthlessly plundered, or even belittled—indeed, it is the reading and transposing of the sayings and doings of the defunct world, and reani mating and blending them in our every day life and intercourse, that seems to lengthen our existence; and it is natural enough to suppose that, while such exercise enlarges our comprehension of the future, it makes the record of the past the fruitful study of the present. Leaving out, then, the question of the truth or falsity of that record, and regarded simply as a heritage of useful precept, it is a blessing; but as the medium for perpetuating old time spite and grudge and feud, it, and all pertaining to it, is a curse as much worse than hereditary disease, that whereas the one only stints and afflicts an individual or family, the other impoverishes and distresses not simply a nation, but a whole race of people, and viewed in many ways, the ill seems almost to overbalance the good. Societies, systems, customs, come down to us festering and putrid with the damning sores of an incurable scurvy, the offspring of a debauchery that would make oblivion charity, and in their most virtuous aspect scarred all over with the atrocities of earlier generations. These, of themselves, are wholesome warnings to stay away, and sermons of surpassing eloquence in favor of repudiation, but, unluckily, with many of these are transmitted the germs of renewed devotion, and the instruments of still further mutilation and with all their "culture," a means of torture still more highly refined. Strange as it may seem, too, these are revealed in the very resources by which we seek immunity, or at least a cure. In other words, we appeal to our Doctors of Divinity, and find them not healing wounds, but irritating passions, and if not propagating strife, at least nursing its offspring. So it is that, in this dilemma, we feel constrained to ask ourselves if we had no "theology;" if we had no "Doctors of Divinity," if we had no records of the past, how should we be affected? Well, we would, in the nature of things, have a religion, but no Creed and then "sin," so far as we were concerned, would be in its infancy; and, without the professor to teach us its pedigree, it would lose one of its most popular claims to aristocratic distinction, and we should feel in a measure restored to the new-born democracy of primitive virtue.

V.

No man can feel a profounder interest in the relics of olden times than I, and yet the feeling with which I regard many of them is, that their antiquity is their exclusive virtue, and so far as the practical utility of the things themselves are concerned, we may venture to affirm they had been better not to have been so old. Amongst these shreds of mummydom we glory, in here a tuft of real hair—there a genuine molar—again a veritable toe-nail—they constitute the only authentic points about history that give a tangibility to the past, and may be regarded as the black dots that punctuate our modern chronicle of by-gone peoples and events—the blank spaces between being filled up, as before noticed, to suit the taste and prejudices of any subsequent age or sect. Curious as are many of these relics in substance, so would be and are some of the more conservative rules of living—customs, dogmas, creeds pertaining to them; but while I yield involuntary homage to the venerable aspect of any one of these, I cannot withhold that sympathy inspired by its infirmities. Chronologically, dead, as it is, I find it impossible to take its stiff, pulseless hand, clammy with the damp of mouldering centuries, and feel in it any of the animating spirit of persuasion and none of the magic inspiration that cheers with " hope of new life." I am convinced there is greater weight, and that we may place far more reliance on experience and opinions, if not contemporary with, at least, approximating, our own special time and condition. It may not be eloquent, it may not be learned, it may not be refined, and yet in the weakest voice that lives there is a power akin to the Mighty—the word then, instead of percolating through the musty catacombs of obsolete scholardom, or through the more modern, but no less irresponsible dust of mouldering experts, comes direct from the living fountain of that human heart which throbs in fraternal unison and sympathy with our own, and which feeds and reanimates an intellect vitalized by that ever-rejuvenating Power, whose finger is upon our pulse, and who sees and provides for the wants of each new second of our life. Hence it seems to me, to engraft upon our feeble and easily bewildered faculties the pestiferous perplexity and ever accumulating burden of abstruse antiquated theory is to oppose instead of facilitating the purpose of its design, besides conflicting with that wise and grateful indulgence which, granting us immunity from the past, also gives to each generation the instinctive attributes incident and necessary to its preservation and well-being both in this and the next world. Nay, it is not on the battered tablets of Time; not amongst the uncertain hieroglyphics of an obsolete age we may seek and find the solution of the exalted mystery of Life and Destiny; but rather in that revelation unfolded to the simplest understanding, in the inexhaustible variety of our beautiful, fructifying World, and we divine and greet the gladsome presages of Fate, not in the extinction but in the eternal reproduction of all things visible! There is nothing either in language or in script adequate in expression to the ways of the All-wise, and we behold the image of the Master only in the impress of his Works. It was through this medium He revealed Himself to the race at a period as far back as the invention of seeing and hearing; and the impression which our doctrinal tutors seek to convey, that the Author of Creation should only have been known and adored since the dawn of our very modern Christianity is a libel as false as the egotism that records it is preposterous.

VI.

History, catering to popular prejudice, erroneously endeavors to make the worship of the Supreme Being not only in primitive times, but in certain alien localities since then, as grotesque as possible; indeed, those dusky days without our sun are made to constitute the darker obscurity which heightens the contrast that glorifies our modern enlightenment. It is only patent, perhaps, to those who take the pains to think, how severe this must be on those who have been so unfortunate as to precede us; and, notwithstanding the immense leverage of public opinion to the contrary, I venture on the assumption that even the earlier inhabitants of our globe, not to mention those like them contemporary with ourselves, were as sincere in their homage to our common Creator, and that they commended themselves to Divine approbation quite as acceptably and as effectually as do we in the present day. It is true their manners, like many other worthy old fashions, may seem to us ludicrous in the extreme, and their forms of worship may have partaken largely of this apparent discrepancy, but I believe it was the fault of appearances only—that their ceremonies, while being simple were heart-felt, and although symbolical were all the more efficiently adapted to the uncouth habits of a people who, with all the damnable characteristics attributed to them, never wanted in true devotion to, nor lacked that guileless confidence in, the scriptless muniments of their faith. We need not, I feel assured, in the superabundance of our pious egotism, carry either our sympathy or our condemnation, or our contempt, back so far, and while pitying and praying, scoff and jeer at those " poor lost heathens" who, we say, knew naught of our God, and perished without our Saviour. In this connection, we may venture, still further in the dangerous role of speculator, and to any one of the countless millions who would conscientiously know what good influence, if any, might have saved these " poor creatures," aye and still succors those like them, and to all those who wonder what sort of a Deity they could have had, and may still have, I would say:—Throw down the stinted volumes that asperse but do not explain the story of their darkened lives—crawl out of the gutters and sluice-ways that feed without cleansing the fetid sewers of your gluttonous " culture;" mount up into the higher regions of sun-light and pure air—up, like Moses did, to the highest pinnacle of some lofty eminence—and instead of shutting your eyes in saintly communion, open them wide and feast your vision on all you see! Then if you forget all about self in the multifarious charms of the varied landscape; if for a time your puny catechism, your stingy creed, your cramped little church, and all the peevish wrigglers that figure there, dwindle away to nothingness, and are lost to thought—if in the rapture of exstacy and awe you exclaim, how grand, how beautiful, how sublime! you shall, in the echo of your own impulsive praise, receive not only the answer as to who was and is the God of the heathen, but also imbibe a truer and better conception of the all prevailing infinitude of that religion which appeals alike to the pagan, the savage, the infidel, and to none more powerfully than to the unlettered, the despised, the abandoned.

VII.

There is a Form, whose outline is the perfect symmetry of the universe, and the harmony of whose parts is the faultless blending of creation. Its spirituality is heaven itself; its substance, the earth. We look up at the sky and see the benign attributes of its beaming Countenance, and in the general aspect of this incomparable Being we behold, in rapture, all the superb phenomena of Nature! This is the God of the heathen, the Creed of the creedless, and they need none of the auxiliaries of classic lore to teach them, It is genuine, It is beautiful, It is Divine! It speaks to them in the thunder of the tempest, It whispers in the sighing of the wind; It prattles in the brooklet, It murmurs in the sea; It warbles in the sunshine, It rumbles in the cloud; It is wafted over sea and land, —up the steep incline of mountain, down into the deepest declivity of valley; It echoes amongst the dwelling-places of the outcast, It searches out the most sequestered haunts of man, and the humblest and meanest require none of the splendid revelations of a learned creed to tell them whose voice it is, and the heathen of ever so long ago (not even excepting those of to-day), could they have listened and felt there was no law, no government, no restraint? No! to the most primitive and unenlightened of our race these echoes were, and are, the mandates of an indisputable authority, and they complied, and still comply, with a guileless simplicity, whose unlettered creed records no high-toned precedent for disobedience.

Finally, let us ask how does our subsidized theology compare with their unsophisticated faith. The geologist amongst the rocks crumbles a bit of earth in the hollow of his hand, and is lost in the perplexity of abstruse analysis—his standard is gold, his dream profit. The "child of the forest," near him, folding his arms in contempt of the grovelling radical, divines a sublimer feature in the grand tableau outspread before him, and raising his glistening eyes in the proud consciousness of a still nobler perception, sees in the majestic profile of the mountainside the contour of the Supreme, and in the uplifted arm of some lofty overreaching crag a gesture of the OMNIPOTENT.

A See-Saw at Sea.

A SEE-SAW AT SEA.

(AN ITEM FROM THE DIARY OF A GREEN-HORN.)

I.

IT was a revelation in destiny too pregnant with fate to call it mere news—those few lines, I mean, disentangled from the inexplicable confusion of the puzzling future, and laid before me in a neat, legible hand-writing, conveying the unexpected, but no less welcome, intelligence, that I was to take up my residence for an indefinite period in London, England, the matter having been all settled that I was to leave at once by the good ship *Sarmatian*, of the Allan line, advertised to sail from Portland, the 12th April.

Some time has elapsed since then; but it seems only yesterday I gathered my traps together preliminary to the journey in question, and having bade adieu to many kind friends, and taken a tender leave of home, boarded the train at Buffalo, with a through ticket in my pocket for the sea-board, *via* Syracuse and Boston. A pleasant and instructive route that way, it is too, as I can vouch, there being an excellent service of trains and a great deal of enjoyable scenery; indeed, whatever one's prejudices may be, he can't well help admiring New England, with the reminder it so charmingly presents of Old England, and though it may not culminate in a climax of such grandeur and importance as that which distinguishes the elder monarchical sire, nevertheless one must admit Boston is an honor and glory to the Fatherland, and although comparatively in its baby-hood, as it is common to consider all cities in the New World, it struck me, in the mere glance I obtained of it as being a remarkably fine youngster. With this preamble, I beg to avail myself of my notes taken at the time, to cull the following items from my diary as a Green-horn.

I was late in arriving at Portland, having stopped over at Yarmouth, but there lost no time in getting fixed up and putting on a disreputable old suit, which I had been given to understand was the correct thing to do preparatory to a sea voyage. Then I fussed about, and was impatient to get off as a champagne cork, and knowing the uncertainty to which all things are subject, the idea of being left behind set me in a perspiration; became nervous at the thought all the rest might have, and probably had, arrived on the scene, and were now discreet masters of the situation, whilst I had recklessly put off making my appearance till the last moment. I was struck in this dilemma with the idea of inquiring, just when the ship would sail; it was a happy thought, and I bounced out of my room in quest of the information. Alas, I could get no reliable intelligence—nobody, not even the clerk in the hotel, seemed to know anything about the matter whatever. I became surprised, impatient, vexed; it did not avail. I importuned and raved, " 'Twas all in vain." Here let me explain:—This narrative is only partially exaggerated. I was a novice. I had come from afar— from a country where the "Allan Line," its ships, and all about them were household talk, and the pride and boast of the people; but here, I bitterly reflected, in a great commercial city, and the port of embarcation, the sailing of the *Sarmatian*, of the Allan line, was, oh, horrors, entirely ignored, and all that I could find out from the different ones of whom I inquired, and I gave them all a chance to redeem their ignorance, and kindly offered them every opportunity to tell me all they knew—I repeat, all they could tell me was,—there was supposed to be an English line of steamers somewhere. This was my first set-back; it was a great blow to the pomp of my expedition, and my proud spirit chafed at the obscurity that seemed to shroud its great designs. In this show of ignorance and indifference on the part of my countrymen, and the land for which I had "fought and bled," there was, I felt, a sense of social oblivion that made me sad. I could have repined; in my sentimental imagination it struck me forcibly that when an ocean steamship was about to sail on a perilous voyage to another hemisphere, freighted with human souls, the occasion assumed an aspect at once solemn and imposing; they seemed like unto a company of voluntary exiles—representatives as it were, of new and wonderful America— called in the grand march of events by some laudable mission to sojourn, perchance, to lay down their lives amongst a strange people afar off in the remote historic east. Moreover there was something to inspire sympathy in a colder heart than mine in the thought that dearly loved "Columbia" recked naught of this departure, and that the handkerchiefs of our prospective band of patriotic spirits must needs, all unobserved, grow damp, not with colds nor moist noses but from the owners' warmth of feeling in the ordeal of parting from kindred land. These meditations occupied some time and were fostered rather than disturbed by my having taken a pretty strong pull at a mug of very mild ale, and thereupon I became a willing victim to the seductive wiles of a most tempting cheroot. These tranquillizing elements had the desired effect to soothe my excited feelings, and soon I settled down to the comfortable enjoyment of a serene spirit. The light blue fragrant smoke as it curled gently and prettily upward, and hovered around, seemed to form a hazy screen betwixt me and the unromantic, unpleasing realities of the world about, and shut in, as it were, apart from the annoyances and turmoil of things in general, there was something in the cosy atmosphere of the " weed," suggestive of cloud land, and straight-way imagination peopled the little sphere with the images of those loved and absent ones whose smiling faces and well remembered forms, blending in a cheery welcome, always lend a ruddy hue to one's thoughts, and while they bring to mind the reminiscences of happy times past never fail to re-inspire one with hopes of good times to come.

Waking with a sigh from these reveries, I turned reluctantly to the business in hand, called a "cab," hustled my traps in and set out for the wharf where it had been intimated the English steamer might be expected. Here too, I was again disappointed. Had been looking forward to seeing an immense crowd of people and passengers nearly, if not all arrived, and all the great preparations and ado attendant on our near departure. On the contrary, all was quiet; a few boxes and odds and ends were being stowed away, and a few listless individuals of the family of tag-rag looking on, evidently without legitimate object or interest, but there was nothing in the general aspect of things to lead one to suppose the ship was not going to remain there in perfect repose all summer. Well, I soon ascertained I had made a mistake in the date of sailing and that I would have to wait over till the next day, so leaving my trunk and other things in a conspicuous place on deck I went back up town to my hotel.

II.

In the evening I went to the theatre, where I heard there was to be a very entertaining performance. The play was "Black Crook," a sort of pantomime, which, in America as in England, means a bewildering exhibition of lower extremities, in which the principal parts are taken by legs; they don't say anything, but, notwithstanding they are mute, the effect makes silence more impressive than words. As regards the attire, I scorn to notice so small and useless an item—suffice it to say, the skirt, in this instance, stood out, and was about the same size and shape as a parasol—aside from this, a close fitting *web* of some gauzy illusion was the only bill of expense art could claim, or cold-hearted economy detect. There was, no doubt, a *spell* in that *web*—and notwithstanding it was of the most doubtful reality, we, all of us, gazed in rapture. It might have been spun in an exquisite caprice of *Venus* from peach blossoms, and was ethereal as the fragrance of roses while to the thoughtless eye of admiration it seemed no more than the lusty glow of health or the *blush* of maidenly embarrassment—aye, Nature might well sigh in envy of the fraud, and old Dame Prudence herself so far yielded to the fascination, that she forgot to frown, and, like in the luxury of some rare, delicious dream, nodded approval, as if, in this uncanny vision, she had seen only some bewitching phantom of beguiled innocence. My bachelor prejudices did not prevent my remaining till the end of the performance, after which I sallied forth into the dreary desolation of the night. Next morning I awoke with the "Lark," but did not begin to fly till about nine o'clock. Meanwhile, a tremendous storm of wind and snow and rain had set in, and struck dismay to the hearts of all who expected, in a few short hours, to have their first experience at sea. On the way down street to the wharf, I bethought me of the "Lemon Theory." With my bump of credulity well developed, even at that early day, I had yielded readily to the influence brought to bear—indeed, was betrayed and cruelly deceived by the unanimity that had prevailed among my nearest and dearest relatives and friends regarding the salutary effects of lemons eaten at sea. From a novice I easily became a convert, and finally got to believing with the rest, that lemons would make sea sickness pleasant. I espied a fresh importation of this agreeable antidote through a shop-window and paused. I seemed to hear the suasive voice of friends in reëchoed injunctions, to buy some, and hesitating only long enough to make a careful estimate of capacity and means, finally hit upon an average of twenty; the idea suggested itself also to add a few for home-sickness also, so I invested in a total of two dozen. Then I had a grand feast of oysters, of which I am especially fond, and managed, notwithstanding my rapidly accumulating responsibilities, to reach the ship in safety. I found about thirty passengers on board, and a great deal of bustle and confusion; my baggage had disappeared; they left me a diminutive hand-bag and hat-box, all the rest had vanished into that cavernous mystery called the "hold." The storm had increased in severity, and there was a strong likelihood of our having to remain in port till it abated. This was not very cheering, and my spirits had not risen with the appearance of the passengers, many of them a rough looking set, who, however, contrasted favorably with a couple of smartly dressed, ostentatious owners of diamond bosoms, who seemed to be local residents of the thriving "emporium" of Portland.

The few ladies I saw, had no redeeming features worthy of note; to say they could have been "adorned," would probably be misconstrued into an unkind insinuation, and might appear envious; suffice it then if I waive all considerations but those most in accord with the promptings of a generous nature, and simply say, theirs was not the vulgar style of beauty one is apt to see cherished outside the home circle. The discrepancy in apparel was attributable no doubt to the economical custom of people going on a voyage to put on those garments which, in a fit of chronic abstraction, they have worn beyond the period which had made them acceptable to decent "charities" or fit offerings, in these days of sensitive vagrancy, even to the most needy. I was in a decidedly gloomy frame of mind when I went below and sought the seclusion of my state-room, but as I entered, my eye immediately lighted on a little package of letters which had been placed there by some good angel. These most kindly and welcome messages of love and affection, had the effect to restore the tottering equilibrium of failing good nature and almost brought tears of grateful acknowledgment to my eyes; indeed, I felt tolerably happy for the rest of the evening. About ten o'clock I crawled into an odd little crevice, nautically called a "bunk," and for the first time in my life tried to feel at home, and sleep aboard ship. I did not sleep—I only dreamt; it was a pleasant night-mare, however, to what might have been expected, and, though I afterwards found the bed and blanket into which I had insinuated myself, a very comfortable sort of contrivance, to get to liking it is no doubt an "acquired taste." In the morning, we found the storm, which had raged fiercely all night, had in a measure spent its fury, and, though it had not cleared off, preparations were being made to get under way. In the meantime the certainty of having to encounter a very rough sea, and many of us for the first time, made matters, in this respect, appear ominous; and we all looked that morning several shades bluer than our average complexion.

III.

We breakfasted in dock, and about eleven o'clock, the tide having served, the order was given to "Cast off." There was a general rush for the deck, I being foremost in the eager throng. Had donned my sea toggery, of course, and now hastening to get outside, where it was snowy, slippery and foolish to be, took up a position and struck an attitude where I was in the way and most liable to be knocked over, and tried to feel I was in for an enjoyable holiday.

The first sensations of "setting sail" were soon over, and I began to lose all thought of self in the interest excited by the lazy majestic motions of the noble ship as she began sleepily to respond to the action of her mammoth engines. We were very soon out of harbor, and had only time to take a good look around before we found ourselves out on the broad ocean. For some time I watched the movements of the sailors and the ship, and glanced again and again at the fast receding land, and thought, not without a pang, that America and "fatherland" would soon vanish from sight.

Although the novelty of my position kept my thoughts busy and my attention occupied for some time, this interesting reverie was, ere long, interrupted by the bell ringing for luncheon. That hospitable call, in this instance, as on former occasions, failed not to rouse my dormant energies, and I prepared to go below. I will explain, that while taking my observations in the manner described, I had found it necessary to have a double grip on the rail, and if I had had claws on my heels I should not have been too proud or indifferent to have made use of them also. We were now right in the midst of a rough, cross sea, which had risen all the higher as the wind went down. The ship, too, which had been so lazy and sluggish in harbor, seemed to have shaken off its lassitude and got, all at once, frisky as a dolphin and light as a paper kite. I thought I was well up in the theory of riding a refractory donkey, but the motion against which I now had to contend baffled all the principles, rules, by-laws and exceptions that might have been, or could possibly be written on the subject of a graceful acquiring of one's "sea legs;" hence I lost no time in snatching at the rudiments of this much neglected science, and in holding fast by main and tail. When I let go, as I did, to make for the saloon, the vessel gave an awful lurch—I made a grab for something I didn't get a hold of, it had vanished suddenly, and I caught instead a handful of air; all at once saw the deck coming right up at my face; stared at it in blank, helpless amazement; then made a push at it with both hands; it sank by magic. Happened to look over my shoulder and saw my tormentor coming the opposite way and making directly for my right ear; instinctively telescoped right leg and paid out a yard or two of left; it wasn't a bad manœuvre at all for a beginner, that wasn't, if I do say so; theoretically it was without a blemish, but chronologically, it showed want of practice; it was a failure in point of time, that was all. I didn't reverse my engines soon enough and the next instant found myself reclining gently but firmly on my right side; there was a pause in the elements and I looked up in considerable embarrassment to see what might be the next item on the programme. My posture was that of the "dying gladiator"; enjoyed a moment's repose in that classic posture, and then scrambled up and resumed my interesting journey, at the same time making greedy efforts to pick up and handle over every thing I could lay my hands on by way of ballast and mainstay. Indeed, it was only by splicing odds and ends as well as I could, to the object in hand, I made out at last to reach the door leading into the saloon.

IV.

Not having secured my seat in time, the one assigned me was, of course, at the further end from where I was; this necessarily entailed quite a long promenade under more difficulties and exposed to more observation than a modest candidate cares to endure, even under circumstances the most favorable. I paused on the threshold to take a hasty survey and to think how nice it was and how very invigorating the sea air. Here again vanity rallied her vanquished eagles; and I determined to make a sensation and give an impromptu exhibition of steady marching. I might have succeeded but the ship behaved badly and made my standing apparatus "a delusion and a snare;" would plunge forward a little way in right direction, then chassé right and left, then bolt. If I noticed any one watching me I would subside immediately, sit down and try to look as if I had arrived at my destination—that I had no idea of going any further. Perhaps when that party looked back again, after a while, to the spot where his impertinent curiosity had left me serene, perhaps, I say, I wasn't there; may be I watched my opportunity when no body was on the lookout, to venture forward. May be this was the case; would not swear it was not. Supposing, however, I was not there, and also allowing that ingratitude, blasphemy and despair, fit qualities, prominently developed to invite interest and inquiry, I should have been found, without a doubt, not far off—I know I should, holding fast on some thing and contemplating in silent anguish the vicissitudes of further progress. Reaching my seat at last I dropped into it like an aerolite and endeavored to look calm, unruffled and at home. Have thought since, I overdid the matter of trying to seem at home, and probably assumed an aspect of more gravity than is altogether in keeping with the enjoyment of such a blessing. I thought, too, I detected an amused expression on the face of one of the stewards, and suspecting the reason, glowered back upon that particular waiter with a look of ill-concealed antagonism; was impressed

with a feeling that it was not an appropriate concern
for a display of levity; said nothing, however, directly;
am opposed to reproving servants at table, and I refrained
now, but in answer to his very respectful inquiry as to
my wants, I said, with considerable asperity, " Lobster!"
While this was being brought I took a glance around. Opposite was the Rev. Archdeacon McLean, of Manitoba, a
robust, happy father, in the midst of a numerous family.
On my left was a Major Pope, of Quebec, a thoroughbred
old war-horse, and to my right, the owner of the diamond
studs. The lobster, with an elaborate dressing and the
tempting side up, was now placed before me; and I forthwith began the manipulation of this my favorite salad.
Was in no hurry, in fact began to think I was not hungry
after all, and that it was rather spiritual diversion than
a carnal gorging I needed most. Indeed there was somewhere in the inscrutable regions of my sensitive organism,
a new-born hankering suggestive of some nameless relish, but in the venal grasp of mere fleshly appetite, the soul
could rise no higher in its conception than to imagine a
tonic in the air Ah, was it the stuffy, soupy atmosphere,
I wonder? I thought it was, there is such a dearth of ventilation in these places—suppressed a sigh, and glanced
wistfully at the sky-lights. Am not sure but that I
had been feeling, for some time, just a little unpleasantness; perhaps I had, but if so, ignored it as a cat
would a mouse. I tried to pass it off as constitutional,
I fought it down with conservative gallantry, and was
bound to " on with the dance." The ship at this period

began to kick her stern up mighty high, then down, down, as if she had no hind legs at all. I was sitting near the tail end, as I said before, and consequently, was in a position to take a deep, I may say, an agonizing interest in these peculiar antics. There is no doubt in my mind it was this diabolical motion that overcame—not my resolution but my powers of resistance. Things began to get confused and dark—there seemed about everything, that peculiar shadowy undulation so charmingly characteristic of marine life, with the additional variety of a rotary accompaniment. I was conscious there was the incipient stage of a revolution in my stomach, and also had a melancholy presentiment of a conspiracy and an uprising amongst the oysters I had taken into my confidence at Portland. It was beginning to affect me badly, and still I bore, not up, but down; even smiled at the Major's last joke, a sickly, ghastly smile, which, had it assumed the rank and volume of a laugh, would have been, sepulchrally speaking, a success—that smile, however, soon went away, it was not wanted by the only one to whom it could appeal for patronage. I had a confused idea that a good many people in the saloon were scampering away—that there was a commotion among the Archdeacon's family—the American was no longer visible, and the Major was silenced. From gazing vacantly about, I had settled upon a wild contemplation of the saloon-door, and the least possible distance between me and seclusion. The boat made another vault up into the Heavens, and collecting my disordered faculties for a mighty effort, I cast off from my seat and paddled for my state-room, regardless of everything save the consciousness that I was about passing through the fearful ordeal of misery at sea.

V.

I ought not to attempt to describe what followed—ought to leave it to be understood; besides, it involves the lemon sequel, and it would seem so much more becoming and generous in me to save those friends and relatives of mine the remorse of knowing what misery their lemon scheme entailed. Let it suffice then for me to say, which I do without malice or reproach, that when the crisis came I went straight for that lemon pile like a rat to its bane—laid hold of one, and with a preliminary, brief, as my wants were pressing, began sucking. I also gave one to a friend and fellow-sufferer—he was a young man, naturally delicate, and as I had done him this little turn purely out of kindness, was rewarded in observing he now regarded me somewhat in the light of a benefactor. I thought how glad the poor boy's mother would be. Soon our mouths were too full for utterance, but in the eye of each might have been seen to kindle vows of mutual admiration and good-fellowship; and on the countenance of the chief lemon propagator, especially, exultation and triumph basked in the full enjoyment of conscious victory. But, alas, that feeling did not endure. Oh joy, why art thou transient! We had sucked on together not to exceed one minute, the picture of infantile gratification, when I observed a great silent metamorphosis stealing over the countenance of the young man, and a whiteness like unto a fog settled down upon his naturally florid features, all of which betokened an unmistakable change in his barometer. I, too, began to feel a death-like sickness, and a nausea which no language can describe; it seemed to seize upon and monopolize, and pervert every natural function. We regarded one another in silent wonder and agony; and there was mute, horrible disgust in the young man's eye, as he fixed its dying gaze upon me, and pointed, with the air of a man conscious, alas, too late, at the lemon I had given him. He, no doubt, thought it was a contrived plan to take a "rise" out of him. I was innocent, of course, but felt, nevertheless, I had lost a friend and forfeited the good-will of a fellow-being. I have a very vague recollection of what transpired for some time after this; am quite positive, however, about two things: first, I was not seen skipping about the deck for many days; secondly, I disgorged all fanatical partisanship in the lemon theory. My poor mortality for six long days was in sore distress, but, thanks to the humanity of all on board, I was an object of profound commiseration. On all occasions during the time I have mentioned, there was an irrepressible upward tendency—an unpleasantness "I struggled to forget." It was not till we hove in sight of Old Ireland, and got a sniff of the fragrant odors of a land-breeze, fresh, sweet and balmy from the heather-clad hills of "Erin," that I began to take an interest in mundane affairs, and to cleave with renewed relish to "the world, the flesh and the devil." As we steamed up Lough Foyle at early sunrise of that fair spring morning, a marvellous recuperation in body and spirit, made life again seem dear. There was a gladness, too, in this first view of long-dreamed-of foreign soil, that conquered all antipathies, even those of illness, and as one poor convalescent looked with admiring gaze out upon the crumbling walls of "Green Castle," it was not simply as a curious pile of picturesque ruin it commended itself to his fancy; nor yet as a warning left there by Time to admonish the overweening strength of bumptious man; but rather the significant exponent of a still greater change, the harbinger of an infinitely more felicitous destiny, which, as a symbol, this is only an inkling, and for which in language, there is no phraseology, save, in like manner, to demolish as expressionless, all the worthless pile of kindless, meaningless, vocabulary, and compress all the pathos of our nature into that one best word, RESTORED.

The Shadow of the End.

D

THE SHADOW OF THE END.

I.

I TOOK up a newspaper the other day, and, glancing carelessly over its contents, was greatly shocked to see the account of the melancholy death of young R——. It seemed to me all the more appalling that it should have happened so near my home; so close, indeed, that the shot might have been heard in the drawing-room. A friend who was with me at the time, and whose attention I drew to the announcement, expressed his disgust at it altogether in terms of cutting reproof. Then he threw the paper down in high dudgeon, and I thought not without a look of contempt, as he regarded my grieved expression. After this, when alone, on different occasions, my thoughts would recur to the subject, and now and again I found myself rapt in a profound reverie, in which I was contrasting my own commiseration with his indifference, or rather, I should say, his condemnation, and trying to deduce therefrom what might be the relative bearing of public opinion in the premises. These reveries gave rise to thoughts, also, having a kindred leaning toward the others, and the following is a hasty and imperfect grouping of ideas following the train of reflection as above.

Although this subject presents some rather unpleasant features, it is not without a fellow interest to us all; not excepting those whose peace and comfort render the thought of it foreign to their speculation. As regards the nature of this young man's death, some people profess to be indignant in reading and hearing of such cases, that anyone can be so unreasonable, so rash, in short, so depraved; especially if there happen to be, as in this instance, a woman mixed up in the affair. They may be shocked in a comfortable sort of way, to be sure, but seem withal not a little pleased, as it brings into more enjoyable contrast their own good fortune. Nay, there is a tingling of self-gratulation at their special immunity, these bad cases, even, being regarded, in one sense, as a not unwelcome reminder of their own superior virtue and merit. People who feel this way, and they are many, no doubt are deserving and especially favored, and as such are to be envied and congratulated; they are, for the most part, married men and women who have slipped easily and comfortably into harness, and, in the quiet hum-drum of every day existence, are as ignorant as brutes, and quite as unconscious of a most formidable misery and danger menacing us all, and which, forsooth, they may have narrowly escaped themselves. Might we not imagine, a pair like these, if they interfered, or let the question trouble them at all, would be the most appropriate and natural champions of the "blessed state of holy matrimony." But here again is exhibited the most disagreeable perversity of human nature in general, and man and wife in particular. Comfortably cuddled up in their calm domestic havens, they have no sympathy, no pity, if they give a thought to those outside the bar, on the billow, in the fog, amidst the storm! Perhaps, I carry the simile too far, I will carry it still further: they will, and do, frequently, even change the lights that guided them to their own safe moorings, choke up the channel by which they entered themselves, and give those outside, who are trying to beat in against wind and tide, to understand they must come in some other way! The conditions, in the awful problem of *eligibility*, are all changed since their time, and parents say, " our children must not suffer what we have suffered;" forgetting it was the trudging together up the steep incline of their early, fresh conflict with the world, that they themselves enjoyed the most. Ah, what was their privation but the edge that fasting puts upon the appetite; aye, and while, in all the crusty biliousness of their later years, they have not found a "nabob sauce" to equal it, yet they say "our children must not suffer as we did." No! the boon that satisfies youth's great hungering rapacity will not suffice. " Live on love, indeed!" and the old set, with the sweeping egotism of overripe wisdom, bestir themselves, with broom in hand, and swooping down on a great wealth of youth's sweet, floral dream, brush the rose leaves from his path. The fact is, it is the scheming and advising and opposing that keep those out of the fold who would otherwise come in, in joyousness and safety; and this is not unfrequently followed by the most lamentable results, as in the case I have instanced. Wrecks at sea are of no account,—at least, we need not concern ourselves about them, they are providential—they are those along the shores that fringe our garden lawns, that are most deplorable, and for these we are all mutually and severally responsible.

II.

As things are, considering all the caprices and breakers and perils to which we are subject in the love period of our lives, it is much to be deprecated, no doubt, that the thousands and millions in the toils like poor R—— was, might not have restrained themselves in time, and been more careful how they indulged their mind to drift into such a miserable state. What a sad truism it is that "the course of true love never did run smooth." The only objection, however, to that saying is, it expresses the trouble altogether too mildly and apologetically; but then again, it is hard to tell young people all we fear, and lay before them all the miserable alternatives that, in our mature observation, commend themselves all unfavorably to our discretion. It is hard to point, with our shaking nerve and shrivelled hand, to the withered fields about and say, the same drought, the same blight, shall visit, except on the most trying conditions, your own sweet flowery land! The tenacity of love, and the hostility it so innocently and yet so aptly engenders, the "crosses" to which it is subject, and the unhappy results of which this subject is an example, all tend to make that "tender passion" the most dangerous element in our constitution; and in inverse ratio to all those sweet conceptions of which it is preeminently capable, it is susceptible to a misery equally exquisite. I pity the man or woman to whose lot falls the latter portion; and, although it is a fate which unfortunately comprises at least half the pain endured by the human race, it is universally ignored or sneered at and contemned, and seems to find no room in the category of ills that enlist people's sympathy. The reason for this stony-hearted indifference, generally, may be found in the relation of well-fed luxury to starving barefoots; take for example the great married world, with them the charm of love's anxious quest has, in possession, been dispelled and their rapture vanished into lethargy. Very many of these, feeling themselves to be in some degree victims of a species of connubial legerdemain, retaliate the delusion—of which they are conscious—back upon the unsophisticated, unsuspecting, legion of youth and credulity. Here, let me confess at once, that, with all due respect for the quality medicinally, I am not one of that numerous following who glory in and extol "experience;" in many cases it is only a pardonable sort of intolerable egotism, with a goodly admixture of prejudice gloomily tinged with superstition, and, so constituted, is indulged and reverenced chiefly on account of the seniority of its claim and its hoary head. But take genuine experience without the other—I was about to say, necessary accompaniment of a venerable aspect to make it estimable—could it be transmitted or were it so, what a heritage of sorrow, what an exploded bubble of pleasure it would present and what miserable joyless models of prudence and wisdom, we should all be! Nay, it seems rather that the illusions of life should all come fresh and blooming to each and be enjoyed by each generation over and over again. The mentors amongst us may see in them none of the golden sheaves that garnish the later and more prudential harvest of autumn; but the "Christmas" genius of youth is, after all, better than that of the old set and without the grey beard of the snow and ice season to commend the brutal crucifixion of flesh and blood, there is, even, in their seeming *want* of experience, the instinct of a purer, diviner spirit shining on and lighting up the way of life's early pleasure with its illimitable wealth of budding follies. It is the radiance of a redeeming grace depicted in those illusions which, gleaming through the freezing lethargy of winter blossom in the fragrant beauties of spring. And what a heritage of wealth those bright fancy pictures are—the birthright of the humblest, they are all that make life tolerable or enjoyable in any sphere, and dispelled, are all that make us in the least resigned to die. Mothers who complain of penniless prospects, what sweeter or more precious dowers than these would you ask for your children? With *them*, reasoning in this way is not philosophizing, it is only the thoughtful use of a little common sense; it is not the second sprouting of a seedy intellect nor yet the superannuated phantasy of "second sight," it's the child opening its eyes in the impulse of sublime instinct and making use of the thankless but inestimable boon of unsophisticated sight, that is all. Am I right? If so, I am encouraged to add my protest against old age and experience, laying bare their wisdom to the juvenile, and pruning away those sprouts and plucking that foliage kindly intended by nature not only to beautify the budding sprig of the young, but to hide and to reperfume the withered trunk of the old. It is only my poor protest which I know is of no avail; and the crabbed asceticism of what is called "maturer years" will continue to set its wrinkled visage against the romping scenes of yore. I can see it in my mind's eye, starting in bilious fright at the very mention of what we liked in the pie and cake and plum-duff period of our life,— I can see it glaring on me as I write these lines, and read my sentence as in the hand-writing on the wall, "exiled from grace!" But turning, like the soldier about to leave the field, I would have a parting shot, and I reiterate, the older set have no business to intrude their dyspepsia on the young; nor, as they would dust the cob-webs from their own antiquated cuddies, sweep the rose leaves out of their path.

III.

As regards the manner of the death of the young man to whom I have referred, and with him may be included all that class of unfortunates who rest under the bane of suicide, it may be thought in bad taste to say anything. While I am far from despising that cautious eulogism which dubs silence "golden," and, while I would not intrude upon that dreadful stillness brooding over those most tongueless and pitiless of all griefs, nevertheless I would raise my voice in unqualified denunciation of an ordinance that makes the transient sin of the living the perpetual profanation of the dead, and against that abominable inconsistency which, while it utters a benediction with its mouth, can with its hand subscribe an interdict, aye, both on one and the same person. These people, the unfortunates I mean, and they are far more numerous than it is customary to admit, belong to a class whose troubles, for whatever cause, make them miserable; they may not be shoeless—they may not be hungry, but they suffer an infinitely worse privation,—it may be in some disaster they fancy irretrievable, or it may be in the possession of faults which in the later stages and especially in the end, isolate them like a leprosy from all human or available sympathy. This grade of suffering offers in itself a very wide field, and is not in that respect, as I have said, confined, necessarily, to the gutter and street and to the viler habitation of the indigent. The sort we see prowling about, hankering for something to eat and to drink and to wear, is bad enough, but that is all a mild sort of bodily discomfort in comparison to what may be experienced in another way; I speak not now of the misfortune of simply being bankrupt in body or estate, but in *mind*, and of being not necessarily insane but altogether hopeless. Some of these cases, could they be seen, as we see others in the spectacle of mere ordinary mishap, would present a picture of mental distress than which there could be none other so ghastly or appalling.

Here we may observe, it is not pleasure alone that has its goal but adversity also, and each of these is the antipodes of the other. In our enjoyment we congratulate ourselves that the latter, the darker one, is far away in another yet unexplored hemisphere; but as in pleasure's goal after which we are all yearning, so in that of adversity which we seek to avoid, we may be in the midst of both and recognise neither. The fact is, there is a Jericho in which we colonize all but what contributes to our gratification, and with these far-off exiles of trouble we communicate, if at all, through the medium of a winged virtue, dubbed " charity." It is a natural aversion, I mean that which we have for the less fortunate ones—and it is a human impulse to shrink away. Some there are whose good fortune it is to enjoy exemption from most all kinds of suffering, and such a respite ought to be, of itself, cherished as the sweetest and most valued of all our carnal treasure. Nevertheless, we cannot by any artifice of our own avoid the dreadful scourge altogether and permanently. Indeed, try, as hard as we may, to keep it somewhere else, it crops up all around, and we do find it desperately hard to build a place for misfortune and its victims, and to sequestrate them and localize them as, in our benevolence, we do poverty and contagion.

It may be, and probably is, a source of consolation that, as I said before, we do not always know, much less respond to, the greatest suffering even when we see it. Wrapt in all the gory paraphernalia of catastrophe, we do recognise it and shudderingly commiserate; but the real pain, like the danger that leads to it, very frequently we utterly ignore. Oftentimes, no doubt, because it does not wear, and in fact it rarely does, the aspect, we are taught, most unmistakably characterizes the direful. Oh yes, it is all so different from what it has been so blunderingly painted, we may even associate with it and not know it; we converse with it, it does not tell us; we wish it a good morning, a happy new year, it thanks us pleasantly and seems to reciprocate our good will. We see it breathing the balmy airs of spring, and basking in the sunshine that lights up and inspires nature's great floral concert, and we think it, like ourselves, participating in the great universal song of rejoicing creation! Ah, there was a pardonable deception in the smile that welcomed our cheery salutation and although, in our careless greeting we did not penetrate its thin disguise, there was in that gay device a veil of tears that screened the good-bye tribute of a broken heart. Still, how far were we from recognising in it all the indescribable pangs the poor fellow must have felt who may then have been on his way to throw off a burden under which he had made, perchance, a plucky attempt to stand and was game to the last. Though it be not orthodox, may we not draw near (ought we not to) and sympathise with these most unfortunate ones? Many, we know, possessed as kindly hearts, as noble impulses as ever inspired a good deed. It is not sufficient to say they lacked the callous stoicism of old age, or the dutiful observance of her pet and unimpressionless pupil, it was rather, they were wanting in the exemption; and promiscuous good luck of those who condemn. But do I believe that in the cursed obloquy attaching to their exit from this world they may not have found the other brighter sphere? No! Some court death in the fury of battle, others in the hopelessness of despair; it is self immolation, the one as much as the other, only in the former case life is ignored, in the latter repudiated. I am aware that to court death, in the midst of prosperity, is heroic; at least, it is deemed so by the same judges who denounced the throwing off of the burden in adversity, as ignominious. However this may be, I verily believe, that, in the sight of God, the latter do not suffer for, or in accordance with the stigma of our Church and Creed. If the seductive influences that betray virtue and honor may be regarded as an inkling of all the world's superabundant charms,—if the effect of yielding clandestinely, be the visitation of all that excruciating remorse which, thanks to the hideous night-mares of the moralist restrains and deters,—then, how contrary and uncongenial to all our natural impulses must be that temptation which inclines us, not to the gorging of appetite, but to the disgorging of the very fountain of all delight within us, and to precipitate, not the "prick of conscience" but the pang of death.

IV.

But here it may be charged reproachfully to my account that I am encouraging suicide. I am not. I am condoling with the mother, that is all. She whom I see so often and so wistfully regarding the great pious banquet for the "crumbs" that do not, and are not, permitted to fall, if the glimmering that lights her cheerless hearth is misplaced, then am I, and, indeed, all of us, astray and deceived in the source whence in distress we borrow comfort. Encourage self-immolation! Say rather discourage the perfidy and cruelty that leads to it; besides, we should require no argument to teach us it is the last thing a sane mind would think of, and then only to be repudiated. I claim no amount of encouragement would in the least incline a man to an end whence he is repelled by all the potent instincts of our pain-dreading nature. But how do "our Charities" regard him in this awful dilemma? They are silent; they, like our "Creeds," subserve a heartless policy, and lack the moral courage to speak; but this is explained in the fact that according to the strict interpretation of a rigid and exclusive orthodoxy, the poor creature is without the "fold," and the earth has no soil dirty enough to receive him. Thus in our pious officiousness we undertake to inflict a share of the sentence of "damnation," which we take for granted has been pronounced; and yet who shall say that that grave, all sequestered and tabooed, is not the object of an especial providence. The mind is subject to even greater calamities than the body, and in the isolation of a great pitiless trouble it is marvellous it does not oftener succumb; but reason once dethroned, and all the kingly attributes of a rational mind awry, who shall say the afflicted one is not the object of the most benign commiseration, and that, turn which way he will, his poor benighted faculties may not detect a glimmering that shall guide him home. Alas, ye poor disordered Kingdom, how sadly desolate, how worse than war or pestilence are the ravages that level thy boundaries, and send Reason a crazed fugitive into the desert of the Daft!! But then, stronger than the first great law of self-preservation, is still left the poor dismantled crown—the last resort—I mean, the all-powerful prerogative of irresponsibility. That is a shield sacred amongst barbarians, and respected, to some extent, even in the refinement of Civilization.

We often hear it said, "he could not have been deranged, he was so composed and deliberate." Have you never, in moments of imminent danger, felt a great calm steal over you? we may speak, then, quietly, coherently, in accents of subdued intensity. Thus, when our perceptive faculties are all alive, our senses otherwise may be entirely engrossed as one in some dreadful trance or in the contemplation of some horrid phantom that seems in its snake-like fascination to charm away all agitation, and to neutralize all resistance. I know it is quite possible to feel that way, and, while these poor unfortunates may appear at ease and tranquil, they are not. It is the fixed deliberation of the somnambulist who glides out upon the roof of a lofty building and moves along the very eaves of the fearful precipice placid and unconcerned! In supreme moments, often, there seems a stilling of all our nervous system so mercifully soothing as almost to paralyze, and outwardly, we may appear, unmoved and unruffled by even so much as the slightest irritation. So it is people are surprised it is possible one can look up with indifference at the gleaming axe which is about to sever his head and say, with the nonchalance of Sir Walter Raleigh, "Thou art a sharp medicine but a sure cure for all ills." Before this can be brought about, Hope must have perished; and that may be accomplished by one of two potent influences, either unavoidable necessity that pronounces one's doom and the awful reality is forced upon one that there can be no appeal, or, dire despair. In the first place it is aggressive, and the inexorable verdict before which Raleigh bowed was "you must die;" on the other hand it is passive, and one's condition, though even more terrible, is not brought about, as in the former case, by a brutal judge, a beastly jury, backed by a depraved and maddened herd, whose cry was blood,—but rather in the stealthy development of inexplicable Fate, surrounded by every kindly and fostering influence—or perchance quaffed at the festive board in the impulse of good-fellowship, and in the dregs of an all too delicious nectar. Thus life may not and need not be destroyed at a blow to morally constitute suicide, but in the more gradual and still no less fatal indulgence in some dreadful habit. Then the mind, inoculated with a virus more deadly than the poison fang of Cobra, seeks with the resistless perversity of a thing that is doomed, its antidote in the very evil by which it is afflicted, and its refuge, in the most appalling of all calamities. Take, for example, one of the thousands whose case corresponds to such a predicament,—the poor fellow was never wholly unmindful of his danger, but seemed powerless to struggle against it. It is as if the Fates had conspired in the production of a beautiful reptile, which while it fascinated was preparing to destroy. There he is with the glittering folds gathering closer and closer about him, and still so dazzled and wrapt in the dreadful embrace that he yields to its sinister charm, and not even biding his time, moves impatiently forward to meet his doom. We see him gliding onward to the inevitable end, may naught be done to save him? may not some kindly hand be raised to turn that dreadful fate away. Rarely is it that affection may not avail when all else fail; especially, when it is only persuasion that is needed, and the ills are those of body and blood and may be comforted. And is it possible this poor youth may have no friends, no home? He has a home, he has a sister! Ah, thank God for that, we exclaim on the impulse, at the mention of so potent a cure. Yes he has a sister whose tender heart in the hush of a mighty solicitude, prays the storm-cloud may pass away, and then, dissembling her own sorrow and despair, she points to the splendid arch reflected through her tears, exclaiming gaily, "'Tis a rain-bow at night, brother, be of good cheer!" There is one brief moment of intelligence vouchsafed the afflicted one; a great light breaks over those pale, wan, harassed features—who shall divine the awful pathos of that look,—and a sob that seems to shiver all the pent-up idols of his little world, breaks the narrow boundaries of long suppressed agony. In that cry the flesh collapsed; its anguish was the expiation of the body, its echo the song of the rejoicing spirit. Finally, in the case of him who severed the thread of life at a blow, let it suffice to add:—the pious sycophants of a fastidious creed, may deny the lifeless, resistless clay, "Christian burial"—aye, they may continue to heap their little mountain of obloquy on his grave; but they may not say to the *daisy*, and the *violet*, and the *lily, ye shall not bloom there*, and round the slab which marks that most desolate mound behold a living vine! They mingle their sweet perfume with the hope thereon inscribed, and entwining the letters in wreaths redolent with blossoms that shall never blight, reveal these lines:—

SUFFERING, HE SOUGHT RELIEF IN PAIN: TROUBLED, HE FOUND REDEMPTION IN TRIBULATION.

Norwood to Beckenham.

NORWOOD TO BECKENHAM.

I.

I HAD a very pleasant walk to Beckenham, not long ago —it is not far from where I am living, and one can just make it out four or five miles away, nestled cosily among the trees and hills of Kent. Imagine it a bright pleasant morning of a Sunday, as it was when I took the walk in question, then, after doing hearty honors to a good breakfast, stepping out into the fresh, invigorating air of the Highlands, for a stroll in the country, with the valley and opposite slope of the Surrey hills in prospect All things above, seemingly afloat in a rosy sea of that peculiar, lazy haze of an English atmosphere; and all below, reposing under that potent spell which the Sabbath, in this country, casts over all the busy doings of the week. One is struck, for a moment, to observe how marvellous it is that the din and roar of London, which, on any other day, is wafted to the ear and sounds like the far-off conflict of storm and ocean, this day is hushed and silent as the breath of a slumbering infant; and of all the deafening babel of its countless multitudes, and of all the uproar of its enormous traffic, nought is heard now, but the drowsy murmur of insects, or the rustling of tiny leaves,—the cawing of rooks, or the far-off chime of village church-bells.

From the heights of Upper Norwood, or say from the Crystal Palace, looking south towards Croydon and Adington, and so round eastward towards Beckenham, there is obtained one of the loveliest views that can be imagined. It would be impossible to describe a picture of scenery adequate to that presented from this standpoint; and ordinary language beggars even simple justice, in an effort to convey to one three thousand miles away, the enchantment of landscape, the superb garb, the numberless winning ways, Nature here dons to greet the eye and refresh the spirit of poor wandering mortality. Indeed, one must have seen and felt, to appreciate, the magic charm, the delightful pang, in that so-sorry-to-leave penalty, which the witching goddess here inflicts on the happy unfortunate found trespassing in this her rural Paradise. The beauty of the palace-grounds, is proverbial and unsurpassed, and I mean now not only these, but the noble range of country beyond, which, from this point, the eye commands for miles around. One is just high enough to get a good view of the valley below, which is about five miles across to the hills of Surrey and Kent opposite. To the right and left of this, the range is extended a long way in the form of a crescent, and within this scope a bewildering variety of most beautiful landscape is unfolded. At the first glance, it looks a bit wild,—there are so many trees, that it appears more like broken forest interspersed with meadow land upon irregular ground of hill and dale. The rich, dark green of numberless luxuriant trees, the wild yet superb profusion of shrub, and the soft velvety verdure of the fields, make Nature, for a time, the whole object of one's admiration. As you approach, however, and look more closely, almost hidden away amid the most charming of rustic retreats, you presently discern the ivy-clad walls of English homes; around which, in all the imposing panoply of brawny arms and abundant foliage, stand, in careless yet magnificent array, that aristocratic phalanx of stately oaks and queenly elms. Nor must I forget to mention,— as we plod along through the midst of this, what always fascinated me from the first—I mean the porter's lodge— that rustic little gem of art and nature ingeniously combined, which guards and embellishes the outer pale of English hospitality. Nay, nor rest content, till I have awarded my humble meed of praise to those models of domestic comfort, the pretty manners, and beguiling airs, which one cannot help admiring in an English cottage. The grass, in that bit of lawn in front, looks so sleek, and is kept so trim; and those shrubs and flowers look so fresh, and smell so sweet; and all wreathed round in a pretty barrier of holly hedge, who can resist its shy, cosy look. One may be puzzled, at first, to understand its numberless corners and its variety of odd, elfish-looking gables, but there is a fascination even about them—they have such a hide-and-seek air, and suggest, to a susceptible "old bach," so many sweet little hide-a-ways within. Then, too, screening these and tucked up all around, or falling like a bridal veil over all, is that most becoming mantle of ivy and jasmine, disguising, to some extent, all that is artful, and only brushed aside, here and there, to make room for those coquettish-looking windows through which the sunbeams glance, and imagination is fain to picture, the image of some fair creature, in all the witchery of blue eyes and yellow hair! I have often thought, when I've come upon one of these, say like those one sees at Norwood, or Stratham, or Twickenham,—I've often thought as I've lingered wistfully, and admiringly, reluctant to pass on and away, what a delightful nook that would be to live in,—and what a temptation it must be, (to one who is in a way to be tempted), to make one's exit from the dusty highways of the world, and leave to the frenzied, panting herd, the continuance of the race for honors, and the scramble after "flesh-pots." In that moment's pause, how charmingly, how forcibly does it appeal to one's good sense, through the voice of one's good angel, to renounce the greedy art of business and all the din and clatter of its dirty machinery, for the peace and joyful solace of this biding place, to dwell ensconced amongst the rhododendrons—there to sojourn through the fickle respite of one's days, with nought to beguile or vex, and all to inspire that nobler and fuller enjoyment which comes from the cultivation and exercise of one's better nature. The partition, just there and then, betwixt heaven and earth, seems much thinner than in most places—just near enough the other Paradise that, barring the chance of plumping right into it, it offers life the sunny side, and we may enjoy it just as we are. So thin, indeed, we may *feel* through, and with all the lusty appetites of our beggarly adoration in full riot, enjoy this rare and delicious proximity to perfect bliss, *with the flesh all on.* I would not be unreasonably poetical in my praise of anything; indeed I have lived long enough to see the propriety of curbing my enthusiasm, and do try hard to be rational. Suffice it then to say, of these good old English dwelling-places, at least, as they impressed me,—they may not be a Paradise,—no, not in an evangelical point of view,—but so far as respectability is concerned, and social enjoyment, and all the countless auxiliaries to pleasure and refinement, they are so near the perfection of Elysium, that I believe the discrepancy is only in us, in our transient possession and want of appreciation, to make our felicity complete. It cannot be denied, that the clumps of precious fruit which poor Faith hungers for in vain, and saints extol in pious rapture as being sweet and satisfying beyond all human conception, may be, and doubtless are, too exalted for mortal reach; but here, forsooth, I am bound to say you may enjoy the comfortable assurance that notwithstanding you are so far beneath, you are just *under the limb*,—aye, and when any of those luscious plums do drop to earth, they fall here and prolific Nature multiplies in all around, delightful tokens that all the scattered sheaves, from that golden harvest of the other realm, are wafted here—borne on soft winds perfumed with the breath of violets and vocal with the song of birds!

II.

It was past eleven o'clock when I got across the valley, and began the easy ascent of the opposite slope; was taking it slowly, moving on up the incline and glancing back enjoying the splendid retrospect over in the direction I had come. While proceeding in this manner, I came unexpectedly upon what turned out to be a very interesting old church. It was just in the outskirts of a little place called Beckingham, and the first intimation I had of being so near, was a glorious flood of music which came down upon your humble wayfarer, and greeted his musing senses with a perfect torrent of sacred melody. Looking quickly round in the direction whence it came, I found myself in close proximity to a quaint-looking structure which, at a glance, bore unmistakable evidence of its great age and sacred character. One, here and there, in the course of long and patient rambles in this country, does happen on these old land marks; and I felt, in this instance, a good deal of that satisfaction which animates the antiquarian, when he unearths some mouldering ruin, or brings to light objects, the design and handywork of an age and people long gone. Feeling rather fagged with my long walk, I sat down on a stile close by, amid the grateful strains of a rich-toned organ, and the blending of many sweet voices. Presently, I found myself a good deal interested in a survey, not only of the church itself, which was odd and monkish-looking, but also of the church-yard surrounding it; where were gathered, in grim, time-broken array, a solemn medley of antiquated grave-stones, jagged monuments, and ghastly recumbent effigies. The edifice was, or had been, to all appearances, one of the few old-time monastic strongholds which still maintain their ground in this ancient colony of Cæsar. They are rare as the relics of Roman occupation, and unique as the dialect of an extinct race; possibly, too, not unlike the language of an obsolete period, may be given a usage and significance that in their own palmy day had seemed grotesque and absurd. This one, built originally of the most substantial materials, it was not at all improbable to suppose, had suffered the chills and frosts of four or five hundred winters, and borne, battered but unshaken, the sacrilegious fury of centuries of bigotry, rebellion and reform. There was, moreover, something in the aspect of those grey old walls, and their association with the past, to inspire emotion, and they impressed me as deserving more than a passing glance. I confess, as a rule, the feeling with which I regard these patriarchal institutions, replete, as many of them are, with sorrowful associations, is not that of enjoyment. There is a species of pleasure, no doubt, in the gratification of one's natural inquisitiveness; but the sensation, in the majority of these cases, is rather too much like that one feels groping about the dingy nooks and cloisters of abbeys and crypts; that is to say, an uncomfortable admixture of admiration and curiosity, together with a very considerable ingredient of dread. They may have, as in the case of Westminster, and St. Paul's, the benefit of every device of skill and art, to make them attractive, but even then, it is only such an attempt to embellish catastrophe, as glorifies without mitigating bereavement; the effect, only one remove less terrifying than the horrors of the catacombs, and hardly less repulsive than those fantastic trophies, constructed from the bones of dismembered skeletons, and exhibited in the vaults of the Capuchin Friars at Naples.

Nevertheless, while there is no pleasure, in the ordinary acceptation of the word, there is an interest, solemn and intense, that takes possession of one's thoughts in the contemplation of things, which, like this old church, have endured so long; for notwithstanding the power of skill to heal, and the magic efficacy of human affection to foster, we read, in tearful eyes on every hand, the sad but inexorable fate of poor human flesh; speedily and surely it is passing away. This omnipotent law is not applied to persons alone, for rarely does the wanderer, in these lands, find a structure that has long withstood that mighty wave of Time, which, lapping up and overwhelming poor mortality, sweeps onward to inevitable destruction all that glittering, heterogeneous mass of things pertaining to the race. It is sad but true that posterity, at this late day, following in the wake of that once gorgeous crest, finds of whatever really belonged to the days of yore, only *air* and *dirt* and *desolation*. It is, indeed, marvellous how few traces remain—here and there, a bit of sturdy granite that *will not yield*—and these, especially where they retain the symmetry or character of the original design, are interesting beyond the gratification of a mere idle fancy. They are the few glimpses of land one gets on the immense sea of events into which are merged and swallowed up all those peoples and things of which we read. They are fast crumbling away, and rapidly being lost in the turbulent rush of "mighty waters"; and soon, indeed, from this modern ark, that vulture *Curiosity* will find, of all those remains of which I speak, no branch, nor sprig, nor place to rest its tired wing—no substance to pacify its hungry greed, in all its flight backward over that great silent ocean of Time!

III.

The power to destroy, is as mighty and we trust as benign as that which creates; was it kindness, then, in Providence, that had sheltered this aged shrine and faithful servant, for there, in the midst of that resistless tide, this veteran has stood firm and endured a veritable "hold fast for faith"—a "shining light," casting far and near, amongst the breakers, the genial rays of its goodly precept. And as I looked upon those wretched deposits of mortal dust around, it seemed they too were blessed; for while so many had been swept onward to some nameless shore, or sank into the bottomless deep, they had caught the gleam of this precious light and clutched at the Cross. They had wrestled with the angry wave, but not alone; the potent magnetism of an unseen Power had been there and succored them, and drawn them, as by some loving hand, within the counter current that eddies round this sacred rock; and there they lie now, stranded on the threshold of a "Christian home,"—reposing in the lap of "Mother

Church." It seems as if this reflection makes the goodly dame look less forbidding and ugly; and, too, there is, about that clinging, sun-lit ivy which has crept as a mantle over her weather beaten walls, and filled and beautified the seams and wrinkles of her stony lineaments, something imparting a pleasant, genial air of fostering love, as closely she gathers under her maternal wing that silent brood of departed spirits, and reflects the sunshine of her precious hope down upon the cold, clayey tenements of her voiceless flock!

Peering in at the vestibule, my eye had been fixed, for some time, on the recumbent effigy of some doughty old knight who was placed there; clad in complete armour, this fierce old crusader, for such he seemed, and may have been, looked formidable in the extreme, and impressed me with the idea he could not have fallen in open encounter with flesh and blood; but seemed, long ago, to have tired of the conflict, and lain down on this earthy couch to rest, and in the grateful respite of some pleasant dream, perchance of home and those he loved, death had crept in softly! How came this martial image here at all, I asked myself; what were his claims to fame, and wherein lay the charm that had preserved the outward form and semblance of this man to this late age, winning their meed of voluntary regard and homage from so many generations. In all the cloistered wealth of our mother land, we find, here and there, the rare virtue of a few uncollected unexhibited relics; they are not the least precious of her obsolete treasure, and amongst them are those simple unartistic specimens of a by gone age, in the shape of effigies. This was one, and no doubt a worthy comrade of the others, if not a chieftain. It does not speak, it does not feel; indeed, one of the inviolable conditions of this warlike proxy was it should be senseless and must be silent. The shadow of its desolate mission is stamped on all its lineaments; it may not even echo the soldier cry of "all's well," and yet there is about this broken and begrimed image an appeal to our intelligence and humanity all the more expressive that it is mute, and none the less pathetic that it is not the most perfect work of art. There are many languages for the living, and they are badly comprehended; but only one for the dead, and that universally understood; one is by voice, the other by sign. Irrespective, then, of tongue, or dialect, or nationality, we read in this crumbling symbol, of wars and conflicts long since hushed for ever, and of feuds and hostile passions, long since blended in a realm of perfect harmony. It bespeaks, too, a being like ourselves, and of a kindly feeling that loved the flesh it counterfeits; for, after all, it was affection, tender and devoted, that in rearing this monument from dust, had sought to perpetuate one who was lost to all but memory, by giving to the senseless clay, to which he had gone, the expression and noble outline of a once loved and gallant form. The music ceased and I rose to go—that glorious hymn of praise which lauds the benignant love and mercy of the Most High, had gone forth on its mission of intercession for troubles, hopes, and fears—and the last expiring echoes of the *Te Deum*, grew softer and fainter as they mounted heavenward, bearing with them the cast off burdens of heavy laden hearts, and leaving with the prayerful ones the happy omen of a blithe and sunny morn.

Our Charities.

ABANDONED.

JUDGE ALLISON'S CASTIGATION OF THE SO-CALLED CHARITY SYSTEM OF PHILADELPHIA--- A REMARKABLE COURT-ROOM SCENE.

PHILADELPHIA, May 27, 1881.

There has been before the Quarter Sessions Court of this city for several days a case of peculiar interest, not only from a humanitarian point of view but, because of the charitable dogmas which it has destroyed. Its sudden ending this afternoon furnished a fittingly dramatic climax to one of the saddest pictures of our so-called civilization that ever was put in words. The facts were, that on a cold, snowy morning during last winter a dead child was found in an area in the rear of a tall tenement house, the upper floors of which were let out to nightly lodgers. Police investigation promptly revealed the fact that a young woman who had engaged the rear room on the previous evening had given birth to the child, and she admitted having thrown it out of the window, declaring that it was born dead. The girl was dragged from her bed, forced by the police officer to walk down three flights of stairs and to the nearest station-house, where she was at once locked up. Brought before the committing magistrate a few days later, she was promptly sent to Moyamensing Prison, charged with infanticide, and certainly would have been convicted had not two young lawyers, who were convinced of her innocence (George Haldorn and Lincoln L. Eyre), come to her assistance. The story of her life is as commonplace as could be imagined: The prisoner had been living with a song and dance performer, in New York, named Edward or "Ned" Aaronson, who, when she was about to become a mother, brought her to Philadelphia, and heartlessly abandoned her. Friendless and wholly unknown, realizing the terrible position in which she was placed, she wandered for days about the streets, until, finally forced by the ravenous and unnatural hunger induced by approaching maternity, she accosted a young girl on the sidewalk, who gave her a few cents and lodged her for the night. On the following day, again cast out upon the tender mercies of the world, she encountered a woman of the town as the Commonwealth fully succeeded in showing, but that her heart was warm the evidence no less clearly proved. In her company Lizzie Aaronson, as she was called in the indictment, for days sought asylum in some hospital where the dreaded ordeal of confinement might be passed. The testimony of Ida Wilson, the girl who thus labored on behalf of another woman in distress without hope of reward, can be briefly summarized as follows:—"I heard of this friendless girl and asked her to my quarters. They were poor enough—only one room—but such as I had I tried to give her. The stranger passed most of her time in tears, and seemed utterly hopeless. Realizing the importance of medical aid for her in the hour of confinement, and being too poor myself to procure it for her, I started with her on the second day to find such a place. Lizzie Aaronson, the prisoner in the dock, was utterly penniless—had been left without a cent." Then follows the story of charity's cold shoulder to actual and evident distress.

THE RULES THAT FORBID.

"First we applied at the Nurses' Home or Lying-in-Charity, as it is called, at Cherry and Eleventh streets. The matron heard the case and admitted that it was a desperate one. She then asked if Lizzie could produce her marriage certificate, and pay $5 per week for her board, but when she learned that Lizzie could do neither the one nor the other the scene ended abruptly. Thence we went to the Homœopathic Hospital, but there was no room for Lizzie's admission. The young physician in charge said she must go the Almshouse. To the Guardians of the Poor, then, we went—to the office in Seventh street. A clerk told us I must take my companion before Magistrate Pole and ask her commitment. We went to the magistrate's, but he refused to commit her unless she would give the name of her husband and swear out a warrant for his arrest, so that he could be compelled to pay the county for her keeping. This, after some hesitation—desperate as was her situation—she refused to do. I advised her to do so. We next applied at the Home Mission, No. 533 Arch Street, in hopes of getting Lizzie a ticket to New York, but the officer in charge would not give her one, although she pleaded piteously for it. He finally offered to sell her one for $1. Neither she nor I had so much money. We then went to the Young Women's Christian Association, on Seventh Street. The matron said, firmly and promptly, that she could not do anything for her, as soon as she saw her condition, asked for her certificate, and made Lizzie cry bitterly.

Finally she said we had better go to the Sixth Ward Relief Association, a branch of the Young Women's Christian Association. There we had almost similar experience. Finally we went to an intelligence office, No. 411 Arch Street, in the hope that she might find some kind person who would take her as a servant, under the circumstances. She there met an elderly gentleman, who engaged her, but, seeing her condition, declined to take her home, although she begged him to and declared that she would work for nothing long enough after her trouble to cover all the expenses. He still firmly declined, but expressed his sympathy by giving her $1. Lizzie and I immediately spent this money in food. I had not eaten anything that day, and she not since the morning of the previous day. When it was too late we recollected that it would have procured the coveted ticket to New York. Then we both felt sorry. But we had been so hungry. At last she returned with me to my room. On several mornings thereafter, seeing that she was a burden to me, as she said, she left. I afterwards learned that as a last resort she pledged her small gold ring—the only article of jewelry she had left—for twenty-five cents, and took the room in which her child was born." This was the last witness for the defence.

A DRAMATIC CLIMAX.

District-Attorney Graham stepped forward and addressed the jury. He spoke of the enormity of the offence, the difficulty of proof, and the doubts cast upon the girl's crime by the testimony of the defence. Therefore he thought it wise, and with the advice of the Judge, to abandon the case.

There was a hum of surprise in the court. Judge Allison then directed the two girls who had been called as witnesses, Ida Wilson and Lizzie Flick, to come to the bar. He gave them seats on a raised platform in front of the jury, and in full view of the crowded court-room. Having first referred to the remarks made by the District Attorney, and commended the wisdom of his course, with deep and evident emotion, he thus addressed the jury:—

"Gentlemen, I have called these two girls to the bar of this court that you may see them, while I say a few words upon another phase of this case. This defendant, Lizzie Aaronson was shown by the testimony of the defence to have come to this city an utter stranger, to have been a homeless wanderer on the streets, without money, without friends. In her utter loneliness and friendliness, driven to seek charity from the passer-by, she accosted this girl here (pointing to Lizzie Flick), and, without hesitation, she shared her poverty with her, giving her a share of the money and comforts she possessed. This other young woman (pointing to Ida Wilson, who, unfortunately, has not led a correct life), however much her moral nature may have been warped in one respect, gave an exhibition of practical Christianity—of practical Christianity, I repeat, with emphasis—when she likewise gave this friendless sister shelter, that would furnish a wholesome example to most of those who are clothed with purple and fine linen. I am sorry to admit that if this poor, friendless girl had applied to nine out of ten of those very people who compose the wealthy classes she would probably have sought in vain the shelter she received from this despised outcast. I, therefore, regard this as the time and the place to make mention from the bench of the kindness of heart displayed by these two girls, and have for that reason dwelt upon their acts, because of the striking contrast which they afford to the conduct of the so-called charities of this city. It has been clearly shown that this defendant, in the midst of her wants, and when the critical hour of her motherhood was near, went from one of those so-called charities to the other, and at each of them sought admission, with the evident purpose of giving her child respectable birth. In this laudable desire she was thwarted at every turn, in consequence of the various regulations governing the so called benevolent institutions, under none of which, unfortunately, was she a fit candidate for admission. At last, alone, in utter squalor, nearly naked, without fire or the most ordinary comforts, amid the darkness of a bitter winter's night, inexperienced and unassisted, she gave birth to her child, whether alive or dead the Almighty and she only will ever know." After an interval, in which the bill of indictment was passed to the foreman of the jury, Judge Allison concluded:—"I direct that you do acquit the prisoner."

Taken altogether, the scene was one of the most unusual that ever occurred in any court-room in this country. The house was crowded, and, strange to say, nearly everybody stood up, hat in hand, as if the benediction of the humane judge was asked for all. The sermon was such a one as will furnish texts for Sunday next.—*New York Herald.*

OUR CHARITIES.

I.

IN common with the rest of poor, ignorant mortality, I noticed certain directions on the guide-boards as I toddled along, and taking it for granted they pointed the right way, followed in the direction they indicated. I saw, it is true, by-paths leading off in other directions, but I stuck to the main highway where I saw everyone else going, and which was broad and pleasant. I took this road not simply because of its superior attractiveness, although I was, I admit, strongly influenced by that; nevertheless, I was conscientious, or tried to be so, but then I had no decided notions of my own concerning certain great questions of the day, and into which, when I plunged, I would be caught up by eddies and twisted and twirled round and round: so I left everything to the guide-boards, as I have said, and plodded on. Besides, another reason I had for taking the capacious and brilliantly lighted boulevard—all so extensive, and so beautifully embellished—was because the narrow paths seemed frequented by a very shabby set, and only a few of them at that; and they looked wild, and haggard, and hungry, and the way looked lonely and quite abandoned, except by these miserable creatures.

Just here, I noticed a very conspicuous guide-board, being, as it were, a combination of several, with certain signs and symbols and hieroglyphics inscribed thereon, amongst which I could make out a hand pointing in the direction of the narrow gauge. It struck me it might prove a good use of time to explore that path, and notwithstanding the uncouth appearance of its habitués, I should, I thought, meet with a less powerful competition than where I was; where everything, while being very fine, and well regulated, seemed under the control of a systematic sort of monopoly, closely resembling, as it seemed to me, the despotism from which I was migrating. It was just at this point I lost so much time hesitating—in fact, I paused some time without making any perceptible progress either way, and lounged vacantly about, though I could not help, in the meantime, taking some observations.

Beside this last mentioned post, I always saw a man who seemed stationed there to interpret the strange writing on the board, and to explain the various ways. This man would be relieved after a while by another, and he in turn by still a different one, and so on. Each of these, as he came along in turn, seemed to me to be a species of emigrant or road agent and official mouthpiece, being apparently well informed about the topography of the promised land. I did not speak to them personally, because I saw, unless there were several together, they took no notice of them whatever, and as application required to be made in lots, being alone, I had to stand aside, which I did—near enough, however, to hear and see what was going forward. As I was looking on watching this agent, it seemed to me he directed the shabby and poor-looking ones that came along, down the narrow, dirty way; but the grand turnouts and aristocratic people either passed straight on, without noticing him, or, as seemed the more polite and customary thing to do, stopped out of mock deference to this functionary—and then it really appeared to me, the agent gave them a peculiar look—I will not say a wink, though it was very like it—and at the same time veered his thumb round in the direction of the grand avenue; whither went all the brilliant part of the throng, including all those who seemed to have any pretensions to greatness. Vigilant, however, as I had become by this time, a bright idea struck me—thought I to myself, I will watch closely to see where the agents themselves go; and in nearly every instance, as fast as they were relieved, and after sending a good batch down the cramped, mean little by-way, each sidled off quietly and gracefully with the grandees; and one, with an especially resigned and pensive look, took the box-seat and reins of a four-in-hand.

When I saw this done so many times, I hesitated no longer, but followed with reassured eagerness "the course of empire"—on the through-ticket system—first class, as the agent advised. I may mention that on this route there are no return tickets; so we are not annoyed by the faint-hearted coming back, and telling us grievous stories of misrepresentation and hardship, and giving disparaging accounts of the prospects ahead.

We see by the wayside, as we pass along, certain wild, beggarly-looking creatures, who shout out to us as we pass, and gesticulate fanatically, and cry "Stop, stop,— go back, go back!" and all that sort of thing; but our mouth-piece tells us not to mind them, that they are poor, daft creatures who have been led astray. They, we perceive, however, are going in a contrary direction. One of these poor things caught hold of my hand, and I shall never forget his look, as I drew it hastily away, having caught the eye of one of the agents bent reprovingly upon me. Our guides are constantly telling us not to mind these people, and to keep a sharp lookout on our pockets. I may mention, too, that on each side of us we see, as we go along, a smooth high wall on which are painted the most beautiful frescoes, depicting the glories and advantages of the country to which we are bound; and all signs of suffering, or want, or pain are kept out of our sight so as not to interfere with the pleasure of our journey. Every now and then, however, from behind the most enticing of these scenes issue shrieks and groans, like of human agony; these reach us frequently in the midst of our comfort and hilarity, and on venturing to inquire as regards this slight interruption to the general ovation, we are hushed up somewhat hastily by the agent, who tells us that that sort of thing is the finest feature in the whole aspect, as indicating exceptionally high moral culture; he also explains that the people who utter these outcries are a miserable class of tramps and malefactors, who are supposed to be possessed of the devil, and who have been taken under the fostering care of the public benevolent institutions, on the easy conditions that they allow certain kindhearted and philanthropic ministers and attendants to gently drive the Evil One out of them; these modern expurgatories being under the full control and auspices of a certain benign spirit called " Charity."

II.

There are many persons and things that have been so long tacitly acknowledged as pure and unimpeachable, that any one who may have the temerity to say ought of them, except in praise, may expect to be sent peremptorily " to Coventry "; and for the matter of that, he has reason to feel particularly fortunate if not more harshly dealt with.

Although the day for branding liberty of speech with a hot iron, may be passed, nevertheless, in this liberal epoch, an instrument just as formidable exists in the more civilized but no less reprehensible means of two powerful influences: Bribery, and Patronage. Whatever we want said, or written, or done, is brought about by "subsidy;" and when the performance is a purely personal effort of our own, to meet with approval and success, it must be such as to propitiate, not so much public opinion, generally, as sectional spite or party interest; and in the effort to win popularity, amongst these conflicting elements, we must and do cater to partisan patronage; and at the same time, we must and do forfeit our claims to the broader, nobler title of "Catholic," or "Independent," or "Liberal." Examples of the truth of the above, are too numerous to mention, and the fact itself too hackneyed perhaps to call for illustration; besides, the bringing up of "distinguished" cases, might seem an aspersion. How far the restraint I speak of may be wholesome, is another question; but it is impossible to find an individual or grade of society that is exempt. The lower orders of people would be more independent, as having smaller interests in jeopardy, but they are even more open to temptation, as they have so much that is needful to gain by patronage; and all untutored as they are, regarding the higher art of dissimulation, they allow their reason and common sense to subserve the logic, and not unfrequently, the venality of the learned, and those in position and authority over them. Thus are they constrained to practise an involuntary servility, as despicable as their mean opinion of themselves is unjust, and as uncalled for, as their reverence and envy of those above them are erroneous and misapplied.

This may be well—it is certainly conducive to harmony and peace, which is preferable to revolution; but to the fact of occasional resistance, are we indebted for two prodigious elements in our progress: Invention and Reform. Conformity, in all things, offers the most tempting comforts, and that page of history which records the triumphs and reverses of the dissenting ones, records also a terrible prelude of persecution, riot and bloodshed.

One of the most honourable distinctions about these men, however, whether we agree with their "crotchets," or not, is that in their disagreement they expressed their opinions, all shackled as they were, in fearless, thankless opposition to established authorities, and not only independently, but in direct repudiation of bribery and patronage.

In contrast with those heroes whose patriotic opposition to high-toned autocratic ordinances has won them well-merited renown, take those marshalled under the same banner, but in an humble way, who only come in conflict with what is termed "well-bred manners," and trivial set notions—they, too, suffer petty martyrdom, and are made to smart for their impulsive sincerity. There may have been no rude or unkind act committed, but whatever be the reason, their not conforming to the teaching and etiquette of the times, is sufficient to make them amenable to that dreadful penalty of social ostracism, which, although it may not include all the terrors of a frozen Siberia, may nevertheless visit a calamity on the victim hardly less intolerable, and all the more pitiless, in the boundless measure of misery and deprivation entailed in that blighting, scathing, excoriating sentence, LOSS OF PATRONAGE. Our every-day business life affords numerous examples of this, and some of the meaner sort, though ludicrous in many respects, afford an all the more refreshing contrast to their graver prototypes.

Let a generously inebriated Hibernian enter a public waiting room or diligence, where, we will suppose, are a number of well-regulated females,—then, with only a hazy, mellow consciousness of his fair surroundings, he begins to soliloquize on a variety of dubious subjects, at the same time incautiously calling things by their right names. Straightway, you will observe the sensitive creatures around begin to assume the *qui vive*. There is a general collapse of all animation, and they set themselves to performing what only woman's witchery is capable of,—that is, they go off into that well-assumed apathy which may easily be mistaken for a trance; and, with all their subtle instincts alive and active, they, in less time than I can write it, resolve themselves into a sort of well-bred spiritual *alibi*. The minds of some find escape out of the window, and are seen gazing fixedly in vacancy; some are lost in pensive reverie; some are conjuring up a new style of hairpin; whilst others precipitately recall some long-forgotten scene in which they are suddenly conscious of a deep and tender interest. In short, they all get as far back into the corner of elsewhere, as possible; and with silent, startling unanimity, these fair dreamers assume an air quite as absent as if they were some marvellous coincidence of so many somnambulists, having met there by chance, and waiting for anxious relatives to come and wake them up. But how fares it with the cause of all this mysterious pantomime? Very soon our intoxicated friend will begin to feel a strange sensation as of frost in the air—a sort of sepulchral dampness mingling in the atmosphere, and thrilling to the marrow of his bones. It is nothing but the manner of his reception, and for having, technically speaking, overstepped, or rather staggered over those dangerous limits that border on propriety. But it sobers him faster than probably anything else could; indeed, he is so impressed with a sense of something amiss, that he looks about him, for the first time, with a puzzled, half-fearful expression, such as a man, of domestic habits and high moral sensibilities, would take on who had dined late and rather heartily, and waked up, after a short period of absent-mindedness, to find himself in what he imagined the boudoir of an Egyptian harem. There is the tingling of the inevitable bow-string about his neck, and then thinking to avoid the fatal twitch, he collects all his drowsy energies in the effort, and makes off at a tangent.

If a man, whose instincts are so blunted with drink, that he can brave anything, is affected thus by the cold freezing attitude of set manners, and established notions, what must be the punishment in the case of a sober man who shall venture on, not a slight infringement of good taste, but indiscreetly, rashly, blurt out something directly and painfully out of tune with our preconceived ideas and hallowed conceits concerning our good men, our immaculate preceptors, and especially " our charities." Of course, the little circle about him that find it out, begin to feel there is no doubt a monster amongst them, whose ideas are outrageously at variance with those generally inculcated, and they edge off—not stopping to think whether he is a ghoul simply, or, what may be equally obnoxious, some one who assumes to be less stupid than they.

III.

Matters tending to controversy which, happily for peace and harmony's sake, have been passed upon and settled years, it may be centuries ago, we do not like to take the trouble or risk to disturb; and thus we are pre-disposed to favour the reiteration of time-worn arguments and panegyrics, all, of course, on the side we happen to be. This is especially the case if the question lacks interest or be of no commercial importance, and not bearing on, or in any way interfering with business affairs; or if it has, then most likely our acquiescence is necessary to invite or to retain that patronage whence we derive our support or prosperity. At any rate, they are about as near the proper thing, we think, as we care to fashion them, or as we are ourselves; so, dreading to be regarded as "sceptical," we yield an indifferent or zealous assumption of adherence, and are counted as supporters of a cause or belief or institution, the righteousness of which may have been disputed through adverse opinion on many a bloody field. Hence it comes about, that the attitude of the modern maintainer, the "latter-day" defender and-if-need-be-warrior, is about that of a fever and ague patient, with a bad case of "shakes," armed cap-à-pie in the clumsy steel armour of some giant crusader. Besides, there are many things we mistrust our ability to improve or our eligibility to examine into, and thus a great part of this enlightened and mature world, yields an apparently helpless or politic obedience to a set of musty ordinances and obsolete customs in which it apparently has not sufficient interest or lacks confidence to think rationally about, or to come in collision with. We may not be altogether satisfied with the logic or common sense of many views generally accepted as right; but we let them pass unchallenged, especially if they are tolerably pleasing or at least not inconveniently obtrusive. They may, indeed, and most likely do comprise the muniments of our pseudo faith—aye, and constituting the grassy bastions pounded periodically by the batteries of adverse opinion, are escaladed from time to time, by the vandal progeny of that prolific bastard REFORM! In this respect, it may be noted that reform stands in the same relation to our old time heritage of creeds, dogmas, prejudices, and forms, as a broom to house cleaning;—with this difference, that, instead of sweeping away dirt, it dispels fallacies. These latter, however, it must be confessed, are not always to be condemned; nay many of them seem a most attractive variety of beautiful ideal growths such as creep spontaneously over everything in the course of time.—It is not always the most substantial thing that saves, and not the least persuasive arguments, in favour of old time institutions, are these sweet appeals to our conservative instincts. They are the blossoms that adorn the crevices of old walls, and we cherish the ruin for the sake of the flower; but as age inspires wisdom, so antiquity hallows conceit, and sometimes we reverence a sentiment for the mere crumbling masonry that, in its creation, earlier generations were ignorant of. So it comes about there are vast quantities of relics enshrined and regarded with that awe and veneration pertaining to sacred things, which had only a very remote reference to what was sacred; so too we see fragments of the cross fashioned centuries ago in imitation of the original, get to be looked upon in course of time as the genuine article, and is elevated and bowed down to as a part of the holy fabric itself. Thus in the transmutability of things are many of the religious observances of the present day accounted for. And it comes to pass we reverence in the coal measure of a fossil period symbols which, like the grey beards of the Druids, are sanctified only by superstition, and hallowed only by lapse of time.

IV.

As regards these ideal growths of blossom to which I have referred, they seem to germinate in some mysterious quality, better than that we find exhibited in the commoner phases of our corporeal humanity. Though they may spring up in the conflict of our worst passions, still their design and influence seem to be to tend most strongly to amity; and while I typify them here as flowers, we recognise them in every beautiful form and fancy, and they not unfrequently find expression in song. Thus the patriot sees in an ideal harp with broken strings, the lacerated chords of that great Irish heart that bled centuries ago; and both here and in the sister Isle, grievances and even atrocities that had their origin and day in a period so far distant as almost to have become sacred, are kept in sympathetic accord with more modern sentiment, through such dulcet mediums as "Erin go-Bragh," and "Scot's wha hae." In this way are they blended in the "green" of those simple leaves, which typify the genius of Celtic liberty, and flower in the sturdy plant that symbolizes the spirit of ancient Gaelic chivalry. In such close affinity to these beautiful growths, that their identity may be merged, are those to which in our more exalted moods we claim personal relationship; and like the others, cropping out of the time-seam of dreary, thatchless ruin, they get their vitality, their sustenance, their fragrance, in certain rare and endearing virtues that sweeten and embellish our moral being. They are unseen veins, as it were, of that living water we have seen ere this bubbling up in all the limpid purity of Horeb's fount, amid the rubbish of some abandoned and tumbled-down old homestead,—among these is—*charity*. In the sense, however, in which charity is made to seem, not only the adorable attribute it really is, but withal subserving and glorifying "our charities," I claim the public estimate of this virtue to be a fallacy, and all its resplendent loveliness a beautiful fraud, that does not even attain to the true dignity and sincerity of a moral illusion, or we might call it that. It may embellish as the blossom, and as such I would foster it ordinarily; but in this case, notwithstanding our splendid assumption to the contrary, it is not the *bona fide* flower—it does not shed its verdure, it does not drop its leaves; it outdoes itself, it blooms perennially, and seems, as it really is, out of all harmony with nature. The fact is, it is not charity at all, and the thing we extol as such is only a weed blooming in lifeless perpetuity, in all the artificial splendor of floral wax!

Now that I think of it, I am almost disposed to humor the delusion regarding "our charities," and shield them from criticism and reform. It is so comforting to foster the presumption, which generally prevails, that the presiding spirit in "our charities" is charity; and by thus incorporating with the name and purpose of the good project, an attribute so queen-like and lovable, exalt the little benefit that accrues in the exercise of our much lauded philanthropy. I say I would humour the delusion, because it has a tendency to absolve us in the uncomfortable feeling we might otherwise have, that we ought to have done more; and not only this, but another important consideration involved in this issue, is the reward. There is no doubt, in exalting "our charities" we get a proportionately higher estimate of our own deserving. I would not decry appreciation, but I protest that our farthing's worth is made to seem a prodigious investment, and our greedy mite of benevolent stock, the ground of ultimate exemption. Thus comforted, as all small minds are with the thought of what they have done, the cry of distress, in the heart-rending pathos of its greatest need, may never reach us; it is effectually stifled within those inquisitorial walls we term "our charities," and rarely penetrates beyond those granite bastions which, reared in luxury to shut out penury, are dedicated to charity. According to this view, the "hand-writing" on these walls may be interpreted this wise—that we seek in our prosperity to propitiate felicity by ostracising misfortune.

I am aware that one only renders himself obnoxious by interfering in these matters; besides there is undoubtedly a certain amount of good done by individuals and communities, and even societies, in relieving distress, which is highly commendable and proper, and I would not disparage their efforts. What I take exception to is not the little good that is done, but rather the virtuous agrarianism, the pious effrontery by which it is so very generally puffed up and appropriated, and also to the atrocious misnomer of calling it by a name so exalted as charity.

V.

There is a strange commingling of good and ill in human kind, it is inherent in the race, and we are come to regard all good deeds as to some extent palliating a stigma attaching to our nature. All share in the credit of what is good, and in the exclusion of what is ill and thus is the merit of the few appropriated by the many; there is about it, indeed, no exclusive proprietorship, and thus do we seek in the individual exception of a rare virtue, a common identity. So it is we rob the grave to monopolize the resplendent qualities of a parent or ancestor or countryman. So also do we rob the cross and appropriating, as by common right, the redeeming traits of the crucified, the gracious attributes of a redeeming Saviour are made to give radiance and character to deeds, which had otherwise left us in darkness, sneaking around on our hands and knees,—not seeking an honest man as did Diogenes, but hiding, fleeing from an infuriated rabble, the demons invoked by our own conscience. Thus it comes about, we see all around us people who do not inconvenience themselves with a higher or more troublesome conception of what is "Christianlike" than an indifferent observance of automatic forms, magnifying these exercises, as they do their benevolence, into a species of pious penance in which one would think the agony of remorse for assumed "short-comings," only second in intensity to that portrayed in the burning, spluttering flesh of the martyrs, and claiming with them, in the meantime, a full share of the atoning graces won at the stake.

As in the case of the few whose noble deeds we applaud, and the credit of which we generally appropriate, I would like to see a reconstruction of the perverted sense of a few noble words, and have restored to them something like an adequate share of the true meaning corresponding not to our upstart pretensions, but to their ancient and honourable lineage. I do not object so much to the monopoly of splendid names in ordinary traffic, or as tokens purely of affection; as in France we see the meanest wines branded and called by the grandest names,—in this case if we do not like the article, we are under no obligation to accept it: the brand, indeed, is only a mild type of a very common fraud of which we are all cognizant. In America, too, we find the shadiest population taking upon themselves imperial nomenclature and exhausting the whole category of great names in history sacred, and profane—that is nothing, it is only a matter of taste or simple custom. Nevertheless, while it would not be proper for a man to call himself by the name of Christ, is it not a still greater outrage to see him appropriating to himself the attributes of Christ, and thus seeking to embellish his brazen image by assuming the sanctity of the "Saviour,"—and yet this is the commonest thing in life to behold. Not only the old things coming down to us from antiquity have put on new disguises, but words have changed, and many of them in their power and expression have degenerated; indeed language we may once have used to praise, now would be opprobrious, and regarded not simply as words, but as names, and particularly those of virtues, their exalted characteristics have become degraded, not alone to the low level of the most commonplace achievements, but to subserve the high ecomium we pronounce on everything we do. It is sickening to observe how magnificently they are applied to little deeds—yes, deeds only actually good enough to save the performer from being ignored or absolutely detested; thus, as I have said, in the mean but natural effort to swell the reward we aggrandize the deed, and most frequently, as we should not know merit but for the comparison to an opposite quality, the temptation is strong, failing our ability or inclination to exalt the former, to degrade the latter.

VI.

The fact is, mixed up and absorbed as we are in

the grovelling affairs of our daily life, our minds and our monstrous assumption of winged virtues are sailing upward and buzzing like flies close under the azure ceiling of the universe,—and there, fastening on to some of the glistening jewels of that heavenly sphere, they stick, and spawn, and multiply, till the object, by the sheer weight of these clustered insects, is drawn down and sinks to earth.—Then, like so many other things pertaining to our boasted eminence, when it rises into light again, as a thing that is drowned, it is brought to the top only by the gas engendered through corruption. Thus have we prostituted the good word Charity, and the virtue it represents has been so twisted and warped and disfigured that now, attired in the tawdry livery of public service, and set up in the jugglery business, all altered and disguised, her own sister, Truth, would not know her. Ah, when Charity put on her new shoes, she left her character in the old ones. Poor Charity, how sadly has the world corrupted thee, and where shall we find a meaner hack than thou! Thy tinselry was never more dazzling, but thy splendor may not shine like the spotless shene of thy lost innocence! Get thee back to the hollow mockeries of whose affluent condescension and sordid selfishness thou art but the graceful menial. Sincerity, in her humblest gown, would shame thee. Seek not, with thy bawdy smile, to ingratiate thyself into the refuge of the persecuted and despised, for the conditions of thy love are harder to bear than the penalty of their transgression. They may seem comforted under thy ministration, and sometimes, indeed, they are benefited, but the little thou bringest them is hampered like the sixpence with the medicine offered to the child. This is no inappropriate apostrophe to the jade we call Charity. But how is it, with all our esteem for what is pure and genuine, we should take pride in a counterfeit so disreputable? There is about the alchemy of words an ideal element peculiarly deceptive and pleasing; and whereas the transmutation of metals only aimed at the production of gold, the prize in this case is the enhancement of our self-esteem. Things that we know are not gold we call golden, and this distinction as regards material things is kept fairly defined, but as in things fanciful the opposite is the case, that which has ever so small a grain of kindliness we call charitable; but that little grain put under a lens as powerful as our disposition to exaggerate, and held up to public view, is magnified, so that a degree of excellence, only remotely pertaining to what is good, gets to be regarded as the good thing itself. Thus, as a clever lawyer often gains a case by the mere turn of an expression, and thereby reverses the whole order of right and wrong, so, like the hoodwinked jury, are we deceived by a subtle play on words, and the slightest glimmering of truth is flashed up into what is made to appear the full blazing orb. Aye, and as we jump in comparison of merit most absurdly from good to bad, so in the reverse order of panegyric, that which is not positively cruelty, gets to be lauded as superlative charity.

There are, it is true, redeeming shades of kindliness even in our pompous display of benevolence, but as the diamond absorbs the very faintest rays of light and flashes them back again great dazzling sunbeams, so have we monopolized the precious name and sublime mission of Charity, that she, like the diamond, may take in our most distant gleams of pity, and reflect back upon us a refulgent glory, not our own. In this way, too, may we account for much of the arrogance of people, and especially that preposterous assumption of superiority over others, which is a marked feature of our "higher life." I am bound to say it is only too often the absurd assumption of a magnificent moral and social elevation, all as ludicrous as to stride a stuffed eagle and imagine one's-self riding on a whirlwind, soaring, with all the brute instincts and incumbrances of the flesh, to an aerie in that virgin realm, whose purity is the perpetual and immaculate snow!

VII.

A poor man has fallen in the street; he may have been drunk, but now he is bruised and bleeding, may be dying; a public guardian takes him in charge and has him conveyed to the hospital, where he will be properly cared for. Is a regulation of this sort, charity? No there is no particle of charity about it. It is simply the exercise of common humanity, and anything less were brutality—cruelty! It may be said they feed and doctor and nurse him till he is well for a merely nominal charge which in case he has no money, is not insisted on. Well, such a provision, while being commendable, is at the same time necessary—it is wanting, however, in the ingredient of option, to make it seem even kindly—and as for its being charitable, it is no more so than any other excellent municipal regulation conducive to the public weal,—as, for instance, compulsory vaccination. Indeed, it is no particular credit to the good word benevolence to call it that, being as it really is, a simple common-place provision for all such emergencies as might be expected in communities priding themselves on their opulence and liberality, and abounding most plentifully, we may observe, where the generosities of the people are made the agreeable hobbies of the more affluent. True, the bill presented the poor convalescent is not exorbitant, it may be a mere bagatelle, but if he have ever so little money, they manage to worm it out of him, and in the case of the decrepit, if they have any work left in their old bones they manage to grind it out also, and that not always in the gentlest and most considerate manner. It is not my purpose, here, to examine the records of "Our Charities,"—they are, it is only too well known, replete with provocation, hypocrisy, and outrage. I simply ask, what constitutes their claims to the sublime title they have assumed? Is it the cheapness of these institutions? Aye, then, they are only such a refuge in misery and destitution, as may, not inappropriately, be termed "bon marché."

But you say, suppose a man build an institution and give it to the indigent and afflicted—now this is considered the "*pièce de resistance*," and anything but eulogy would be construed as downright blasphemy—well, is not that charity? I may seem obtuse, perverse, prejudiced, but I must emphatically say—No! The man who is able to do such a thing, has hoarded up his money and when he finds he cannot possibly use it to afford him the gratification he expected, he feels disappointed, chagrined; it loses its charm, and he says in that dire perplexity that baulks the most successful schemer—"What shall I do with it"— as a man would who is trying to run away with more than he can carry. He is just generous enough to decide not to bury it, as he would have a legal right to do; he knows he will not live long, and as founding an institution is the only way a man can decently build a monument to himself and live to enjoy it, he builds this monument, and the world bows down to it and calls it Charity, and the man a philanthropist; at the same time this good man may have brothers and sisters and aged parents grubbing through a miserable existence and suffering absolute privation, whom he utterly ignores or aggravates with some slight remembrance. In this connection, we may mention that a monument does not require the substratum of human dust to make it a memorial, and many of these, instead of being simple columns, are reared in the form of an edifice, or something that may be utilized, and as such serve a two-fold purpose,—they may be useful and beneficial to a community and at the same time memorize the person by whose bounty they were erected. So it is, now-a-days, when a large sum is given by way of "charity," the donor is rather prone to require it to take this shape, and seeks to make the gift the price of an enduring souvenir. Now, to give this amount away in small sums to the distressed, as we would administer medicine to the sick, does not seem to answer the purpose of the modern philanthropist, so he founds or endows an institution with the professed object of ameliorating future distress. This would be all very commendable, leaving out the question of motive, were it not that we have too many buildings of that sort now; besides, the public "benefactor," in this case, must inevitably have passed so many in the travail of great immediate want. And, why may we not quote in this connection, "and sufficient unto the day!" Nay, had the individuals referred to given away what they did in less noteworthy items, they might and probably must have done without a splendid "charity" monument, and the wealth therein entailed had been swallowed up in that great troubled sea of hungering humanity.

Again you say, can we hope to find anything more benevolent, more charitable, than our Romish and English Churches, together with their splendid group of affiliated institutions. It does appear that way and no doubt with a certain amount of desert; but we can only judge these institutions by our knowledge of individuals. I have seen men, and they were much above the average lot, who were sympathetic and "charitable" in a distant view of those objects and situations which are supposed to inspire such sentiments, and their voices, often raised in random commiseration, were a power of benevolence. I do not say they were not sincere, I believe in their way they were, and so far it was all well enough, considering the objects were sufficiently remote to allow them to conjure up cases they thought worthy of their approbation. But, mind you, it was all a charity of fancy,—a spectral comforter rising in the midst of their cheerful surroundings to make them flush and smile in self-gratulation,—a blooming exotic, with, however, insufficient fragrance, leave alone fruit, to overcome the first doubtful sniff of a conflicting smell. Their sympathy and charity was all invented on ideal, pattern principles to correspond, NOT to what misery *is*, but what it *ought* to be; and these same men brought close up to some disgusting novelty in the way of, not physical deformity, but real mental and bodily suffering, in nine cases out of ten, detect an odor about it or its history that displeases them, and they are, all at once, possessed with an insufferable repugnance—a positive aversion. The fact is, we are all humanitarians in the abstract, but bring us in actual contact with all the objectionable details, and the whys and wherefores that lead to trouble and down the hill to want and degradation, and it cools us off immensely, and the cucumber in our bosom is no longer a warm responsive heart.

So it is when a wrong is committed, the perpetrator, evincing a depravity actually only a few degrees below, not our fancy standard, but the real moral average, and a great hue and cry is raised,—the poor victim is regarded as a monster, an abnormal exception to the rest of his species, and as in the " reign of terror" during the French Revolution, so now, in our social intercourse, we dare not, if we would, sympathize; there is such a ticklish mistrust of self and of others' opinions of us, we think, we profess a becoming abhorrence of the criminal by approving and advocating an implacable and excoriating sentence, and in the chorus of denunciation no voice is heard so loudly vociferating *à la lanterne* as that of the "charitable" and "virtuous" *snob*. It is by such delusive excesses as I have attempted to describe, and by making up character by false and responsible estimates, we arrive at those grand results by which we swell the train of our pompous pretensions. It is thus we are exalted above ourselves, above regret, above pity, above penitence, and find so much that should excite our deepest commiseration, unable to commend itself to our overtrained and hackeneyed sensibilities. It is thus, too, we evangelize conceit, and canonize luxury, and make the slops that ooze out of the gluttonous ceremonial the boasted tribute we dub charity.

VIII.

In the lukewarm spasms of pity that flit in the sputtering tallow of our hearts, behold those beacon lights that radiate afar; but instead of warming and cheering the dingy refuge of the poor, they are made rather to shed a halo of pious benevolence around those ostentatious monuments we call "our charities." Our charities, forsooth! If these two words mean anything at all, then what a world of pent-up sympathy do they comprehend for the human race and for all the ills that "flesh is heir to,"—what inexhaustible reservoirs of loving, forgiving commiseration, not for the sweet-smelling and beautiful only, but for the most repulsive and the worst kind of tribulation and distress. There is, I admit, a halo of good intention surrounding these institutions; but perverted with fanaticism, fettered and chilled with theology, they are become a species of splendid advertisement—the good work, a competition of of rival sects for converts, and a conflict of bigots for souls. Here, poor broken-down humanity is prepared for dissolution by being put through the throes of exorcism, and all the comfort eked out of charity is pricking and bleeding in an agony of "thorns."—Symbols of benign intent moulded in stone, our charities are presented to the public in the splendid guise of imposing architecture, and yet to the poor and hungry their good cheer is as the feast of Tantalus, and their towering symmetry not less repulsive than the grimmest spectre of destitution.—Monuments of superabundance, rising sphinx-like in a desert, they smile down in gloomy grandeur, and while assuming to be hot-beds warming in tenderest sympathy, are, with rare exceptions, gilded refrigerators, which, while dripping tears of pity on the outside, are congealing within in an atmosphere of frost and ice.

As we have observed, there is a general tendency to sublimate not only petty deeds of so-called charity, but other things as well, which, while enhancing, to an absurd degree, the importance of acts which are simply humane or politic, gives a relative degree of respectability to others which, if not down-right despicable, are at least only mediocre. Thus, praising to the skies the performance of a simple duty, makes the omission to do what we ought to do seem, if not laudable, at least excusable. In saying aught against anything held in such jealous esteem as are the institutions to which I have referred, it may seem to many like scoffing at the Divine,—if so, my apology is they are not divine. Moreover, yielding the sublime tribute of charity to all that comes under the head of simple benevolence, however gratifying it may be to the giver of "alms" and the founder of memorial palaces for the poor, indicates, in my humble judgment, three things:—first, the fulsome puffing of our puny virtues; second, a vulgar estimate of the attributes of the Most High; third, the righteousness of protest. I cast no slur on the true spirit of religion; and in all I have said, I have failed to make myself understood, if I have not succeeded in inspiring the feeling that, on the one hand, we should set a higher estimate on all wise precept, and, on the other, cultivate a clearer, purer conception of all things pertaining to those virtues which go to make up the elements of a truly noble and ingenuous character. In the bearing such sentiments have upon my subject, I have sought to give them expression in words which, in justice to the effort, it must be confessed are weak and ineffectual, when compared with the more powerful and pathetic appeal of visible proof abounding on every side; and in this connection I may mention a tableau that often presents itself to my mind—I mean the sight of charity shivering on the steps of "our charities."

In conclusion, you may ask, what is Charity, then, to one so sceptical? I confess the answer is difficult. It is much easier to reply in the negative and tell what it is not and I may say emphatically it is not the thing we see paraded about, banqueted, and aggrandized, and apostrophized as such; indeed it is something more refined even than the extreme opposite of what is barbarous and cruel. Ah, but then you say with a little more deference for what the good word means, but all the more persistently, *who* is Charity? I answer, no one can tell. We may define the word but not the spirit. Indeed, to say she is the rarest and sublimest of all the virtues does not describe her, nor do her any manner of justice. Those who have felt her touch may know her by that—it is grateful and pure as the first reviving kiss of fragrant spring upon the cold marble cheek of poor frozen winter. We may feel and yet be powerless to define, and were I a Gainsborough, in word painting, I might have the desire but not the ability to attempt her portrait. Suffice it then as the most lovable if not the most beautiful of all the graces she had made a conquest of the heart of Christ, when He kissed Mary Magdalene, called her "sister," forgave her, and bade her "depart in peace and sin no more."

First Experience Under Fire.

FIRST EXPERIENCE UNDER FIRE.

A REMINISCENCE OF THE AMERICAN CIVIL WAR.

I.

ANY one who has never heard the "long roll," particularly in time of war, in camp and in close proximity to the enemy, has missed one of the most, I think I may say, the most stirring of all alarms. It is a continuous roll of the drum, seeming to increase in volume and intensity with each successive moment, and is kept up for some time, according to circumstances. It is never resorted to except in cases of extreme danger, and then, while it never fails to inspire the liveliest apprehension in the minds of many, the emergency calls into requisition all the silent, questionless alacrity of the soldier. The meaning is, "to arms," and the crisis almost warrants the assumption that the enemy is in sight and advancing to attack. Then comes the quick incisive order to "fall in," and straightway each company commander and subaltern, each sergeant and private, vies with the other in the credit and honor of being first in "company" and on "battalion line." Every thought, every business or diversion other than that pertaining to the new and startling situation must give way, and yield the most prompt obedience to that inexorable summons to expectant combat, the issue of which is life or death, and the near approach of the dread alternative is unmismistakably proclaimed in that fateful roll and rueful rumble of the drum. The change, then, from the monotonous routine of every-day camp life to all the necessary preparations for attack and defence, can only in a very slight degree be imagined by those whose good fortunes have "cast their lines" far away from the arena of bloody strife, in those pleasant ways of peace and harmony where nothing more serious disturbs the quiet serenity of social life than the occasional uproar of an anniversary, the discord of a domestic squall, or the sudden jar of an unfriendly knockdown. Some are reading or writing—not a few telling stories or playing cards, and many lounging about homesick and listless. Not the least displeased, too, of the many who find this change of programme objectionable, are those engaged, as quite a number are likely to be, in the popular and highly commendable process of preparing the coming meal. It may be that which is welcomed so gratefully, either in the bracing, appetizing air of early dawn, or in the hungrier, more sumptuous hour of noon. Under any other conditions, cookie's time-honored prerogative of exemption had held its ground inviolable and supreme, but none better than he knows, in this great emergency, how sweeping and inexorable that imperative summons, so significantly heralded, of "All fall in." If, then, he stops to remove from the treacherous fire his little feast of savory stew, his tempting roast of beef or fowl, he does so in frantic haste, and at his own proper peril.

I believe it was in the autumn of '63 that the event to which my narrative refers took place. We were encamped near the little village of Suffolk, in Eastern Virginia, and had been having a very "soft thing" of it, with very little to do, outside our regular drill, but ride about, get up games, and have our photographs taken; not a few of us at this time developing a faculty for correspondence we didn't know we possessed before, but it was of the "spicy" sort; our reading too, was not the kind to win us promotion, being of the order yclept "light;" history, it is true, we patronized, not, however, as consumers, but producers. Our *ménu* was rather scant, and we alternately fasted on "hard-tack and salt-horse," furnished by a none too liberal commissariat, and feasted on the boxes of good things sent from home. We used to have occasional marches out for a change, but so far had hardly exchanged shots with the enemy, having honorably managed, some way, to shy round one and other, and there had been nothing of what might be called fighting with our regiment, although some of the others had had a little "out-post" exercise, not unattended with bloodshed. Thus far I was not able to boast of having been under fire, and the little narrative of my maiden engagement was still a thing of the future. Indeed, up to this time I knew no more about the music of bullets than had been obtainable, in a rudimentary way, in cautiously avoiding the range at target practice. From this, it may be inferred, I think correctly, that I, for one, was not "spoiling for a fight;" nevertheless my turn was coming, and not long to be delayed. I remember the day, but not the date; had that evening received a box from home, full of all sorts of luxuries and lots of good things to eat, drink and be merry over; such, indeed, as but one woman in the world can devise, and she I always claimed to be my own mother. We did have a grand feast on this occasion—a regular tuck-out, and one to be recalled subsequently in many a trying interval of starvation and hardship. When the banquet was over and our little band had wished each other good-night, I got out my pipe to smoke a "nightcap," and think of home, and of the one especially to whose affection and forethought I was indebted for such good cheer. Then it was, I think, I began to feel a bit gloomy, and, in my absent-mindedness, let my pipe go out, which, with me, is a bad sign; am not sure but that I had the least shade of a presentiment of something about to happen, of a nature unhappily contrasting with our evening's entertainment. Before turning in, I poked my head out to take a look around—"taps" had sounded some time before, and with the extinguishing of lights, for which they are the signal, had come an end to revelry. The camp was hushed and dark, and the convivial orgies of the eight hundred men who composed out battalion, had died away into silence and repose. I had hardly lain down and commenced the harmless exercise of snoring, when I was aroused by a fearful rumbling sound, which grew louder and louder till it seemed to grapple my drowsy senses and shake them wide awake. Then I was able to distinguish the tramping of feet outside, and the confused hum of voices, amongst which could be heard the harsh, guttural word of command. At this moment there was a sudden spring from the bunk next to mine, and the voice of my old chum, West, exclaimed impulsively:—"It's the long roll, by Jove!"

II.

It seems our pickets had been driven in, and, of course, we had been ordered out. From this point in my narrative we may pass lightly over what transpired till we near the scene of action and of my first experience under fire. At any rate, owing to the confusion, I do not remember much of what occurred until some distance had been traversed on the march out. Our direction was across the Nancimond river, westerly towards the Blackwater; the latter stream was some eight or ten miles away, the former just outside our line of fortifications. This was the route whence the alarms generally proceeded, and which we generally took; it led right into the enemy's country, where there was understood to be a large force assembled, threatening our stronghold—in fact we had been expecting to be besieged every day, as indeed we were, later, by General Longstreet. The night was dubious, and gave rather unpleasant indications of a storm—a star twinkled fitfully here and there through chinks in the clouds, seeming to give eyes to vapory monsters that looked down upon a darkened scene, lighted, from time to time, by those fantastic flames and phosphorescent flashes peculiar to the swamp regions of the south.

The roads, which were, as might have been expected in that part of the country, miserably bad, led nearly all the way through bog and bush land, being crossed by numberless little streams, but no bridges. I always feel rather "skittish" in the woods at night; I don't mean frightened but fidgety, though in the day-time no one can be more ready or willing to take refuge there, and well do I call to mind the dash and energy with which I have penetrated their recesses in quest of deer or partridge. But this was quite a different sort of game; heretofore, the shooting had been all on my side, now the honors were to be divided, and I confess the change was not so agreeable as might have been supposed by those who are descended from a warlike family, and from ancestors to whom fighting was at once an agreeable pastime, and an anti-dyspetic exercise. Without feeling, as I remember, any special desire to meet the enemy, I had managed to appear pretty fairly and becomingly indifferent; but the nature of the low lying, swampy, woody country, hedging us in all round, was suggestive in the extreme, and more than once I found myself calculating the chances of an ambuscade; but that was unpleasant to ponder over, so I tried to think of something else. It was no unwelcome diversion that I began to feel about this time a bit hungry, and my thoughts recurred to the box I had received and the good things, all snug in camp awaiting my return, and a renewal of the feast. It is always cheering to anticipate the keen appetite one will be sure to have after so much marching and fasting; on these occasions, too, one's mind turns back to home and friends, and now as we marched silently along, I believe those amongst us who had any body to care for them, thought of the place far away, where they had said good-by, and wondered wistfully what a night might bring forth. My thoughts, at least, took some such

FIRST EXPERIENCE UNDER FIRE.

a turn. I was a mere boy then, but it all comes up in vivid retrospect, how I thought I saw something in dear old mother's anxious face that made me uneasy; indeed, I think then I wished myself well quit of that night's business, and was quite willing and ready to exchange all the romance of war, or at least that which was likely to accrue to my heroism, for the more precious assurance of an undiminished length of humble, prosy biography, in that hill-side home which, under the circumstances seemed so incomparably " the dearest spot on earth."

III.

Our column was composed of one brigade of infantry, two regiments of cavalry, and one battery of artillery; * also, I may add here, a company of sharp-shooters, though they never count much in a fight. As we approached the place where the enemy was thought to be posted, we were constantly being startled by false alarms from the front, and though these were somewhat of an annoyance, and not a little strain on our nerves, they kept us from being as drowsy as we otherwise should have been, and as one is apt to be in a lonesome tedious march at night. In this way we had been trudging along for over two hours in constant apprehension, and without discovering any sign of opposition. It was not the first time we had been routed out of our comfortable beds, for what turned out to have been a

---

* 69th, 99th, 130th New York, and the 13th Indiana regiments, Infantry; 11th Pennsylvania Cavalry, and 1st N. Y. Mounted Rifles; an Indiana battery, together with a detachment of 5th United States Artillery.

midnight "wild-goose-chase," and there was already some show of grumbling in the ranks. Meanwhile, am not aware I was particularly disappointed to feel our chances for a meeting were growing slimmer, and the prospect of a "brush" dwindling away into a tedious countermarch back to camp. Any uneasiness I may have felt at first however, was rapidly subsiding, when all at once the stillness of every body and every thing around and amongst us was broken by the sharp detonation of a dozen shots fired in quick succession—these were followed almost immediately by a volley, and then another and still louder discharge, all of which rang out with startling distinctness on the night air.

This little by-play took place at a point about a mile or so distant in our front, and the intelligence was flashed back upon the whole length and breadth of our weary, listless column that at last we had struck the foe,—we knew, then, that the chorus of rifles still ringing in our ears, was, as it turned out to be, our advance guard in contact with and driving in the enemy's outpost. If my memory serves me right, I am correct in saying it was not found necessary to issue the order that all dreaming should be temporarily discontinued. We were all thoroughly aroused, and having been halted opened out nimbly in two lines to the right and left of the road. This was to make way for the General commanding, (Corcoran), who galloped up smartly from the "rear," and proceeded to the "front," closely followed by his staff and the battery

FIRST EXPERIENCE UNDER FIRE.

of artillery all *à la pêle-mêle*. Then we closed in quickly behind, and resumed our forward movement.

From this time on, till under fire, I felt a strange tingling sensation, together with an all absorbing but not unpleasant interest in what we knew was coming. The feeling of dread, all had no doubt experienced at first, had yielded directly, and was superseded by a general impulse to rush forward and do something, anything, to relieve the fast growing eagerness and suspense. On our way, as we passed the spot where the picket firing had taken place, I got my first sight of a wounded man; he was lying down partly stripped, in charge of the surgeon who seemed to be endeavoring to trace the course of a bullet which had penetrated the region of the lungs. He was a mere lad,—I caught a glimpse of his face by the light of a lantern, it was pale and ghastly looking,—but he was quiet and resigned, and seemed only weary and faint. This tableau had rather a bad effect on my nerves, and I believe just then my face indicated symptoms of early and rapid decline, or that, at least, I was not in my usual robust health and spirits. The spectacle of the wounded and dying is a severe ordeal for men advancing to share in the vicissitudes of an engagement; indeed, it is the season of probation, that besets people in every sphere in life, only under the circumstances of which I speak it is greatly condensed with the travail of spirit proportionately intensified. There may be immunity from it, but with some it is the toughest strain they have to bear.

IV.

We had struck the enemy under General Pryor, at a place called "Deserted House," and the fight which ensued was simply an artillery duel over a field, say eight or nine hundred yards across, environed with forest and swamp. The position of our regiment, after deploying, was about fifty yards in rear of and "supporting" the artillery, and while taking post I did not fail to observe we were being brought right fairly within the focus of our opponents' fire. Sometime before we got settled, our battery, a tidy instrument of fifteen guns, had commenced the the exchange of preliminary compliments with the enemy, who, as it was afterwards ascertained, had about the same weight of metal. Both sides now opened the ball in earnest, at point blank range over a bit of meadow land smooth as a tenis lawn and flat as a billiard table. The gunners, too, roused as they had been from the lethargy of a chill night air, had unlimbered and gone to work with even more than their habitual gusto, and each piece served with a skill which, through long practice anticipates dilemma, when the emergency comes, it dispenses with deliberation, and acting at a glance, the precision is easy and faultless as the puzzling aptitude of a deft " cue."

Now the darkness which had before enveloped us, began to give way to the incessant flash of burning powder, and the sulphurous smoke all threw over the scene a lurid glare, not unlike that we may have witnessed on the stage in incantation scenes of Druid worship. We could see the cannoneers at work, bringing up bullets and ammunition from the caissons, and loading and firing, and they seemed for all the world like those demons of the Catskills who performed at nine pins, and gesticulated with such elfish glee, before the placid Rip van Winkle. Notwithstanding matters began to assume an air so business-like, still, I confess, for a while I did not, in any degree, realize the situation in all its solemn and dreadful aspect; even attempted an off-hand joke, not so much to appear funny, as that I thought it would indicate a becoming nonchalance, and so exclaimed :—" Boys, I'm thinking we'll have lights to-night without candles!" Had hardly got the words well out of my mouth, when what seemed to me an uncommonly solid shot struck the top of a tree which had spread its protecting arms over our heads, bringing down a shower of leaves and broken limbs. I may add here, I joked no more that night—felt admonished levity would not be tolerated. Soon after this, the order was passed to lie down; in the execution of this simple manœuvre I gave the example to the rest of the men, and had presence of mind enough to select low ground.

V.

The cannonade quickly reached its climax, and the crash, to my unaccustomed ears, was simply terrific. Besides, the discharges followed each other so rapidly as to seem almost a continuous roar, except now and then, a simultaneous explosion altogether, not unlike we occasionally hear in a mild sort of way, in the irregular clashing of cathedral bells,—then, the earth trembled with the thunder of a salvo, after which came a momentary pause, worse, even, in its tiresome unstringing of nerves than the concussion itself. They were no empty, meaningless, compliments, those giant detonations,—all so like and yet so different from the frolicsome hubbub of noisy anniversaries,—nay, pat-shots were those huge, plunging, shrieking missiles of death, and skinning the ground so closely too, as they seemed to me. Our adversaries' range for a while was, as is almost invarably the case in firing, too high, close, but not close enough; they were not long, however, in discovering the defect, and set about, as only skilful workmen can, rectifying it; then down, down, down, came that awful trajectory! I say I lay flat, but how I longed and shortened and squirmed to get flatter, aye, and for the superlative degree of flat. How lovingly I cuddled that damp, cold ground, I never can forget, and I see now before me, as plainly as if it had just happened, the eagerness and frantic despair, or maybe I ought rather to say, presence of mind, with which I sought to find a less exposed place, at the same time keeping as low and as quiet as if all but my extremities were paralyzed. I see my hands and fingers gliding about me now, to find that devoutly longed for dimple in the ground, and no pitying mother, caressing the bruised and tender bump of a firstborn could have been half so persistent and yet so gentle,—no blind man, spelling out with his fingers' ends the gladsome hope of restored vision, could have had a touch more exquisitely sensitive than mine as I felt about me for that priceless indentation, that microscopic chasm wherein to take refuge and to alter, by the fraction of a hair, the awful chances of that gradually sinking parabola of fire. And oh horrors those louder explosions seemed almost to raise a fellow up! The night was cool and even frosty, and yet there was a closeness about everything, and the very air seemed tainted with a belligerent odour that was suffocating and oppressive in the extreme.

I have no hesitation in affirming that had I been the owner of Chatsworth, I had gladly given it to have been at the north pole in search of the toothbrush and shirtbuttons of Sir John Franklin. I could have been buried alive, indeed, and sphinx-like looked out upon the battle and enjoyed it, but as it was, there I lay all night right in the focus of hell-fire. At one time one of our caissons blew up, and at another, I remember, a shell struck directly in front of where I lay and ricochetted over our heads, splashing the dirt up in our faces; of all that interested crowd of watchful spectators I don't believe one " ducked " on this occasion, they hadn't time. Those bullets come on so precipitately, and take one so confoundedly by surprise. Presently came my experience of " first killed," I mean in our immediate vicinity. A solid globe of iron, propelled at a velocity of something less than five hundred yards per second, plumped like a shadow right into the line of crouching, shrinking, shivering forms. It had grazed the ground quite near where I lay—ah, I hear it now, and it sounded in the uproar then, not unlike the scratching of my pen, and the impression, in one way, is similar to that we are so familiar with when a cricket ball at Prince's, or the Oval, taking the direction of the grand stand, lands amongst the ladies' petticoats: there is a thud and one imagines a muffled sound as of yielding garments,—a murmur, too, as of stifled sobs, and then all is quiet till the roar of the battle, which seemed hushed a moment, rushes in again.

VI.

That shot killed two of our best men and wounded several. It was more than I could bear calmly, expectantly. There was in our company a German sergeant of very extensive proportions, indeed, when he sat down he was able fully to monopolize a small sized pew. The bulky veteran was then lying near by. Here was a chance—this was the moment that came to Wellington at Waterloo, and that Ney missed at Quatre Bras,—I mean the happy nick of time caught in a glance of lightning rapidity,—that subtle period between perfect fruition and incipient perishing, that one requires to strike, to win the prize, dame fortune, in a fickle mood, allows to gleam an infinitesimal space of time the unguarded prey of those eagle perceptions which, like Napoleon's or Nelson's, seem rather to divine than wait the full development. I ordered the sergeant to creep up to where I was—he should have been there anyway, although he was not skulking, being, as I can vouch, a brave soldier and a worthy man. I now put him in the front rank, the post of honour, and modestly settled myself flat down, directly in rear of, and close up to his antecedents. After this stage of the battle I became more tranquil and resigned. Meanwhile, my friend Captain Taylor, who commanded the next company on our left, had not fared so well; his courage had been high enough to raise him on his elbows, where, with his head cocked, he had been watching the rapid play of the rival batteries. We learn by experience to judge danger by certain signs, and under the circumstances of being "shelled" at night, as we were, an important indication of mischief was the light of the fuse which the enemy was then using; if stationary in its flight you might consider yourself directly in range, as any other than a direct line would give it motion. Whether poor Taylor had watched these fire-flies till he had become emboldened or whether he saw in that stationary glimmer a horrible, resistless fascination that rendered him powerless to avert his doom, will never be known; on comes the fatal slug, a hissing, shrieking, precursor of destruction—a dull, heavy concussion is heard,—there is a splashing of earth behind the captain, who, turning quietly but quickly over on his back, looks up to the blue arch above, it might have been in the mute consciousness of having, in soldier parlance, escaped "a close call," and as if in the silent depths of unutterable gratitude he would have said for the little ones at home and the anxious prayerful wife far away,—"God, I thank thee!" His brother by his side sees his white, ghastly face near his own, and shakes him in the rude impulse of a dawning fear,—then, shrinks away! Alas! that once manly form and robust physique had, in a flash, undergone the dreaded metamorphosis of death. The ball had disembowelled him completely, but he was not otherwise mangled. I noticed, next day, the gilt buttons of his waistcoat were quite flattened as if with a hammer, though none of them, that I could perceive, were detached. Some excitement in the ranks at one time seemed to attract the attention of my sergeant (the one I before referred to) and he commenced gathering himself up as if he contemplated a change of base; this new intention on his part was far from meeting my approbation, but, whatever his plan was, I did not suffer it to ripen—I "nipped it in the bud." Raising myself slightly, and calling the the sergeant by name, I said, (throwing at the same time all the thunder into my voice I could spare):—" Sergeant, if you move, you are a dead man;" and then I added, in a tone of gentle reproof,—" we are holding a position of great importance, and our country calls us to be firm."

Later on, when I had become a trifle more used to this sort of thing, I went with Lieutenant West to another part of the field, and chance threw us into company with the Colonel of our regiment. We were walking along together when a shell dropped and exploded with a deafening noise close at hand; indeed, it seemed right at our very feet, an appearance which I afterwards found was deceptive. I did not "start"—no, that expression is not quite strong enough—I jumped, I leaped right up into the air, as if every nerve in my sensitive body had been probed, and for a moment or two I thought the breath had been knocked right out of me. It was not so much fear either as that I was surprised, and I think the Colonel, a bluff, profane old veteran, saw it in this light, for he swore at me in his gentlest, most considerate tone and manner, and in language too terrible to be repeated here, philosophized as regards that awfully hot place to which, had that shell been intended for me, I must inevitably have gone ere I had time to jump.

VII.

Towards morning the enemy's fire slackened, and we found at daylight, when our line advanced, their main force had retired beyond pursuit. We had quite a number of killed and wounded; one poor boy, a bugler, I noticed with more than common regret as having received his quietus that night. He had been a marvellous mimic in his way, and had created more amusement for the regiment than all the rest of our humorous talent put together. They called him "Banty," and many a drenched and dreary bivouac had the exercise of his peculiar faculty made to pass the more cheerily. This eventful morning, however, found him sitting up against a tree—I thought at first he was asleep—the poor lad looked as if he were only tired of making fun, and had relapsed, as such characters often do, into an uncommon fit of seriousness, but alas, poor Banty! a fragment of shell had entered his brain, and he was quite dead.

Apropos of casualties, I may mention, that it is erroneous to think, as some do, that the wounded and dying in an engagement give vent to their misery in loud cries of agony and supplication. When a man is hit, he drops —that is if badly hurt—but it is no rare occurrence that a strong man will keep right on loading and firing, although severely wounded, and in his excitement not even notice it, till he falls exhausted,—not from exertion, as he thinks, but from loss of blood. The mortally wounded sink right down—saying not a word, and passing away without evincing much if any pain. But while in those hard cases, there is a kind and mercifully soothing sort of numbness, which makes the blow comparatively easy to bear, there is a way of being hit, which, while there is no particle of injury done, the effect is altogether most painful and terrifying—I mean in the case of a "spent ball"—and then it is not at all uncommon to see the bravest men behave like children, and set up a most pitiful wail although the missile did not even penetrate the skin, and was nothing worse than a "stinger."

As regards first experience under fire, I believe the sensations I have attempted to describe were not exclusively applicable to my own case, but are felt to a greater or less extent by all who participate, for the first time, in that especially rough game of war,—and who, in their fresh, blooming novitiate, find themselves situated as I was, in that most trying of all predicaments in which a soldier, though he be a veteran, can be placed,—that is, inactive, within easy range of a well-served battery, and right within the focus of a well-sustained artillery fire of shot and shell, with now and then the spicy novelty of a sprinkling of "shrapnel." In the ordinary affairs of life, we not unfrequently pass through emergencies of a most dangerous character, but under such circumstances that we realize but a small fraction of the risk involved, and, only mildly admonished, we are enabled to appear quite indifferent; or we may on occasions of a senseless fright swell with the bravado of a false alarm, and humoring the solicitude of others to the full extent, appreciate the danger ourselves only so far as to appear comfortably heroic; and this, I believe, is the commonest and, I have no doubt, the most popular test of bravery. I do not flatter myself in saying I had always, up to the time I speak of, enjoyed a full gift of nerve necessary to sustain me unflinchingly in the ordeal of the somewhat hackneyed but still much applauded "hair-breadth escape," and on the strength of this reputation I am emboldened to admit, frankly, that when under fire for the first time, lying supinely on the ground supporting that battery of ours, I was the prey of very grave and troubled thoughts. To be so near the belching mouths of the enemy's cannon, as almost to feel the scorching fire singe my hair, brought me in rather unhappy communion with the spirit world, and instead of all the convivial pleasantry of habitual companionship there seemed surrounding those ponderous globes, as they sped shrieking and spluttering on their death errand, a shadowy group, which fancy clothed in all the uncongenial paraphernalia appropiate to the occasion. It was playing football with devils (that is what it seemed like to me), and on the very brink of that fathomless abyss whose bottom is an infernal mystery! I only draw it mildly when I say in my first battle I was wanting in the enthusiasm necessary to make my share in the sport a success. There were certain restraining influences that kept me, much against my inclination, tolerably firm at my post, or I am sure I could have run away—gone back ingloriously to the rear—anywhere, in fact, to get out of the way of that "iron hail." Such a retreat, then, indeed, seemed embellished with all those ineffable charms incident to existence, and I felt I could have reposed in such a goal, fully rewarded for the absence of the blood-stained laurels of war in the undisturbed enjoyment of those other dearer emblems of peace!

Thus it is in imminent personal peril we realize most vividly *that the grandest position in glory is a little kingdom whose monarch is Death! and the meanest refuge in security a gorgeous World, whose sovereign is Life!!*

Granite and Ashes.

GRANITE AND ASHES,

OR GLEANINGS FROM THE SEPULCHRES OF GREAT ENGLISH STORY-TELLERS.

I.

IT was once my good fortune, to sojourn a short time in the South of Ireland. In the midst of that charming scenery which has given to Erin the characteristic title of Emerald, are embosomed those fairy lakes of Killarney. As I sat musing by the shore, one beautiful moonlit evening, there came stealing over the lily-capped waters that exquisite strain of melody from Balfe,—"Then You'll Remember Me." I took the music somewhat to heart, and the turn then and there given to a train of naturally sentimental reflection, gave rise to this essay.

In our twilight communings with the spirit, there comes up at times a mute but pathetic appeal from the "flesh," and the query, how shall we be remembered, how soon forgotten, finds its expression and answer in a sigh; the though itself is one shade nearer the nightfall, and obtruding its sombre visage like a spectre, casts a shadow over the gladness of life's earlier, brighter dream. 'Tis then we shrink from the contemplation of our phantom future, and turning to the more genial and instructive survey of others, and what they have done to be remembered, we regard with eager interest the impress they have left of earthly ties.

These reflections, commingling with kindred observations, have led to the following imperfect sketch and to such a grouping of ideas as were suggested by the refrain of that sweet old song, and by the conjunction of two significant words—Granite and Ashes.

There is about that cruel word oblivion, an import so dreadful, that, although we do not realize it, the very thought of it may well make the abode of the damned, seem, in contradistinction, an asylum if not so agreeable and satisfying as the poet's dream of Paradise, at least a most acceptable substitute; and even a condition of pain hereafter, notwithstanding all that is said against it, might then appear an exquisite and grateful relief taken in connection with the boon of restored life, without which we could not suffer; and tenacious as we are of existence, such an issue of all our hopes and prayers, untoward as it may seem, may, nevertheless, gladden out hearts, as when some loved one, crushed and maimed, is aroused from a death-like insensibility, and opens his eyes and moans.

As in our thoughts of after-life, so in this do the humble as well as the great naturally aspire to oppose as much as possible such an all-devouring blight as would lap up and swallow every trace of their bodily existence; and in this trying emergency we are indebted to the handicraft of two representative fellow-beings, both of whom cooperate in succouring what would otherwise perish forever away—I refer to the conservatism of Art, as demonstrated in the sublime labors of two of Nature's greatest admirers, and man's most earnest workers—the *painter* and the *sculptor*. We point to a portrait by Vandyke, and the form and features of Charles I., who has been dead over two hundred years, look down upon us in the fresh prime of life and in the lusty zenith of his robust health and manly beauty! So, too, in the lapse of three centennials from to-day, as the posterity of the patriots of Bunker Hill gather together on Boston Common, to celebrate the birth of liberty on the American continent, they will look upon a life-like statue in their midst, and hail in pride and admiration the imperishable image of Washington.

The products of great masters in Art, these likenesses may have cost much of the nation's treasure to secure; but in the case of the "sovereign" George, as we, the loving children of the "father of his country," take the true impress of his noble lineaments to our hearts, who can find it in his mind to say, the price was too high; and as for the monarch Charles, what a puny recompense in exchange for even this species of perpetuated mortality, the fleeting trinket of royalty,—the dissolving bagatelle of kingdom.

While we may not all have nor expect a splendid memorial,—which, as a work of art, may survive to the latest generations,—nevertheless, though shorn of all the costly splendor that enriches the more princely mausoleum, there is a quality inherent in the record of the simplest life, and commingling with the humblest dust, even sublimer and more effective;—it is that element of memory which, clinging to deeds, suffices in the prolongation of existence to enable one's virtues to outlive his faults.

To "let the dead bury their dead" was all very well in primitive times and in the days of leprosy, when to bury a man out of sight, to forgive him for having lived, and to forget him was the last best service the living could perform; but it seems to me, things have changed somewhat since such an interpretation of that injunction obtained. There are many, and among them our best men, who require to be long dead to be known and appreciated.—Moreover, for centuries, Enterprise has identified those rare intellects so closely with Progress, that the short time allotted our great men to live amongst us is found too short, and the influence they may still exert, too powerful and abiding, to "let the dead bury their dead"—so we hand down their effigy and their example from generation to generation.

While the masses, and among them many good men, seem destined to sink from obscurity into oblivion, others there are who never die, and in this sense are never buried; they are become identified, it may be, with some project, the grave seems but one stage of the work, and death, in its application, like sleep, only to supply a defect in our organization requiring rest; that is all,—and after the pause twixt sunset and sunrise, the work goes on with the same master minds seemingly alive and animating. Thus great and needful undertakings are carried on over a space of successive lives to completion; consecutive generations, in the spirit, have hold of the rope like sailors,—with here and there a voice, a living voice, to give the word—and they pull, those phantoms, and heave together till the sails, catching and filling with the cumulative impulse of the wafting breeze, the great social ship of human affairs, cleaves onward!

Here, we may observe, in qualification of the above, there is a certain conceit strutting abroad, and appropriating much of the credit that ought to be shared in common with those who are no more. This age, particularly in the new world, is become egotistical in the extreme, and it is simply erroneous to attribute to it, alone, the advancement we see at this time. The works, or at least the principles upon which they were wrought, were planned and put in operation long before the unfurling of our "starry banner,"—long, indeed, before the "Jack" of England had suggested the economy of union, —aye, when the seed of our national greatness was in embryo, and when the great-great-grandfather of our Franklin was a skittish boy, the philosophy of our republican institutions had been chewing its cud for over two thousand years, and in moral and political isolation and disuse, had grown old, and stale, and obsolete.

II.

The case of our grand Republic, in the above connection, reminds one of the apprentice who, stealing the ideas and designs of the master, and absconding, sets up shop on his own account, ignoring altogether the old firm, and the tutelage of generations acquired in mother land. In this manner there is engendered a feeling of contempt for the past, its wisdom and counsels, such as one gets to feel for preceptors and old men. We may notice further, that among communities and nations, there is a tendency as strong as human selfishness, not simply to utilize results, but to claim at the same time a monopoly of the credit in the means by which these results have been obtained; of course, in the same ratio as we belittle the achievements of those who are gone by, do we aggrandize our own efforts; and thus, is the principal glory and applause, appropriated and enjoyed by modern apostles and contemporaries.

The history of invention and improvement, not only in mechanical industry, but also in state policy, is prolific in trial and persecution,—in obloquy and repudiation,—toward the early pioneers of modern triumph; and with no feeling of sympathy, and still less esteem and gratitude for those noble hearts and great intellects, that, in a long weary struggle expired on the threshold and in the very shock and awe of prodigious discovery,—we eulogize and aggrandize those who, in the robust impetuosity of juniors, come bustling later in upon the scene. And so, in the predisposition to patronize what is contemporary, the productions of our generation, like fruits in season, commend themselves in preference to what we are most prone to regard as the fossil deposits of antiquity. Hence, I reiterate, that notwithstanding an affected admiration for "old masters," the tendency, as I have noticed, is strongly to ignore, if not to obloquize men who lived long ago, and whose works are remembered only to be contrasted with the so-called superior attainments of our day. In some respects, this discrepancy may be justified. If we take, for example, Literature,—that mighty medium through which we are enabled to communicate with the dead world, and to obtain, as we think, a correct knowledge of the past—here, the *outgrowth*, not so much of ideas and principles as of their *expression*, and the peculiar manner of their conveyance, necessitates, for the convenience of our understanding, new works. It must be admitted that nothing in the light of wisdom can be, or has been, added to the philosophy of Socrates, the logic of Aristotle, or the metaphysics of Plato, to make them more complete, but we have so far outlived their language and times, that the subjects on which they treated in a manner never since equalled, much less surpassed, have afforded material to immortalize a host of successors, who, had they lived in those olden times, had possibly never been known.

It is not so much, indeed, the great flood of original light shed in modern times, as the obscuration of old ideas and expression through lapse of time; and thus, in the tendency of all records to outlive their true meaning, it comes about, that in the more modern recast of old time thought, "savants," (I mean by them, delvers into the murky mysteries of the *recondite*), and from them that imposing phalanx of the mechanically illuminated, (I mean those tutored parrots we esteem as our "educated," our "professional," and our "public men"), are enabled to substitute themselves and take, in a manner, undisputed precedence over their predecessors, and in our better understanding of their fresh, living phraseology we gratefully accord some of them, at least, the partial virtue of "new-light."

Here, too, we may note in behalf of the living, that the virtues of a few of the defunct set have grown abnormally with age, and through the medium of reiterated praise, have attained for individuals an atmosphere of glory, that owes much of its hallowed splendor to a glamour of purely extraneous fancy. Then, it is the *nimbus* with which imagination encircles objects that are too remote for "ocular demonstration." Practically, however, taking men of note in literature, standing successively each behind the other, and reaching from a late, back into an early period, we find those comparatively in front, enjoy the largest patronage. But this, as we have noted, is because there is hardly a train of thought, the latest expression of which does not appeal the most strongly to our sympathies; and yet, the great wealth of wisdom on which they draw, is the brains of past generations—and a comparison of epochs, and a glance into the great silent world of the obsolete, reveal the fact that the literary spawn of the nineteenth century, like the designs of that prolific goddess Fashion,—and the plethora of books striving to keep pace with the newspapers, and shed with the fecundity of fly-blows on raw meat, are, for the most part, only a clever modification of old ideas recut, and turned, and dressed up to suit new and later styles of thought and expression. And to the commendable efforts which have been made to simply emancipate some of these from antiquated prejudice, and to the comparatively humiliating process of remodelling others, do many of our "distinguished men of letters," to-day, owe their envied and much lauded reputations. And the ignorant and thoughtless call these men great, and the age in which they live mighty, and bow down and worship them; but, however much aptitude and even talent, we may see displayed, it is, after all, in its most ancient and honorable aspect, only such astute old politicians as Lycurgus, and Solon, transmitting with the stamp of their individuality the lessons of still earlier civilizations,—and later, true to the classic example of Xenophon fathering the scriptless wisdom of Socrates, we have the venerable More, manufacturing "Utopia" out of the "Republic" of Plato,—Chaucer revelling in the alien wealth of Boccaccio,—Spenser blowing the sparks that light his imagery from the ashes of Ariosto,—Luther fulminating the train laid by Wycliffe,—aye, and Vespucius filching immortality from the story of Columbus!!

In this manner do the works if not the teachings of the old set become, at least so far as the generality of people are concerned, obsolete, obliterated, forgotten,— the palm of originality is passed along and enjoyed as *spolia opima* of later generations of men, and hence it is so many of our granite memorials apply only to present times, new men, and fresh triumphs.

The reason for the order of merit being in a manner successive and largely exclusive, is in the outgrowth before mentioned ; and this is regulated, not merely by fancy, but by the immutable law of change. Everything is in a state of restless, tireless transition.—Words, idioms, *vernaculars* are changing,—and language, in which is embalmed our knowledge of events and characacter, in its variable meanings and chameleon-like ways, presents all the puzzling shifts of the kaleidoscope.

Impressions and chronicles of past occurrences, presented and imbibed in our younger days as sober, historic fact, we are assured by the same kind of unimpeachable authority, were but the offspring of fancy, a misrepresentation of truth, and perniciously false.—Opinions that obtained a century, a year, a month, an hour ago, are turned and twisted out of all semblance to the original, and this even on the very same statement of facts.—No two events ever did or ever can occur under exactly the same conditions, and those stereotyped formulas applicable to one case, can only be approximately so to others, and are made available by modification and change.—An outgrowth of fealty is engendered, and insensibly but irresistibly we attorn from the old seed to the new fruit; but so gradually does the metamorphosis steal over us, we think we are cleaving to the one when we are conceiving and maturing the other. —Much of what we were wont to hold sacred, is become apocryphal and absurd, and forms once reverenced with jealous devotion, are come to be regarded only as customs or idle spectacles; and, as in the case of the early drama, ceremonies, commemorative of religious events and made the objects of pious observance, have degenerated,—as did the Saturnalia of ancient, and I think I may add also, as has the Christmas of modern times.—Enterprise, Reform, in all the sturdy greed of their lustful impulses, are opposing Conservatism, demanding change, and in order to build new structures, deplete old ones.—Progress, Utility oppose duration, because improvement necessitates substitution and involves annihilation; a thing may be a welcome novelty to-day, and stand forth as the perfection of a wonderful revelation, to-morrow, it is set aside for a more acceptable substitute. Nay, however precious a thing may be, so long as avarice is a ruling passion, the lasting properties of any structure is measured in a great, degree by the magnitude of the temptation to destroy and is apportioned to the value of the material.—Nature yields, but recuperates; Art, however, in the monuments of antiquity, has so far succumbed to this flaw in human kind, that all Greece could do in that way to preserve, availed naught, at least, when she left the impress of her incomparable genius, on any substance more precious than clay or stone. Our laws are changing, and the completest code ever devised by the wisdom of man falls as far short as did the triumphs of Justinian; and renewed legislation becomes a constant want, an ever-appealing necessity.— Our hearts, our loves are changing, and if not so ostensibly, none the less surely, those granite barriers that gird our coasts, and with which we seek to perpetuate our memories, are dissolving, crumbling, changing. The idols and temples, religions and creeds pertaining to our capricious worship, form no exception to the omniscient rule; and the idea that those most invulnerable bulwarks of faith,—the Bibles of nations,—can remain any considerable time unaltered and unrevised, is as impossible and unnatural as for the rocks to resist the potent and salutary influences by which we have acquired the fertile strata of our soil and the means necessary to supply existence.

Though we may not preserve the past in all its living integrity, we may now and then reflect sorrowfully, gratefully over the few disfigured landmarks of a once struggling, loving, perishing people,—and as we call the roll of honored dead, accord their heroes at least a portion of that coveted tribute of remembrance, which we, in our turn, would fain solicit of posterity.

There is a potent spirit prevailing over the minds of men; all are the humble instruments of the All-wise Designer of the universe, but in the progress of the great work we call civilization, it has been (and is) the good fortune of some to have become individually and conspicuously identified, and although it may have been only in the beginning, they are not to be despised because they labored without the easy systems, and ingenious appliances, that grace and propitiate our efforts. So, Numa, in establishing the religious and civil laws of Rome, deserves an even greater glory than Constantine, who merely affixed his august signature to the remodelled works of his predecessors; so, too, Artaxerxes may claim, in the task of evangelical reform, a goodly share with Theodosius. Zoroaster with Confucius, and Mahomet with Erasmus; but while no one of these may claim at once, the high distinction and exclusive credit, of interpreting and executing the Divine will, nevertheless we may presume that each and all, together with the humblest of their followers, in their own time and way, performed their allotted stint; and could we read aright, we should find the record of their faithful service on such memorials as the Sanscrit, the Zenda-Vesta, the Talmud the Koran.

III.

While the monuments of a nation's dead, may be regarded in some degree as an index to its glory, they are not always a true exponent of merit, and rarely an exclusive tribute to the man; on the contrary, it is, in the case of many of our finest, a distinctive idea breathed through them that is aggrandized. Speaking as a cosmopolitan I may, say:—there is in that towering shaft reared to O'Connell, a species of Hibernian spunk and a granite and enduring defiance of England—it typifies the spirit of Irish intolerance, rising in its power and majesty to repel British aggression,—and yet every stone used in that magnificent memorial might be engraved with a different name, and then many a patriot leader treasured in the Irish heart, but whose sentiments find significant expression in this silent bulwark, would be left out. O'Connell, as a partisan, monopolizes the whole edifice, but as a man, a single solitary brick would suffice. Journeying toward the metropolis of England, looking towards London, one sees through a vista of haze and smoke the grim outline of a giant form looming in the clouds! 'Tis the hero of the Nile! But here again it is not British love for Nelson,—he was not a man either to love or to be loved,—it is, rather, Britannia, claiming for England the empire of the wave,—and British bulldogism, saying to the outer world and to posterity,—REMEMBER TRAFALGAR!

English Conservatism may form a commendable exception to the rule, but it is sad to note in other countries that even these granite columns are, after all, but the transient commemoration of a fickle triumph: indeed, mere personal renown although identified with national aggrandizement, will not suffice to counteract the withering blast with which Time and Passion sweep down as with the " besom of destruction " our fairest Babylons.

In the rapid march of events, other Waterloos, other Trafalgars will be fought, and while new triumphs and new defeats will change the whole order of hero-worship, those names now blazoned over, like the "N" on the Louvre, with a nation's pride, will be erased, despised, forgotten,—or survive, perchance, only in the musty records of faded leaves.

After all, what is renown? It is the accident of ability and opportunity combining to make a man conspicuous for the successful performance of some extraordinary undertaking, and that regardless of motive. Aye, but the true greatness of any deed, so far as the author is concerned, is the *motive* that inspired it, so far as the world is concerned, however, it is only the advantage it confers. In the former case, of all actions, the noblest are unselfish and disinterested, and they are the rarest and most obscure—they may win friends, but do not necessarily confer either profit or distinction. Accordingly, a man may be a profitless failure before all the world, and at the same time possess a character and manhood which, although shut out from the laurel field, would entitle him to the highest rank in the unhonored legion of nameless and undecorated heroes. It follows, the humble may envy the great, but they need not always feel humiliated in obscurity. So, too, amongst all the monuments of men, the simplest are those of true worth and affection, and they are the dearest and best.

In looking back over the past, we find the greatest men have no monuments at all, and the landmarks by which we trace their existence, are their works. Some, indeed, have been denied even the menial rights of decent burial, and have done without the temporal boon of a grave; but the atrocious meanness that would have consigned their memory to opprobrium, has, nevertheless, defeated its object. And here we are reminded that the most striking, if not the grandest memorial in England, is a certain, simple tomb, situate in an obscure corner of old Westminster:—there, in close proximity to the finest of all the mausoleums of English kings, despoiled of its human dust, exhibited as a curiosity, the vacant sepulchre of Oliver Cromwell remains a reproach to his countrymen; but as we regard the roughly tumbled earth whence a regal envy extracted his mortal relics, we are reminded of the apostrophe wrung from the heart of a great Roman general,*—" Ungrateful city, ye shall not even have my ashes!"

In proportion as a man's works contribute to the happiness of a people is he likely to be remembered. O'Connell may have done much to give tone and character to Irish politics, and if so, the world ought to feel thankful, and especially Ireland. We must all honor his patriotism, but if we find it difficult to see, individually, wherein this great politician has contributed to our welfare, how much more discouraging the effort to eke out comfort and felicity from the smoke and carnage of Trafalgar or Balaklava— ah, what a joyous pic-nic ground in retrospect, the bloody deck of the " Victory," or the gory trail of the doomed " six hundred"! Nay, I protest that is not the sort of fame either to covet or endure—it is too sectional to last or to merit approbation—it is the triumph of antagonism, that savage exultation which makes aliens of countrymen— that conflict amongst brothers which makes mothers mourn and sisters weep; it may win a throne,—'tis a joyless trophy, and the enjoyment, such as might be expected in the isolation of a splendid triumph wrought in competition with mankind.

---

* Scipio Africanus.

There is no satisfaction in the contemplation of life, or after-life, from those dizzy heights to which popular clamor has raised, *in memoriam,* the effigies of men,—elevated as they have been, more in the lust of party aggrandizement, than as a personal tribute of love or respect. There is no kindliness, no tender sentiment, commemorated; and one feels a relief in getting down from those snow-clad summits where the eagles perch, to the sweet smelling vales of the violet and the cuckoo. Aye, how much more genial those grassy glades of Stoke,—the grazing herds,—and that humble mound beneath " that yew tree's shade,"—cherished memorials of the ".Elegy" and of Gray.

IV.

There are works boundless in their humanity as love, ever-green in their beauty as affection, and precious in our need as the happiness they inspire; there is a sublimity in the attainment of such results,—they shall not perish, we cherish them, and the author lives amongst us, and with our children, and remains for ever the friend and brother of mankind!

Dearer to us and to Ireland, is her Tom Moore, who gave to the world those triumphs of pathos which touched a chord that shall vibrate for all time, in every land, in every heart! Worthy compeer of Shakespeare, and Handel, and Burns, and Byron, I greet thee in the names of millions who would do thee homage! Such men are not the mere chieftains and champions of a division, or sect,—their language, their deeds, inspire naught but the kindliest emotions, which, under the potent spell of melody, proclaim a welcome truce to discord, and bring all within the great universal brotherhood of mutual dependence and sympathy.

Regarding the labours of these men, we may remark,—there must be a great deal that is fictitious in Romance and Poetry, but while they people our minds with the names of many who never lived, and whose adventures and troubles are purely imaginary, yet they are not all false, and to be condemned for all that. They are fictitious, in the main, only in proportion as they are not in accord with such vicissitudes as would be possible to happen us if similarly situated. Many things about them are highly idealized, no doubt, may be extravagantly so, but they are all the more charming and interesting as a welcome and instructive diversion, and quite as rational, too, at least, many of them, as that confidence in perfect love or friendship, which, though it may not exist in all the rigid exactness of a demonstration, and fact, and proof, might undeceive us, still it gives us pleasure, and we feel better to cling to the delusion, while the truth would make us miserable. So like words in song, they blend with the music of our better thoughts, and harmonize our impulses.

Ah, who could find it in his heart to say, I would I had never read "Tales of a Grandfather," the " Vicar of Wakefield," or the "Arabian Nights." But it is said that they unfit us for the sterner realities of life,—well, when these realities oppress us, as they are sure to do, do not these old friends solace us? They may not exalt, although I think they do, still how gently, how cheerily, do we welcome them in our restful hours, and with what grateful fancies, and even softer minstrelsy, do they accompany us down into the "valley and shadow." Surrounded as we are by so much outside affectation and deceit, where shall we find a truer or more natural impulse than that which claims genial fellowship with "Tam o' Shanter," "Robinson Crusoe," or "Rip Van Winkle." And the minds and hearts whose creative power they are the offspring, how kindly, how lovingly we have thought of them ; how many spectacled men of science, indeed, and blue-visaged historians must it take to rival, in our young hearts, just one name —Defoe—or that other nameless one who tells with such pathetic humor the story of Sinbad.

V.

Nay, then, are the shrines of some of these old companions worthy a pilgrimage ? In the course of a somewhat wandering and not uneventful career, I have come across the marble and ashes of a goodly number of these men, and the interest with which I have always regarded them, has in no stinted measure recompensed me for the privation and sacrifice which the old adage visits with such exceptionless rigor on the "rolling stone."

In exploring the remarkable burial-places of the old world, and especially those of our English fatherland, we are led thither by that peculiar charm inspired in our reading of the careers of great men,—warriors, statesmen, and authors, of whom we have heard and thought so much,—heroes all, whose story has excited our admiration, sympathy, and interest, and whose lives history, biography, and romance, have made us feel as familiar with as if we had lived in their day, known them personally and enjoyed in their society the rare privilege of intimate companionship. It is not mere idle curiosity, then, that impels us forward almost reluctantly, as it were, in the solemn quest of their last earthly resting-place; nay, it may be the only tangible relic of an existence endeared to us by the benefit and happiness its works have conferred, and the feeling with which we would regard the hallowed precinct, partakes rather of that kindliness and emotion which is stirred up only in the recollection of things we have loved.

It must be confessed, however, in the commemoration of those, or many of them, who have planted amongst us the germs of so prolific a harvest of moral and intellectual enjoyment, ashes which should have been garnered up and treasured in proud and grateful remembrance, seem, on the contrary, not only miserably neglected, but, in many cases, altogether abandoned; and if we follow the trail of the most illustrious foot-prints, we find, not unfrequently, they lead out of the broad, splendid avenues of life, of fortune, and of fame, to terminate in the gloomy, dreary labyrinths of death and deprivation, where we behold, hidden away in tangled weed and wild-wood, the poor, discarded rubbish of our once choicest mortality!

This would seem a dreadful shame, and may be it is, but there is a peculiar significance even in the all too apparent absence of any effort to hedge them in and nationalize them; indeed, the fact conveys of itself a tribute which bespeaks, not merely a nation's pride of relationship, but what is better,—it implies a kinship to the world, and such a brotherhood with all mankind as to preclude, as belittling, all exclusive national control or distinction. The obligation entailed, we tacitly feel, rests alike upon the whole race of man, and the absence of all local signs of sepulchral aggrandizement, only indicates that what is nobody's work in particular, is all the world's, and what all the world may not perform is left undone.

If you will imagine yourself in England, for a short time, I will take you to see for yourself; and making London the starting point, some of the objects we have been speaking about may be found within the reach of an easy stroll. But whither away? Well, it is not to that magnificent cenotaph in Hyde Park, I would lead you,—that is not a monument in the sense I mean, but rather a questionable work of art, reared in family pride and connubial affliction, and dedicated *in memoriam*, to a prince whose quiet virtues and unobtrusive accomplishments, it out-dazzles and obscures,—leaving, indeed, the artist the greater hero of the two.

In passing this tribute of royalty, however, I am reminded by the contrast, of one less princely I saw at Melrose, in Scotland. In the ruins of the divine old abbey there, one sees a bit of earth that may once have been a mound, but now it is settled down and is hardly distinguishable from the ground around. I do not know what there can be to keep us from walking right over it, but some way we do hesitate to plant our foot on that particular spot, and at a second glance we notice a plain, pine stick with a piece across, together, not much larger than, nor unlike the symbol worn at the girdle of a monkish devotee; but what is that bit of writing,—is it worth while looking? We stoop down in the impulse of careless curiosity, and give a great start,—then look again more eagerly and closely to make sure, and feel a thrill as if the iron gauntlet of a Plantagenet, or a Wallace, had been laid upon our shoulder—would you wonder, for there we read—"Here Lies the Heart of Bruce!"

VI.

In an expedition like that we propose, one cannot help inclining towards Westminster Abbey, and now, the temptation is strong, to make this our destination; we shall at least pass through, as it is directly on our way, and there, moving reverently along the dim aisle leading past that magnetic corner consecrated to the Poets, we pause a moment to look wistfully at a few well-remembered faces.—Ah, they almost incline us to curtail our walk, and one fain would sidle off on the sly and abandon the project of going further. Many is the time before this, I have lingered there, and as I've looked around on that silent company of the world's and my precious idols, it has ever been with hopeless longing, yet yearning desire that I might recall the life, and breath, and smile, to those marble effigies, and, claiming the privilege of membership in the great common brotherhood of man, embrace them in the flesh!

These fellows take one's heart away,—and how can we carry a single tribute of our puny store past them.— Wordsworth, Pope, Young, Southey, and a host of others! They cannot speak, and yet each recalls some pathetic line, some verse, or thought, that at some time has given expression to feelings that even we had no language to utter; but verily we feel we shall get melancholy if we stay much longer, and suppressing a sigh, we, in the effort to rally our drooping spirits, are almost disposed to play a joke on Sheridan,—pounce upon him and dun him for a little bill, but are diverted by a glance at the benign features of " Oh rare Ben. Jonson," and afraid to trust ourselves further, break from the spot and hurry on our way.

Suffice it then for the abbey, on this occasion to add:— as we cast a parting glance over its mural wealth of kingly entablature so grandly arrayed, there seems about it all a species of knighthood, that makes this superb congregation of voiceless, lifeless nobility, appear a veritable House of Lords,—a Peerage, to which a sovereign intellect raises the great commoner after death. Great men and good we find here, and they seem in their proper place—a nation's pride can do no more; but it is not here lies the object of our quest—it is all too grand, the atmosphere too courtly, and the frigid air too much like the high latitudes of Phœnix Park, and Trafalgar Square.

VII.

Taking the direction past Whitehall, we soon find ourselves in the Strand, and later leave any of the incense of the abbey that may yet cling about us, in the still more odorous regions of Long Acre, and High Holborn.

Yet stay! we are forgetting an old friend—we must not slight *him*, so we get back into the Strand, again, by way of Drury Lane, and proceed along to Temple Bar. Here we turn down a narrow alley to the right, where we find all at once, like Ali Baba, we have plumped almost involuntarily, not into a den of thieves, but into a hardly less sinister looking locality, whose shabby antiquated rookeries, intersected in all directions by stealthy, hide-and-seek passages, are known to the initiated as the old English "Inns of Court." This place may be regarded as John Bull's antique conception of a judicial paradise. But what is there pertaining to our project to interest us here? it does look more like the *tomb*, than the *cradle*, of English Common Law, really, and here probably lies, pigeon-holed, centuries of mouldering material for a resurrection in Chancery. But stop! do you see that gray old edifice, round like a cheese box? that is the "Temple,"—it is famous as an ecclesiastical resort in the time of the Crusaders, and people attend there now, on Sabbath days, to worship its antiquity, but it is not to that I wish to call your attention—look closely over there to the left into that opening between the walls,—do you not see a plain rough stone, raised a little above the other flags, but with no other protection from the hurry and scurry of busy feet? That, my friend, is a grave and within it lies all that remains of a Prince of English literature,—the author of The Vicar of Wakefield." *

---

* Oliver Goldsmith.

It would seem as if the old man had gone to the church with a half yearning desire to go in, but had paused just outside and hesitated as if in childish perplexity to think it over,--then, reclining his feeble old frame to rest a bit, was soon lying prone,—and soothed, perchance by some soft strain from the choir within, a grateful drowse had stolen over his harassed spirit and he slept!

One fain would think it was rather a feeling of reverence and tenderness not to disturb the old man that they let him lie just where he was.—Ah, we reflect sorrowfully over the magnificent intellect extinguished there and of that still greater heart—always oscillating, yet ever true as the pendulum,—loving all the world, yet forgetting to care for self—at once the most useful and noblest of men, and the least frugal and most worthless of vagabonds— prodigal in giving pleasure, and yet denied one happy hour! As we turn from the spot, would that the slab and sod that cover him now, were changed for a mantle which like our memory of him might be as the grassy verdure of never failing green—not forgetting a sprinkling of violets, and daisies, and loving hands to tuck him in.

VIII.

It is not without reluctance after all, we leave the Temple and its vicinity, replete as they are with interesting reminiscences; but we have a pretty long walk before us, so turning away we retrace our steps in the direction of High Holborn. In the interval of meditation, our thoughts fly back again towards the abbey to mark a contrast, but our destination is another part of London—not the superb quarter, basking in the opulent splendor of royal patronage, hedged round by ducal mansions, stately parliaments, regal palaces,—but a mean, shabby, filthy part, so easy to find and so hard to lose as some of the inferior localities of London are, where instead of the other accessories of grandeur, we find breweries, soap factories and smoking furnaces, all betokening the sweat and toil of active physical industry.

It is in such a vicinity, we next find ourselves trudging along a not very inviting thoroughfare called "City Road." That name sounds rural-like, as in the case of St. Giles Fields, but it is deceptive, like the "Heathen Chinee," and odors, that powerfully remind one of the absence of clover fields, offend the nostrils at every step, and the eye appeals wistfully, yet hopelessly, to those begrimed, unwelcoming walls, those close packed dwellings and slimy pavements. It is not so bad as Wapping, but one must needs be a resident to distinguish the difference; however, it is a satisfaction to perceive from the surroundings we are near the end of our journey.

London, is an exception, as regards the monotony one would otherwise feel in wandering through those endless, narrow grooves called streets; and the more we know of its dingy habitations, the more agreeably are we impressed with the fact that nearly every one of them has a history, or story, connected with it, really worthy of record; many of these being intimately associated with persons and events that have played an important part on the world's great stage, and lent to the imposing drama of the past, its delicious fund of inexplicable mystery and tragic interest. An instance could be cited of this or that place, which we have already passed on our way hither, that would be as entertaining and instructive, perhaps, as could be found in any similar field of exploration; indeed, places you would ignorantly go by without noticing, you would, if you only knew, retrace your steps for miles, to catch another glimpse of; the one to which we are bound, being, in its way, a fair illustration of this.

But here we are at our destination. A sombre, vacant space two or three acres in extent, meets the eye on the left; an uninviting looking spot it is, too, jagged over with rough, stone slabs packed close together—all old and out of fashion but still on duty, holding with sturdy rigidity their several lines of demarcation. Some, we observe, are thickly covered with tiny patches of a greyish shell-like appearance, that seem with a sort of tenacious energy to attach themselves to whatever cannot readily be devoured—they are the barnacles of time, that feast in death and fat on dissolution!

I am afraid you will be disappointed, after all, in the place to which I've brought you, and I may find it difficult to satisfy you for coming so far; indeed, I am almost afraid to tell you that that old Cemetery is Bunhill Fields, in the anxiety whether you may not feel, after all, sorry you came; but you must be indulgent, and bear in mind our expedition is not altogether the sort of stroll we take when we are in for a "lark."

K

Ah, but what of Bunhill Fields, you say, with an air of distrust that makes me almost wish we had stayed in the Abbey. Well, the people living round about this dreadfully decrepid and evidently long disused old receptacle, no doubt regard it as a plague spot, and smart under a consciousness of being, thereby, misrepresented if not maligned. I feel sorry for them; but it is possible they are too high-toned, and that the soap factories, and distilleries, abounding in this neighbourhood, have had rather too much of a purifying and refining influence. They want Westminster Abbey, up here, and some of the worthies who have taken an indefinite lease of the "Poets' Corner;" they covet an item of the ashes of defunct royalty,—a monarch or so, with say a sprinkling of the hallowed dust of smothered princelings,—a Guelph would do, although they would prefer an older pedigree. The Fates, however, are inexorable, so they have to bear with what they have; and poor old Bunhill Fields, where the mortality of London went, for centuries, to scrape its feet, must suffice.

Here lie the excommunicated and voluntary exiles of the Romish and English churches,—here, covered with wounds, the veterans of religious strife, have dragged their weary frames to lay their bones in peace; and with them, too, no doubt many of the ragged-band that followed them,—the "lame, and halt, and blind," the "moral leper," and all the conscience-stricken riff-raff that required to be spoken to as "Man never spake before."

We enter and look about us. Not far from the entrance is the tomb of Isaac Watts, and around him are clustered a goodly array of dissenting preachers; all in accord now, it is hoped, like the pious ditties of their chief. Quaint inscriptions and sepulchral oddities, may be seen all around; but there is a dread about this sort of thing, and as we pick our way amongst them, we feel a gloom that even the bright sun beaming down, does not with all its cheering influence seem readily to dispel.

IX.

But "whose monument is that," you ask curiously, "so modern and fresh-looking, as if it had not stood there long?"—(Pointing to a simple shaft about as high as an ordinary ceiling.) Ah, you have discovered one of my heroes! and do not feel too disappointed when I tell you it is only Daniel Defoe. He shivered long in the cold, before he got those new clothes, but people took compassion on him and dressed him up a bit, that he might not appear quite so shabby even among the ragged set surrounding him. It was a contribution in "penn'orths" from the children of England; too small a sum to have been compatible with the dignity of those who built the monuments in and about Hyde Park, and Trafalgar Square, so it came as the gift of the children,—those whose fresh young hearts had not out-lived the memory of dear old Robinson Crusoe. Ah! as a tribute from them, we feel reconciled it is not in St. James' Park, ten times as high, and surmounted by a bronze figure to perpetuate and recall a form and feature, which, as a shaggy, elfish-looking creature surrounded by his animal friends, is better known, kindlier thought of, and more heartily sympathized with, than any name in all the kingdom of storydom.

It is quite in keeping with this abandoned spot, this Bunhill Fields—all ignored in the high-toned map of regal, Christian London—to feel we are indeed so near the virtual hero of that far off deserted island; and here too, blending with his dust, is his "man Friday." The story that made the immortality of these men one, can it be possible it were all a fiction? How we have sympathized with them in their troubles, grieved with them in their misfortunes, or rejoiced with them in those gleams of hope that bade them cheer! How kindly, how lovingly, even in our later life, do we recall those gatherings round the fireside, where the question whose turn it was to sit on father's knee, was of greater import to us than were to cabinets the deposition of emperors or the accession of kings! And now behold the interest, the delicious blending of terror and wonder with which they listen to the oft-repeated tale of those two cast-aways!—Watch the sparkling eye, the glowing cheek, the quaffing of each word, the boyish gulping down of whole sentences!—How ill they brook a pause, how jealously they glance sideways at the old black pipe, on the mantelpiece, whose interruptions they know of old and each moment hoping, yet fearing the exercise of its sovereign rule!

What a gush of sweet memories, even now, sweeps over us with the thought—and is the story of Crusoe all an illusion? Granted; but it is true to nature and inspires this picture which is real. A shouting in the street outside arouses us from our reverie, and we look around rather startled; some of these plucky old dissenters, we remember just then, died hard and long, and they do tell awful tales of ghosts and spring-heeled jacks resorting in this vicinity. We feel pretty brave in the daytime, but we must confess we are interlopers, after all, and you know live carcasses have no business here; but the voice that might have bid us begone is hushed, and we edge a little further in.

Are you not getting tired and hungry? this sort of exploring is not like those jolly rambles in and about the flowery vales of Twickenham, and Hampton Court, is it? and what a desperate appetite it does give one for sandwiches and beer. Well, we've only one more visit to make and then—but look, do you see that pile of old stones there—ah, here we are now close up to it; you can't very well make out the inscription, it is rather obliterated and it all looks so awfully old and crumbled. Well, I've been here once before this and studied it out and now I know who is there; possibly, you might have heard of him, I think you have, for the world knows him well, and even that most exacting goddess Fame, was so enamoured of his homely visage she wreathed round the brow now pillowed there a garland of her choicest immortelles! You may guess whom I mean—it is the author of "Pilgrim's Progress"*:—In life, buffeted in turmoil—in death, sequestered in repose.

---

* While the author is at variance with Bunyan in a doctrinal point of view, that does not prevent him from feeling and expressing the highest admiration, not only for the honest preacher, but for a work which all must concur in esteeming as one of the few finest and most original productions of the imagination extant.

X.

Four rough-hewed slabs breast-high, form a rude inclosure, and on the top of this is placed the recumbent effigy of John Bunyan. The sculptor must have thought John a very homely man, for certainly a more uncomely likeness it would be difficult to imagine. This tomb and its whereabouts is poor and mean, regarded in the light of in any way an adequate remembrance; there is no tribute about it at all. No more has been done than common decency required, unless, perhaps, the effigy, which may be regarded as an item extra. Perfectly in keeping, however, with the unpolished simplicity of this man's life, so was his death, and is his resting place.

Why repine that Westminster Abbey may not contain the ashes of this illustrious plebeian! this once rude, illiterate, vulgar tinker! Well, it has most of our great dead, but the greatest it lacks, and amongst them this poor tenant of Bunhill Fields. This place, it is true, is hardly in keeping, if we take into account the beautiful and priceless heritage which he bequeathed; but then it must be remembered, that gratitude does not always express its thanks magnificently, and precedence, you know, in England, and especially "conformity," goes a long way; besides, it must not be forgotten that Bunyan had undergone no monkish manipulation of "hands," and really had no Episcopal authority for bringing his "Christian" into the world at all.

It is none the less a consolation, however, to reflect that, any effort to rear a monument adequate to the resplendent reputation of the author of "Pilgrim's Progress," would be simply impossible, and serve rather to stint the sentiment which his memory and his great work inspire. We may deck the mausoleum of pampered princes, with the grandeur becoming their rank and state,—it impels the admiration of gaping crowds, posterity is dazzled, and royalty maintained; but this man was the artificer of his own greatness, and that wrought in the envenomed teeth of a persecution where none durst say, "God bless him!" There is no splendid Invalides, no bronze statue here—none of the dumb* accessories of Buffalo, and Lion, and Camel, and Elephant—we behold, indeed, only the cast-off habiliments of a great man's mortality; but up form his ashes rises a form, not princely, it is true, and yet sublimer in its Doric simplicity, than the jewelled majesty of kings.—Unlike the artificial light that comes down and melts in a flood of mellow flame *on* the tomb of Napoleon, there shines *out* from this rough stone urn, a refulgence that casts its grateful beams broadcast over the earth.

It is just as well there is no lofty pedestal, no granite monument with spiral steeps, to seek and stint the acme of his fame—his peerless work is his memorial—and here, despite all the detracting influences of mean surroundings and abandoned ruin, we behold in his very isolation an individuality all the more clearly defined, and virtues all the more absolutely his own. No august† dome rears its regal arch over his head,—nought to intercept the smile of

---

* Albert Memorial.
†St Paul's.

heaven or break the glancing rays of sun, and moon, and star—out in sunshine as in storm, amid the twittering of birds and the rolling of thunder, he sleeps now, calmly, blissfully, THAT SLUMBROUS REST WHICH BIDES THE GOD OF DAY TO BID HIM RISE, AND BE MARSHALLED WITH "THE SPIRITS OF THE JUST MADE PERFECT."

Imagination.

IMAGINATION.

I.

IN commencing this article, I desire, in the first place, to apologize for giving it so grand a name, and to explain that its objective feature is, in one sense, the opposite of what its title would indicate; it being my intention not to confine myself exclusively to the ideal, the handling of which requires a tangibility which is found only in a contrast with the real. In other words, while using the word imagination as a heading, it is not my purpose to attempt an elaborate analysis of the mighty and complex elements which it comprehends; on the contrary, I appeal to the splendid luminary whose name I have borrowed only for such glimmerings as may be accorded my poor but earnest efforts to illuminate those other darker phases of existence which I shall bring up for examination, and whither I would direct those searching rays with a view to contrasting the relative influences of two great opposing elements, the *real* and the *unreal*, on the ups and downs of life.

The title, then, rather denotes the source whence comes that rosy flame which, drawn by fancy pinnacles from the darkest clouds, lights up not simply the aimless, beguiling labyrinth of mere reverie, but also that other path, beaten hard, winding its tortuous way along the steep decline—through time seam, and mountain gorge— down the hill-side into the vale.

Here let me say that whatever eulogy I may feel like pronouncing on Imagination, I would not have it regarded as an exclusive virtue, comprehending in itself all the requirements of happiness. The natural obstacles to its free healthful exercise may be, and doubtless are, many; but the fewer these are the greater our enjoyment, and the unwise multiplication of them has the reverse tendency to make us miserable.

In keeping, as I propose, within an easy range of the two extremes of Reality and Imagination, I shall leave it to others to say where the line between the two should be drawn—the most I shall attempt to do is to suggest; but while in my predisposition to favor the ideal, I may fail in justice to the real, it will be found the burden of my lament is largely a protest against the frantic zeal evinced in the universal mania to realize, and against the sleepless anxiety, as in the case of the holder of a note on a doubtful bank, to redeem ideas and to materialize thought.

Apropos of favoring extremes, we may observe that, practically, divinity as well as wisdom lies somewhere between what I was about to call the narrow golden strip, but it is not golden, at least not in our vulgar sense of being adorned, but all undefined, exists a mysterious borderland called by that good word moderation. There is, indeed, a medium in all things that to some extent falsifies and puts to shame extremes ; to find the former, however, it is necessary to have a proper appreciation of the latter, and although there is no easy method by which this may be accomplished in all cases, yet it is about the line drawn midway between these two opposites, the happy goal lies, the exact estimate of which is our highest conception of right, and the reward for its observance, the corresponding measure of felicity. But these extremes are capricious and beguiling—they are as drifting sand or the confusing glamour of a mirage, and often lead astray the most unbiassed and sober judgment.—Peace may be a mere respite from war,—the breathing spell of a nation recuperating from some stunning blow, but the people of which are, or may be, secretly planning retaliation.—Then it is Vengeance hiding his lowering brow under the smiling mask of reconciliation.—Between these extremes rises the sublime image of the Reproving Angel, and before Her they shrink back abashed.—Her dominion is maintained by a power more potent than the sword, and less susceptible to mistrust than the "olive branch."—Her sceptre is the pivot on which is balanced the magic scale of right and wrong.—Her tranquillity is better than peace, it is neutrality, and Her triumph the majesty of conscious strength reposing in the midst of contention !

Thus, too, save for disbelief and inability to comprehend, the soul would shrink back appalled at the extreme spectacle of writhing bodies in an eternal Hell of quenchless fire and it is equally a blessing that even Imagination is dumb and expressionless to adequately appreciate the contrast between that and the opposite extreme of perpetual and perfect bliss. Indeed, the realization of either, in the slightest appreciable degree, would be overwhelming; but the comparative stolidity with which we listen to all extreme preaching, indicates not so much our indifference as that we are mercifully constituted and constrained to imbibe only the more moderate view; and, in the prodigious issue involving our salvation, *that* is as much as it is possible for poor blind mortality to realize, or even partially to comprehend. Thus does finite Purgatory, take a stronger grip than infinite Hell, and while Reason, in religion, as in the most petty affairs of every day life, lies between extremes, the finger of Truth points inward from the outer verge to the true goal of Equity and Justice. Instinct, Humanity, Conscience may teach us our true bearings to this haven; but when they are the result of calculation a contrast of extremes is necessary, and the effect, as in the harangue of zealots to the same end, is all the more marked that exorcism, by way of comparison, introduces elements so widely at variance as to seem hostile. Fanaticism is the confounding of these extremes for the means—it may be on the right road, but moving in the wrong direction.—I claim, however, its devotee will reach the goal at last, though it be in a contrary way that prolongs the toil without barring hope; and, furthermore, that any departure from the true way will bring us back in the spirit to the shrine from whence we started. Indeed, it is not unfrequently the case that the heart of the most perverse and persevering in vice, is entwined in certain reclaiming influences which cropping, insensibly, out of depravity itself, the outcast is conducted through inexplicable ordeal to the spot whence he began his downward career. The place, in our moral compass, is hallowed, then, as the threshold of home to the returned prodigal; and wounded in the conflict 'twixt right and wrong, the scarred veteran in crime sinks vanquished before the altar of bleeding memories.

The idea that all true political and social reform is progress directly opposite to and away from the condition whence it dates the new order of improvement, is erroneous and fanatical, and comes of that propensity for antagonism in human nature which, instead of reconciling discrepancies, sets them in conflict. Indeed, it is the misapprehension of progress that makes the people of the nineteenth century exult in an exclusive wisdom and righteousness all their own, and sneer at the so-called sensuality and impiety of earlier generations. Reform, however, generally advocates extremes,—it progresses and retrogrades,—it surges as in the throes of a mighty wave,—it inundates a country and then subsides into old-time channels.—Aye, as lightning flashing through a pent-up atmosphere, and dissolving its inky vapours into grateful showers,—disappears,—so Reform, opening up the flood-gates on filthy Conservatism, and cleansing humanity of social and political scurf, evaporates; satiated in turmoil, it is assuaged by the very agony itself creates, and as tears coursing down the grim profile of mountains, and along the jagged slopes of hills, it rushes down in torrents into the valleys, and is lost in the sluggish, almost imperceptible current of "mighty waters."

II.

First, then, let us inquire, what is Reality—what is Imagination. In their connection, and according to the view herein, realization is as the lead that probes the briny blue depths of crystal ocean, and tells the anxious mariner what is beneath the buoyant wave; the bits of sand, or rock, or slime adhering, being the facts that bespeak to his practised eye what sort of anchorage he may expect, and what are the dregs of Imagination.

Again, measureless as the fathomless sea would be the volume of language necessary, ever so briefly but adequately, to define and explain Imagination; and here it must suffice to say, it is the family name of that innumerable progeny of angelic visions that people and beautify the gorgeous realm of the incorporeal. Its mission is not to tantalize but to comfort; and in this re-respect its fancies are not all mythical reasonless phantoms to be despised and repelled, but kind, ever thoughtful, and faithful friends, whose virtues, unhappily, we are too prone to imbibe in the spirit and falsify in the flesh.

The purest, the most delightful and fascinating of these ideal attractions, not unfrequently, are found where Reality presents, in contradistinction, what is most unprepossessing and repulsive;—sympathizing with the flesh, they fraternize only with the spirit,—gratification is the cloud, the blurring mist that obscures them,—this, desire dispels, and in adversity or want they assume a loveliness preternaturally sublime, and shine down upon us in the full splendor of midnight stars.

As in music there are no refrains so sweet as those which are attuned to pain, so in imagery, our brightest conceptions of life are the gleanings of its darkest hours. But while the most splendid dream of the poet is born in deprivation and agony, and mutilated in song, the highest realization of the painter or sculptor is comparative deformity, dumb, senseless, spiritless—and hence, the *chef d' œuvre* that typifies Liberty in her most perfect symmetry, is not perched, as we see it, on the capitol dome of a free, opulent people, but pictured rather, in the imagination of the fettered and oppressed—radiating the heart of the galley slave, or set in conjuration against the dark, slimy walls of hopeless incarceration.

All the pleasure, all the pain in life are summed up in two words—*Imagination,—reality*. I would fain leave out the pang of the latter, and confine myself to the bliss of the former, not simply for the brief span of this hastily concocted article, but could I exist a thousand years, live, and think, and write in the delightful task of sapping to the fullest extent a subject so vast, so resplendent, so sublime as Imagination. That may not be, I know it cannot, and yet looking out upon its magnificent expanse, I am inspired with an ever increasing awe and adoration for the beauty and grandeur of this superb attribute of infinity. Standing, as I feel I am, in the obscurity and silent solitude of the aborigine, gazing out on that glittering sea, a sentiment not altogether vain, makes the temptation strong to take the plunge and swim or sink. There are trophies there, in which, though all may claim participation, none but august minds may grasp and secure possession; and while I am restrained by a knowledge of the pitiable doom of the legions who have yielded and been engulfed, I confess to no slight envy of the chosen few who found in those limpid depths an ineffable delight—a blessed immortality! Could one dive and not sink forever, what a "Lethe" in its oblivion it would be to all trouble—what a delicious unconsciousness of all reality and vexation. One takes courage in thinking, as I do in the handling of this subject, that he will not risk himself far out nor where the water is very deep—that he will avoid the breakers—the conflicting tides—the treacherous undertow—and then, in the effort of the shrinking flesh to follow the soul into its native and most genial element, the most intrepid, all shivering in abject fear, dips the ends of his fingers in and lets that suffice.

But though we may forego the plunge, how longingly the poorest and least eligible of us looks further sea-wards.— There, in yon blue depths, we know, are scattered countess hoards of ungarnered, unreclaimed pearls, and yet the world has decided on the possessors of that exhaustless store.—Ah, we sigh to think to venture there were to impeach the validity of titled deeds, and by impugning the integrity of hallowed records, we should disturb the well-merited repose of those great Leviathans whose clement it is. Indeed, the very thought of venturing, were a sacrilegious ignoring of those giant intellects whose appropriate dominion it is; and although they might not resent the intrusion,—they sleep, but their dreams are amongst the triumphs of an ever wakeful, jealous World.

True, we may not fetter nor circumscribe even the humblest thought, nevertheless, it may not range through the universe of letters untrammelled by any consideration for others, or where others have been; and even in the airy sphere of imagination, all are constrained to yield to lordly minds, that exclusive proprietorship which comes of hard wrought mental exploration and discovery.

In this connection, however, we may observe that even in the case of those whose attainments, in the ideal realm we glorify, how puny may their best efforts justly be considered, how stinted and inadequate, in comparison to the boundless store on which it has been their rare privilege to have drawn. In yielding then, even the poor tribute of my submission, to the universal and omnipotent rule that grants us glimpses but denies us Paradise, it is consoling to reflect that the greatest have not been altogether an exception,—nay, nor so far removed from those humble ones, who like myself, while yearning for exemption, can offer no better plea than that of conscious disability.

While all may enjoy the pleasures of Fancy, it is doubtless a luxury to the world that they do not require to write all they imagine. It is easy enough to construct a vision in the mind, but to transcribe it without marring, in fact without mutilation, is not so easy as throwing one's hat over a butterfly; and let anyone, even the most cultured, sit down and attempt to write on Imagination and he will soon begin to feel uncomfortably oppressed with the magnitude of thought which the word suggests. It is a sublime subject to think about, but a puzzling one to handle, and difficult and guideless in its immensity.—Its horizon is ever receding—indeed, its scope is boundless, and as the very means by which we seek to compass it are those by which it is inflated, so does its beauty beguile and its elasticity bewilder. But while it cannot be described, nor measured, nor confined, it blends in reason only when associated with what is real.

In the manipulation of such an element, I am not unmindful of the peril involved.—A chemist, experimenting on the volatility of gas, may be caught up and carried away by the very contrivance he uses to explain its power; and to grapple with Imagination, even with the usual care and precaution, might expose the most expert to the mishap of getting entangled in some hidden coil attached to the buoyant bauble, and then, whatever satisfaction might otherwise have been felt in an illustration so emphatic of its elevating tendency, he would appear to those looking on below, dangling in mid-air or shooting with meteoric velocity sky-wards.

III.

It must be confessed that whatever charms the Ideal may have, it is so far from true we cannot ignore the Real, that it is the hope to realize which constitutes a special, if not the chief attraction. Indeed, realities in their inception are phantoms of the Imagination, and those beautiful islands we see studding the placid waters of the ideal, and all so charming in the distance, become in actual impact a reassuring evidence, it is true, of our substantial existence, but alas for the magnetic charm that attracted and beguiled us! it is gone. Our insatiable love of possession, however, and the spirit of discontent we call Enterprise, will not let us rest; we follow from one to another of these infatuating objects, and in each are we successively and invariably disappointed. Hope reanimates Despair, and onward through many a perplexing labyrinth we drag our weary limbs in pursuit of the delusion.—We meet friends and those we love, we enlist their sympathies, and they join eagerly in the chase.—All are fascinated, maddened,—and emulation degenerating into rivalry, the expedition becomes a race, a struggle, a contest! And all for what! Echo sends back the usual provoking refrain, "and all for what!" With those in front whose speed has outstripped the others, we hear the anxious query, "where is it?"—and those behind, overcome in the agony of feeling the prize is lost, fall with the mournful ejaculation,—" Ah, I have missed it!" But the cry whose pathos penetrates above the babel is "*what is it?*" It bespeaks volumes of the trophy, as " ah, I have missed it!" does of the vanity of human wants and wishes. Oftentimes it is mute, but we interpret its appeal in the eloquent physiognomy of Hope and Despair, and, though it be not uttered, we note its silent impulse as it gleams in the eye, throbs in the heart, and pants upon the tongue!

In the ennui of luxurious homes,—in the hungering haunts of the poor,—it is the novelty and splendor of that mysterious, "what is it" which at one time vexes, at another charms and eternally beguiles. It is the motive power in conquest, in enterprise and in love. The vanquisher stands in full possession of the citadel which has so long withstood the ordeal of an arduous and gallant siege, he ransacks its treasure, but finds it not.—Those who have achieved the highest distinction in politics, art, or commerce, look about them in the midst of their triumphs, and remarking its absence with a pang, wonder where and what it is! Aye, what is it. It is the subtle humor of life's nameless yearning. All feel it; the infant in its first troubled wail indicates a guileless inkling of the inexplicable want, it is soothed in slumber, but when it wakes it cries.—Youth, in the blushing nudity of unfledged confidence, plumes himself he knows "what it is," and slyly revels in the tempting vision of waking love,—then, threading the rosy labyrinth that leads him to his goal, beholds in the incarnation of his dream the charm is fled! It was only a glimpse he had of the fleeting fugitive, entangled for a few brief moments in the warp and woof of Imagination. Alas, it was only the sweet image of a mirage, cast in the amorous deception of a spell. Like him, we struggle forward,—the vision vanishes further away; we pursue it all through life, and find it always and for ever fled. Its flight leads through a shadowy vale, along the darkened trail of lost love and of faded beauty— its refuge, that elysium of spent harmony where blend in angelic chorus the receded echoes of music and of song.

IV.

In opposition to, or rather in prostitution of, the Ideal, it is a marked characteristic of this clever age to materialize, and we have now come to regard not only profit as the main object of production, but also the market value as the measure of merit. This applies not only to things in fancy, but in flesh, and not alone to substances, but to persons.

Here we may observe, that so far as the utility of a thing may commend it to the wants of a community, patronage following approval makes the reward not only an evidence of merit, but a substantial mark of public favour; and he who confers this requirement on society, may be satisfactorily recompensed, not in gratitude, but in money—not in public thanks, but in national funds. While this is the practical return commonly preferred as offering the strongest inducements to labor, nevertheless, regarded as an all-prevailing incentive to exertion, it is a humiliating fact that such a compensation is wanting very materially in those finer attributes calculated to encourage and develop the higher nature in man.

It requires no effort in imagination to conceive such noble deeds as may have no price, no money equivalent, but how far short of this do those schemes fall wherein merit depends exclusively on pecuniary success; and the discrepancy herein does not simply indicate the exception I have taken to the market value of merit, but it explains away the shabby raiment in which we not unfrequently find the miserable creature of good impulses.

It requires very little knowledge of the world to have perceived that any product or project appertaining to abstract worth, though it be of rare humane and intellectual desert is, if not openly tabooed, left to suffer such a discount in the public mart as virtually to languish and all but starve. At the same time, designs subserving the most vicious propensities of a people are in eager demand at a high premium.—So true is this that we may approve and neglect one thing on abstract principles, and, though condemning, patronize another from motives of avaricious policy; but then, it is only in view of profit we consent to countenance what conscience reprobates.

Thus, while in the realm of letters, the finest works that embellish our book-world have emanated in the privation and penury of profitless ideal, titles and fabulous sums have accrued to the invention of big guns, murderous torpedoes, and to such political bravado as leads to a periodical rupture of the iron-clad peace of nations. So it comes about that the best thoughts, the purest motives, the most disinterested projects, while endowed with the noblest qualities and the highest integrity, are for that very reason wanting in those elements necessary to render them profitable, and as such must submit to what, in a money age, is a worse stigma than crime—pecuniary failure. At the same time, while it might be expected the possessor would, in one sense, be regarded as a moral triumph,—he is not, as society is at present organized, even a popular example of the notion, commonly inculcated, of the abundance and sweetness of virtue's reward.

In this connection we may notice further, that while public opinion, though frequently in error, offers in the long run, a fair trial of merit, that test of public esteem which is obtained in the knocking down of a thing to the highest bidder, is to make merit turn on the caprice of a prejudiced and oftentimes depraved taste. Besides, the boon of even such a faulty judgment, is practically forestalled, and public approbation anticipated by go-betweens,—men whose duty it is to propitiate patronage and cater to the general appetite,—and who, though professing a latent appreciation of abstract merit, find their verdict, like their service, controlled by an exclusive regard for the momentous question of profit and loss.

These censors exist, and many by this means subsist in every conceivable form and capacity. Indeed, in their omnipresent character, any act or expression which attains beyond the privacy of one's own thoughts comes, one way or another, under their scrutiny, and is subjected not simply to their criticism but arbitrament. Then, while no sentiment is thought of much consequence, unless stamped by regularly constituted authorities, ideas that do not bear the unquestionable " Hall mark," are regarded with suspicion, not to say contempt; finding that difficulty in passing current as does a bank cheque that is wanting the " cross " or magic " initials " which, in the mercantile hierarchy, denote the extent of its endowment with the redeemable essence of the God of Bullion.

V.

Not unlike the bold Procrustes, who lopped off or stretched out all subjects to suit his peculiar notion of a good fit, the modern Inquisitor, who, in a minor capacity, is reflected in every sphere and walk of life, evinces, in his plenipotential character a hardly less depraved taste. It is true he exhibits his knowledge of what is wanted in a manner somewhat less cruel than his ancient prototype, that is, he neither *lops* nor *stretches*, but he prunes and eliminates just as heartlessly, and though he may not mutilate, he repudiates all that does not come up to a certain specific gravity whose omniscient standard is GOLD.

Suffice it, however, for these to say—they are the proxies of public opinion, with their office in the vestibule of posterity; and it is to them we are indebted for such a grotesque misconception of the abiding sentiment of ages as declined Goldsmith's "Vicar,"—till the old man Johnson, obtruding the weight of his colossal indignation on the scene, forced the bid up only to such a starvation price, as hastened the demise of the author, whose energies, we may add, expiring with the immortality of the "Traveller," and "The Deserted Village," a portion of the paltry income that had otherwise been needed to reimburse society for the (to him) extravagant luxury of a more prolonged illness, went as an appropriate fund for the partial liquidation of funeral expenses.

There is no doubt, the business of life is getting to be exclusively to make money, and a man's ability to accumulate wealth, or the extent of his property, is taken as the popular measure of his respectability and usefulness. Now-a-days, in our pious adoration of opulent virtue, an individual without a good bank-account gets but scant benison, and this, notwithstanding he be the pink of moral indigence.—A son who may not have the knack of making money, is deemed, even by his parents, abnormally deficient in the purposes of his existence—a providential misfit and a useless incumbrance. So too, a daughter, a dearly-beloved daughter, whom we have reared in accordance with these golden rules, who cannot or does not marry a fortune, or at least considerable property, strikes a death-blow to family pride, and is even a worse failure than the son.—She has "thrown herself away," we say, and wantonly prostrated in the dust the gilded fabric which her doting parents and admiring relatives have reared, aye, and commenced holding up to her dazzled but delighted vision, almost from the time they first taught her to lisp her wants.

Everything, in fact, of any utility is come to be looked upon as a promise to pay, and the person or thing that does not pay is held in about the same esteem as the drawer of a protested note. Verily, it is hard to conceive a more sordid state of human depravity.—Religion, with all her high-toned accessories, is contaminated, and the question "will it pay" is marching and counter-marching the great army of modern crusaders, who look more anxiously to the New Jerusalem for redeemed paper than for redeemed souls.—Friendship is contaminated, and we can conceive no noble sentiment to sanction what is shabby and profitless.—The music and sunshine of life's sublimest heroism, Love, is contaminated, and now Mammon says brusquely, to the living embodiment of our loving heart's ideal, "come," and she follows,—and behold the tender but sensitive chords, the blossoming vine, and floral lace work that woman's witchery has inextricably interwoven and embowered our shrine, droop and fade, and fall, under the gleam of that yellow blight, like autumn leaves,—and the idol of a worship all too divine, unmasking the hidden Paradise of our yearning faith, reveals the mean imposture by which we have been beguiled.

The poor girl is not altogether to blame, in such a case, it is rather the fault of her tutors; and the generation of the present may in turn shift the guilt back upon others who, having transmitted the curse, passed away. And here we may observe, if these early ones burn, as we are told, till all accounts are sent in against them, they will wait and linger long in turmoil, for crimes which they only bequeathed, and the evil of which they ignored, but the misery, consequent, endured centuries after they had vanished in dust! Thus, we might expect the responsibility of sin to be divided and mutually borne, and it would not be unreasonable to suppose the beginning waited on the ending, but for that divine proclamation of amnesty to the mouldering and dying races of man, —"let the dead bury their dead."

VI.

I cite the amassing of wealth as an example of the prevailing passion to materialize, and the consequent impatience and discontent with which we regard every thing in a transitory and imperfect state, lead naturally to our contempt for the ideal, which is looked upon as opposed to the real. Our business and our triumphs now-a-days are not, we think, with the incorporeal, which is rather the bug-bear against which we bar our doors and windows, and close up all the avenues of our treasure. Despite our caution, however, we may not lock our hearts—they may be the grim, tenantless rookeries of bachelordom, but they are all the more eligible in imagination, as the sequestered haunts of love's piracy and passion's lawless witchery.

Still the cry is for the substantial, the tangible!—The etherial is not solid enough, it won't bear the beating, the hauling, and squeezing that comes up to our ideas of a real trophy; so we push on and hardly stop to breathe till we have reduced our ideas of earthly treasure into hard cash,—our thoughts of an abiding place into brick and mortar,—our dreams of love into wives, and then all restless and fagged, we lose appreciation in the drowsy daze of disappointment, and Dame Fortune, tired of our service, says with Delilah, "The Philistines be upon thee!"

We have progressed so far in our material civilization, that we measure character as we would gas, and purse and credit are synonimous terms. So too, happiness and misery are bargained for and against, and sold and doled out by the ounce, or ton, or dose, as is wine or physic and the consequence is, we are either in the frantic intoxication of artificial excitement or reduced to despair by a pernicious reaction.

Meanwhile, racked by these contending elements and debasing influences, we are expected to imbibe, and actually profess to practise, withal, a righteous sense of living, and to make and apply all the subtle distinctions between right and wrong. A feat of mental equilibrium, the performance of which requires our utmost sobriety, and the exercise of our keenest moral perception, and even then, our best attainments, in reality, are only worthy of the rare distinction of being pardonable failures. Indeed, the most energetic and successful workers for good, triumph actually, only so far as to at last struggle and fall on the right side of the neutral line; but while some drop with only a leg, or an arm, or a finger over the magic boundary, we pray some pitying spirit may help them the rest of the way.

It may be urged in extenuation, that, owing to the high standard of propriety professedly in vogue, we are forced to dissemble for appearance sake, and we submit—it is to be hoped, with commendable reluctance—to cloak our debauchery under the proud assumption of better living. In this disguise then, we strut abroad with the dazzling concomitants of wealth and so called refinement, conspiring in our honor and protection; and thus too, our pretensions pass current in the eyes of those we meet,— not however, in the impulse of mutual esteem, but as two individuals (I will not say thieves), encountering in some lonely place at night,—each suspecting the other to be a rogue, they pass one another with that deference and civility engendered by mutual distrust.

VII.

I would not deny the caprice of better-impulses, those choicer strains of virtue that keep on trying to tug our baser carcase along in the direction the spirit prompts; but I fail to see in a prescribed, formal reiteration of good resolves and in that orthodox, ostentatious "mending" of people's "ways," any higher efficacy for the cure of the evil of which I speak, than such as makes abstinence an appetizer, and such a fasting for a day as gives gusto to feasting of a week!

This may be a discouraging and in itself a depraved view of human nature; but while it may be regarded by some as an intemperate and exaggerated criticism, it is proffered in good faith as a sober, and, as I think, rational estimate,—the colors, only, being touched up, here and there, to suit at once the ideal and the real complexion of Truth. So it is, without doubt or scepticism, I most emphatically reaffirm, that to any one of the virtues we profess to patronize, our sphere must appear simply a pandemonium of carnal riot; and in our drunken, sensual conviviality we must seem, at best, what we really are, the agreeable perfection of all that is most depraved. Regarded in this light, then, it follows, that in the remorse of sober reaction, and in the chagrin of prostituted homage, we should revenge outraged humanity on each other, and malign, harass, destroy. So, too, even in the much glorified efforts of some to relegate these evils,—stripped of all fulsome panegyric, what is there to extol? Why a man whose surfeit of debauchery makes him ill, sneaking away to find relief, calls the filthy mission Reform; again, he sees, with the sated eye of the gourmand, poverty starving in the street and, returning to the festive board, recalls the vision only with the sympathetic pang of a keener relish. Meanwhile, WANT covets bread and PLENTY calls the hankering Communism!!!

VIII.

But you say, why introduce into a subject like this such glum phases of our social existence, or pass in review such scurvy evidences of our defiled humanity; why recall the battered and stinking characteristics of our meaner mortality,—what have they to do with imagination, unless, perhaps, to deodorize the sweeter graces of Fancy. I answer, they have everything to do with it; in comparison with the ideal, they are the dismal range of bleak-hill and dusky mountain banked up against a rosy sunset.—They figure in the gloaming of dispelled fancy, chinked away inside the partition that divides the earthly Day from the celestial Morrow, and though screened and embellished constitute the inner lining of dark between two gilded walls! The result of the all prevailing mania to subsidize, is the rapid accumulation of these time scars which it requires no over-keen perception to see grouped in a dim shadowy array of grim Realities.

Against the sombre shades of this darkened background, Imagination rears those magic illusions which though intangible, are real as the emotion that calls them into being, and though defective, in comparison with the

Supreme, are faultless as our highest conception of all perfect loveliness. These are not all portraits, some are pictures of life which we people with the forms we like best, and enact scenes wherein Love, Friendship, Devotion, each plays a favoured rôle in some pet drama in which Affection has written the story of cherished memories, and in which Hope blends her spice of untasted joys.

Artists, highest in the art of portraying pathetic scenes in life, have won imperishable fame, and justly so. While I would not presume to detract from their laurels, nevertheless with all their great works before us, offering as they do, the highest evidence that the knack of transferring the ideal to canvas, was known and practised long ago by a few of the old masters, it must be admitted, notwithstanding, by those who take the trouble to think, that the grandest achievement of the greatest painter can only be merely suggestive. After all it is God's own handiwork wrought in the imagination that gives it its splendor, its spirituality, its life! In this view, the corresponding ability on our part necessary to make it admirable, renders those sublime touches of Art a mutual success—not alone an exclusive honor to one, but a general triumph in which the humblest may claim participation.—Aye, and so the mendicant, crouched in abject adoration before that master-piece, "The Transfiguration," might, if he only knew and appreciated the high estate pertaining to his being, rise in the dignity of his manhood, and shaking off the trammels of mere social abasement, assume an indisputable share in the pride and glory of his brother Raffaelle.

IX.

Reality may be defined in many ways, and in its relation to things animate, may be regarded as one stage in life which infinitesimal space of time marks in our progress towards the end—evolved, as it were, in a complex system of whirlpools, round which we are propelled by all our inclinations, and the focus of all these minor pools is the bottomless vortex which we call the grave.

That we should take to these fateful stages of our momentous journey so willingly, comes about in that delightful exercise of the ideal which, by magnifying and radiating these friction sparks of time into a variety of pleasing forms, the period of fruition, becomes devoutly wished for epochs, to which, in perspective, we cleave lovingly. It is characteristic of our nature, as well as of the times, to want to draw near reality; I mean, the consummation of wishes and plans by which we are expecting a legacy of pleasure. All our faces turn that way, and there is a magnetism as well as a fascination about it that we cannot or do not resist. In fact, we are so far from simply submitting to be borne along, we use every means in our power to propel ourselves forward, and out of all patience, even with the rapid flight of time, in our contempt for its too tardy habits we cleverly ignore intervals,—opening our eyes only at certain periods, indicating we have arrived at this or that stage of our journey, which we are consoled to feel, is being expedited by the accelerated speed of lightning express.

These intervals which oftentimes we doze away and count as naught, constitute the ever perspective season we term *Anticipation*; the stopping-places being the *Reality*. The former is the blossoming,—the latter the fruition, of life; and thus classified, they represent respectively, pleasure and disappointment. It is no doubt true, with many people, this order is reversed, and they impatiently fret and fume for what they believe to be felicity, not in hand but coming, and they postpone their enjoyment till the happy period of arrival. But even then, our modicum of pleasure is doled out in anticipation, and to expedite the meeting we hasten forward in advance—like a bridegroom to meet his bride—rejoicing, indeed, rather than tiring as we wander, year after year, in a vain search for an affinity existing only in imagination.

X.

These intervals of waiting and longing, we all too frequently count as an ordeal of probation and self-denial to which we yield of necessity but most grudgingly. They are to us a tedious tension of mind and body, an agony of suspense which if we only outlive we think will usher in an ample compensation. Aye, and we bide the time as children do, itching and scratching through the interminable age twixt Christmas Eve and the tardy dawn that signals the sweet assault on socks.

Ah, how we long for the goal and that precious period of banqueting and love-making!—how we strain our mental vision to catch a glimpse of it ahead; but we will wait, we think consolingly, and not take anything in the meantime to spoil our appetite. And yet how impatient we are of our speed. We would outstrip Time. The one who drives the fastest it is taken for granted will get there first, and so we say, put on more steam, apply the whip, faster, faster! Old chums pass us in the race,—we congratulate them as they are hurled past; rivals go by us exultingly,—we envy them and are chagrined to be left behind.

If we have a dear and anxious friend with a film before his eyes, just a gauzy partition, say, between him and his promised land, we wrench it away feeling we have performed for him an invaluable service. But, great Heavens! we exclaim in alarm and consternation, what ails him now? he seems transfixed in terror—broken in grief. What have we done? Nothing we need mind about, it is what all the world does, it is a way they have; we waked him up, that is all. We thought it was the station where he wanted to stop, and in waiting for which he had been in such eager suspense, or perhaps we only informed him of something which we thought he ought to know and of which he was in blissful ignorance. Now, however, there is a change of aspect. Our disinterested performance was to him the unwelcome signal of some dread calamity, or may be only some lesser misfortune or vexation; but the contrast to present pain makes the retrospect seem as if it might have been delightful, and may be it was. Perhaps, our kindly office was a duty; still we say—though it may sound like the policy of the sick-room—we had done much better not to have disturbed him.

Who says nay, I care not what his belief, is the fanatic who issues forth in pious frenzy into the tranquil night of so called heathendom, and in the assumed voice of the avenging angel cries, "Fire! Fire!" when there is no fire. It falls upon the startled ear of the slumbering devotee, and wakes him to the carnal apprehension he will be burnt; and with no higher instinct than the mad impulse to save himself, he sees the opening where the light is let in—it is made to seem the only means of egress from his perilous situation—he jumps and then he falls into that lethargic state of new-fangled evangelism, whose boasted liberality is only too apt to be the arrogance of bigotry, the serenity of apathy.

Whatever orthodoxy may dictate to the contrary,

I believe there is reason in the indulgence that inclines in such a case to give him back his dream. I admit that dream may be all erroneous, but then if it be happy, it is as good as right, and if serenely confident that all is well, it is better than wisdom, it is faith. In making such a startling affirmation as,—if it be happy it must be right,—I mean that in following the simple promptings of humanity, all have the benefit of a monitor whose kindly suasion is not only in unison with the finest instincts of our nature, but also as nearly in accordance as it be possible to conceive, with that Divine will whose exponent, incarnate, is the human heart.

Would I approve the immolation of a fellow being as a sacred rite? No. Why? Because the instinct of which I speak condemns not only that horrid custom, but many others for which we have to thank, not the will of the people or of God, but rather the ordinance of a heartless Hierarchy, that they ever prevailed. We have exalted evidence of the fact that the worst atrocities in all the black roll of crime have been perpetrated in the name and misconception of right; but that does not disprove the view above enunciated. Nay, even in the tableau of the unhappy Abraham, sacrificing his own son, we see a further illustration of the common sense of making peace-of-mind the indicator of right doing; and the atrocious triumph of the saint over the father, on that occasion, is only redeemed from universal reprobation by the God of Silence having broken the spell of speechless wrath to bid him stay!

We may add, furthermore, that many of the doctrines we would substitute, are neither enlightened, peaceful, nor humane. There is no sense, no justice, no love in the abominable expedient of cruelty,—all virtues are opposed as with one voice to vengeance,—and the theory of a lake of fire, is no doubt a crude and glaring example of the sensual tendency of this and an obsolete age to materialize. However politic its use may have been in an early period, it is needless to inquire; but now it is not simply illogical, it is vicious to maintain, that to eke out the reward of spiritual felicity, we must needs not only be threatened with corporal punishment but have, as we do, this sweet fore-taste of fragrant Paradise, made at once redolent with the odors of appeasing incense and stifling with the fumes of purgatorial brimstone. Indeed, it can be regarded in no better light than as a sacrilegious monstrosity, the effete virtues of which are conceded only by those who have the brazen effrontery to profess what they do not believe,—and, without wanting in ability to apprehend, are lacking in manliness to condemn. I reiterate, it is a pious leprosy transmitted, despite the disinfecting fumes of incense, through the contagion of putrid generations. The effect being worse than in the darkest days of bigotry and intolerance; for without the faith that then obtained to dispose us to purchase absolution, we save our money and in the oblivion of its luxury enjoy a comfortable indifference erroneously dubbed liberal piety

XI.

Reality is the wreck of Imagination; and we see the evidences, all too sad and true, that Time has cast upon the shore. To a great extent, this is inevitable. We are all drifting on that rocky *portage* which, looming in a black barrier against the sky, betokens at once the end and the origin of the turbid waters of life. Well, let it come in the gradual progress of events; and why I raise my voice is to expostulate with that mad seamanship which, crowding on all sail and steaming directly for the land, precipitates catastrophe. The ambition of people in these fretful, enterprising times is, as I have said, to reduce all things pertaining to the ideal to the real—this, too, as quickly as possible—and therein, I claim, lies the secret of much tribulation, as well as the cause of that withering blight which, falling in the budding spring-tide of life, heaps upon a barren strand, joyless mounds of drifted leaves.

While the dream of happiness should not be awakened simply because it is a dream, the dispelling of anything so absurdly pleasant as many of our illusions may be, not unfrequently invites a worse deception in the fact that proves it a chimera. Besides, too, ideas nursed from their inception with parental tenderness, will attain later, the strength and maturity of reason and utility; whereas, to force their growth, as we do, is to invite decline and precipitate disappointment. Indeed, it is the cultivation of anticipation,—long drawn out, that becomes, in its gradual ripening, a fruitful source of happiness.—It does not perish from day to day as the shrivelling flesh, but fructifies in the spirit, and makes the ordeal of final dissolution only the birth of new life and the perpetuation of uninterrupted joy.

Here we may observe that, while consummation comes as the natural sequence to the hard wishing and toil preceding it, nevertheless, its tardy approach may be felicitated in the reflection that, the last blow struck in the completion of any work dispels the charm that made the idea of its origin the delight of its creation. Mere sensual gratification is, as a rule, the mainspring of all our plans and actions; but it is only in the exception, and that rarely, we realize expectation, and to find the true secret of happiness, we discover, when too late to enjoy, we must set about undoing, or at least repenting much we have done. This, too, notwithstanding our achievements may have been counted by the world a success.

In the labor of retrospection, we not unfrequently find those works by which we set the least store, assume the greater prominence and reveal the most worth. And in this connection we may note, the attainment of anything that is a mere contribution to our own pleasure must be distinguished from the performance of a duty, or some act of pure benevolence or kindness in behalf of others. In the latter case we may go about it with a degree of deliberation bordering on reluctance, and think wistfully of more genial tasks we have put aside for this work of self-abnegation. It is, or appears a sacrifice for which we may not expect much return, but now the pleasure, in the reverse order of the former case, instead of being the antecedent glow or thrill of greedy impulse, comes to lighten the retrospect of which I speak, and is, in effect, happiness sown for subsequent enjoyment—the recompense, the abundant gratification of a perpetual harvest.

In opposition to the real, one feature of the ideal is that it assumes persons and things to be better than they are, and more attractive than they would otherwise appear; and to this peculiarity are we indebted, not a little, for peace-of-mind under adverse circumstances. Indeed, it is not too much to assume there is no misfortune, taken in the *bona fide* course of events, that has not, as herein, its attendant and adequate balm to solace and recuperate.— We may go a little further even, and say there is no condition in life that has not the latent and natural, although wanting in the ostensible and material attributes to make all men equal and all things well.—That while the world is naturally as enjoyable for one as for another, the discrepancies that seem at variance with this are, for the most part, brought about by an improper exercise of nature's gifts; or, at best, by such a misconception of our duty as to make much of our boasted enterprise, greatly, if not wholly, at variance with the higher plans of a most kindly and impartial Providence. These plans for our happiness are neither difficult nor obscure; at least, they would not be, did not our schooling and enlightenment make them so, and our advisers, instead of guiding, mislead us as regards what constitutes the true treasure and correct object of life.

It must be confessed some may appear more bountifully favored than others, but so far as worldly goods are concerned, while appreciation makes the poor man rich, avarice makes the rich man poor. Physically, however, the above exception would seem to obtain, but even those cases are endowed with retrieving graces of the mind. Besides, the man who carts his body around with him every where is under the muscular dominion of appetite, and is beguiled by something worse than the vanity of his own shadow. Then, too, while the exercise of our corporeal being is conducive to pleasure, it is equally susceptible to pain: youth favors the former, old age the latter. Now while we labor professedly to provide for the infirmities of the one, our efforts are really to supply the appetites of the other; and the store, however tempting it would have been in our early days, seems, on the contrary, more especially adapted to the punishment of a Tantalus than to the succoring of our enfeebled energies. So it is, old and incapable, we find we have succeeded, by exercising all the keener instincts of the gourmand, in realizing the dream of the voluptuary; but in the attainment of a luxurious establishment, perfect in all its appointments, there is still one drawback.—It is, indeed, an elysium for youth, but the very opposite of an asylum for old age, and pestered with the cruel inconsistency between the armchair of the patriarch and the goal of the juvenile,—poor, miserable, chagrined,—we turn from the gilded fraud, a wholly ineligible candidate for the temporary use, much less the unrestricted enjoyment, of our own possessions.

XII.

The measure of misery which a thing may produce is in inverse ratio to the pleasure it is capable of affording. Though we derive exquisite enjoyment from the FLESH, it is only in the exception it is not made the instrument of our suffering; meanwhile a little of that observation bestowed on less worthy objects discovers this mistake,—that we set our chief store of happiness by it. As, however, we may not blind ourselves to the fact that it must perish, we become the natural prey to a well-founded apprehension and, instead of rejoicing, lament in the midst of our material triumphs.

Why the poorer classes are not happier is because they are not educated beyond the satisfying of mere brute appetite; and amongst the wealthy and more cultivated the same animal propensities are only the more largely but gracefully developed and exercised. So, also, the use and discipline, and not alone the exaltation and praise, of those higher faculties which would raise them above the dread of petty failure and a shabby living, although professedly observed to the letter, are virtually ignored, both in spirit and practice, or at best patronized only for effect.

In other words, the so-called refinement we see paraded all around us, and bought and paid for, is to man what a brush or curry-comb is to a horse—a means for showing them off to greater advantage. But being, in the former case, adapted especially to the embellishment of prosperity, it does not in any degree develop those other latent qualities and deep-hidden gems, which, constituting at once the glittering regalia of man's innate royalty and the patent of his nobility, go so far to win homage and respect even for the refugee in adversity.

The truth is, we do not foster a proper esteem for the idealistic. Nay, and the time stolen, as if in shame, from the all too engrossing cares of business, and dedicated grudgingly to the seemingly unprofitable cultivation of that beautiful and prolific field, should not be, as it is, the fag-end of a idle hour,—a dusky intrusion on a wearied spirit,—and, altogether, the peevish tribute of a vexed day's old age, but rather a goodly share of that period which gladdens the first springy impulses of restored nature—I mean that golden border to the night when the mellow flame that lights our dreams merges in the rosy blush of dawn—that nick of time when starry Eve, rising in sweet embarrassment from the arms of Morpheus, yields with maternal instinct to the ever recurring infancy of elastic morn, and,—vanishing,—we still behold the imprint of her kiss in sprinkled dew-drops sparkling on the baby face of the new-born day!

XIII.

Youth is supposed to be overflowing with romantic visions, which it is presumed by the older ones to be their duty to dispel, and so they belabor themselves in hacking and pruning and trimming. Give us, say these knowing ones, corn not roses, and the flower they encourage is the kind they eat. This reminds one of the fanaticism of the reformer or pioneer, who cuts down and clears away every vestige of tree, and shrub, and vine, in his contempt for what he styles vain and profitless ornament. Later generations, however, frequently find that what their extinct daddies prudently condemned as an extraneous and worthless growth, was not all a superfluous production and a mistake in nature, and thereupon invoke bountiful and ever-forgiving Providence, to restore the grateful luxury of this old-time heritage. Then it is the bushy chestnut and the leafy oak, the ever-green hedge-row and blossoming gorse, once so unceremoniously expelled, are recalled and reinstated. Then, too, as the scions of an ancient noblesse in the gorgeous pageant of a restored dynasty, they are pointed out with pride and love, not only as amongst the courtly graces of a benigner *régime*, but also as the most admirable tokens of an improved social polity.

Generally speaking, in our treatment of the mind, we seek to sow only what will mature quickest, and as regards expeditiousness in yielding, are 'rather disposed to favor the example of some of the lower orders of animals. We would, if we could, make production simultaneous with conception, sowing and reaping all in the same stride. The variety of production aimed at, being that which will the most readily contribute to the making up of what is termed a "living," beyond this we have in view what constitutes our highest conception of an earthly EL-DORADO—it is comprehended in an article and a substantive, and this noun, together with its adjunct, is about all the great majority of us ever realize of " A FORTUNE."

In this manner the minds of our children are "trained," only in such teaching as, like the wares of a common huckster, can be the soonest realized in the market; and thus, with all the ridiculous gravity of learned baboons, we apply ourselves to enlarging their understanding, by warping their aspirations. The one all-absorbing object in life is money-making, and to accomplish this end we subordinate both the uses of Education and the purposes of Existence.

Nor are the higher systems of what is erroneously called "University" education, without such warping characteristics as make them like the "religion" of sects, catholic only in name. We might have hoped (might still hope) to see our universities convalescent homes for diseased prejudice; but instead of that, they are contagious resorts, where healthy minds are sent to be inoculated with the prevailing distempers of the age, and are graduated invalids physically,—and mentally, maniacs on every subject pertaining to the liberal doctrine of common sense. Education, however, ordinarily speaking, is largely the result of a hasty cramming, and mechanical committal to memory, of numberless text-books—many of which are "garbled," and the true meaning of the original perverted and mystified. Its use, the dexterous application of certain rules and formulas, not in the commoner business affairs of life merely, but in those professions where the ministering of these forms are become lucrative occupations and crafts for the exclusive benefit of the few, and to the impoverishment and general hardship of the many. Beyond "coaching" the intellect to profit by and maintain "professions" and "cliques" which are already become a grievous public nuisance, our process of "culture," inculcates no more liberality than is observable in the arrogance of the pedant, whom we see delivering himself with such sententious gravity and *aplomb* of his unimpeachable "authorities." Here let us observe there is nothing, speaking within bounds, that the human mind in the exercise of its natural energy and foresight, does not possess the faculty to analyze and test. Without doubt, too, the truly ennobling part of knowledge is the real hard study and thought by which it is originally conceived. But this effort of mental brooding and hatching, is impossible, when it is considered the number of rules, regulations, and exceptions one must be able to rattle off in order to stand high in his class. So ignoring our own self-producing faculties, we take and pay for the intellectual food prepared for our consumption, and, with no thought of the altered conditions of life, shut our eyes and blindly swallow.

In this way it comes about, the youth aspiring to collegiate honors is set to the routine of acquiring knowledge when he is not considered fit for anything else; graduating later, literally stuffed with ideas not his own, he astonishes an ignorant community by fathering conceptions whose real parents are as old as the Pyramids.

XIV.

In athletics, each different exercise brings into requisition new sets of muscles, all of which become stronger with the strain. This applies as well to the mental, as to the physical organisms. In the former case, however, these combinations, rightly exercised assume, through the medium of fancy, all the brilliancy of pyrotechnics, together with the changeful splendors of the kaleidoscope,—this, too, with the additional and fateful charm of that vitalizing essence which, instead of conveying to the senses the marvellous phenomena of pleasing and wonderful colors only, endows those coruscant flashes in the ideal heavens, with the highest perfection of human virtue and intelligence. Then it is, that in the sublimity of their conception, and in the infinitude of their variety, we identify mind with soul,— and, stamping thought with those regal attributes of primitive creation, blend the likeness of man with that of the Supreme, and unite mortality with immortality!

In confining ourselves to the more grovelling affairs of material advancement, our greed, in the effort to plunder others, overleaps itself, and we pass indifferently over the fact that each and all of us possess immense territories in the mind, which, though we regard them in many cases as of no particular value or utility, are only veiled in a mystic wealth, whose hidden veins of latent riches intersect our ideal being. While these only need a little exploring and opening up to be brought most agreeably and beneficially into play, they are permitted, nay encouraged, to lie fallow; hence, though ignorance may sometimes be bliss, it is not economy.

There is the impression we have already noticed, which is, if we leave the Imagination free it would run riot; sober teaching, it is claimed, is necessary to keep it within bounds. So they clap on the brakes and set the young mind, not to grubbing always, but to copying after the example of certain models so antiquated as to merit the unique title of "classical." Barring, however, their opportunity to thus discipline the Imagination they do what is considered by some the best, and by many the next best thing,—they hobble it. Later, forsooth, the highest conception such a stinted mind can have, is to get rid of its shackles; like the poor cripple, whose dream of bliss is to be rid of his deformity.

Generally speaking, time, labor, and treasure spent in the imbibing of certain so-called knowledge and doctrines invariably secure, if not our belief, at least our acquiescence in the truth and infallibility of such acquirements. Our puny intellects have wrestled with the mighty works of famous masters, and we come out of the scholastic tussle mental athletes in the handling of the ponderous problems and prodigious ideas of other men. We are easily made proud of our achievements, and the refined world applauds; but what are the acquirements of which we boast? Some, it is true, may be genuine trophies won in the bloodless warfare that is waged with all the pomp and gallantry of the mock-heroic against that vandal Ignorance; but the most of them are ideas plundered in the anarchy of conflicting theories,—pratings, cribbed in the abstraction of adverse opinion.

Some of these mental offshoots may and do bear transplanting, and taking root, on the principle of the graft, find sap enough in our heads to be kept alive; and though they become a surface growth—the ivy of wisdom only— are both highly ornamental, and admirably adapted to the difficulty of fastening their delicate tendrils into the hardest and most opaque substances. But here we may indulge the conceit suggested by the thought that, in the donning of this sort of apparel, if Nature was as obliging to the lower orders of animals as with man, we should be treated to the edifying spectacle of the male of the goose assuming the brilliant plumage of the peacock, and the female of the baboon decked out in the incomparable splendors of the bird of paradise. I do not intend to enter into a lengthy critique on such acquirements; while being capital in stock to the possessor, they are in many cases the mysterious fountain of professional reverence and success, and as such cannot be too highly prized or too zealously sought after. Satisfying, in this view then, the purposes for which they are intended, it is not surprising that, despite the imposing amount of erudition upon which Progress and Civilization are supposed to wait to get their authority and impetus to go on, how often we find amongst the votaries of this species of knowledge, if not the most bigotry, at any rate the least originality. Then, too, many minds supposed in this way to be most abundantly enriched, are rather hampered and weighed down with a mighty load of fossil trumpery, impeding the free activity of the Imagination which, instead of being allowed to swim, like a fish, propelled by the graceful unity and combined symmetry of all its parts, is packed like a donkey and made to climb. Thus, with a limpid sea before us, of myriad springs of living waters, and with the mind's heaven of peerless blue, in which Imagination mirrors all the jewelled wealth of the other starry realm, we confine our thoughts to commerce and to skipping, like flies, over the dank, fetid moisture which sepulchral ages have accumulated in the foot-prints of pigmies!

XV.

Many things we know by heart, we never took the trouble to ascertain the meaning of, and the true merit of which had we known, we had never taken the trouble to learn by heart. To various forms of this sort of rubbish are we lashed, as was Moses in the rushes, and thus swathed, are sent out into the world, not simply to battle for life, but to perform a certain task which is to make money, and to get possession of our neighbors' property, without actually robbing him.

This dowery of antiquated lore is supposed to keep our moral being afloat, and we are enjoined by the guardians of our intellectual welfare to stick to it for dear life. Then, when we are aroused later to rational consciousness, *that* is the sort of stuff to which we find we have been clinging as do sailors to the debris of a shipwreck. In some respects this may be all well enough, but in others its ludicrousness is exhibited in the spectacle of people, who never see more than water enough to wash themselves in, walking in rugged ways miles in-land, lashed as I have said to these grotesque moral life-preservers. Thus it is that the manners of the Nineteenth-Century assume the characteristics of the Deluge, and the grand avenues of our boasted free-thought and free speech retain all the tortuous windings, which in a primitive age was traced by the meandering path of some blear-eyed, crazy, old goat.

While this may be regarded as an exaggeration, there is no doubt that many of the teachings and writings with which we burden our memories are to day highly venerable specimens of obsolete nonsense—admirably adapted, no doubt, to the circumstances that gave them birth, but may we not presume they have served the purposes of their creation, and ought to be allowed to become extinct; instead of which, their general and eternal application to all similar cases and requirements are not simply taken for granted, but rigidly enforced. Thus, emergencies in the lives of our piously revered ancestors, whose vicissitudes partisan History in its efforts to glorify has obscured, and who lived too long ago, either to excite interest, or to be known, are kept in a state of perpetual and mock resurrection. In this way, too, the crime, heroism and conviviality, which, together with their concomitants anguish, cowardice, and heart-burn, that disturbed the peace of individuals thousands of years ago, are made subjects of religious tuition and kept alive, fostered, and moralized.

Again, if we take the man who in his early youth was shortened or pulled out to suit the Procrustean measure of " useful knowledge," and has used his intellect like a tread-mill. Is he struggling for "creature comforts?" Well, talk to him about the virtues of the idealistic, and you will either excite his contempt or scare the life out of him; at least, he will suspect your sanity or designs. He has become so as to feel that anything outside the items regulating his hire and subsistence, and the routine of his departmental duties are a "delusion and a snare." Or let us presume he has plodded into "a fortune," and that all his aspirations and efforts have been enlisted and absorbed in the work. Well, in the zenith of his triumph he is a monomaniac,—neither can he stop even to taste in peace the fruits of his labor. This man went in exclusively for the substantial, not the idealistic, and as the incentive to exertion, so the measure of the reward partakes of the nature of the body and not of the spirit. Talk to him of the trophies of an ideal realm, and you only excite his derision. It is true he may ape an admiration for some things pertaining to Art, and even condescend to patronize them, but his "forte" is business and all his energies are focussed on the prospect of accumulating property. He can't bring his cramped abilities to bear on any thing else, and though not originally a brute, he has gone in for and must be satisfied with the enjoyment of the brute.

I don't say he may not enjoy a certain amount of gratification in his way, so long as his treasures stay by him, but these do not rise above the dignity or satisfaction of mere chattels, and on them he is as helplessly dependent as a child. Indeed, in the case of him or any one else, whose life objects are embodied in his possessions, loss of property is the most pregnant source of misery. Even though he secure his means against reverses, then, since his wealth cannot be taken from him, he is tortured with another still darker apprehension,—may not he be taken away, kidnapped as it were from his wealth, and removed beyond all hope of restoration from that which has catered so fondly to his appetites. This phantom stays by him to the last; overshadowing not only his own future, but also that of his children, whose happiness he may think, and has taught them to feel, is dependent on the same grovelling and penurious conditions.—Ah, it is a spectre only to be driven away by the lusty exercise of a superabundance of animal, or as is most frequently the case, of alcoholic spirits. So too, consistently with this man's manner of living, the anniversary of his dissolution is the serving of a bountiful feast,—a most sumptuous spread of costly plate and tempting viands—and at the head of the table, in the great arm chair of domestic state, sits enthroned a bleaching skeleton. Then straightway, his bones are hustled away as are the debris of a Christmas banquet, and the routine of twixt holidays goes on.

XVI.

I have no doubt if you could have met this man in his more clammy moments.—I mean when the steam of a hardly contested competition had condensed somewhat—he would have assured you in the vacant contemplation of an absent mind, he was not what the world thought him—a success. That he had made a great mistake in life, and in his own private opinion, his career had been a failure.—That business vexations, from which he had ever been powerless to claim exemption, had always kept him dissatisfied, perplexed, miserable; farthermore, he doubted whether there was any such thing as happiness except in the fevered visions of extatic dreamers.

Well, I do not favor any more than he or anybody else the apathetic dozing away of precious life; but what I do object to is, on the one hand, the chaining down of the mind to the exigencies and vanities of a mere body-service; and on the other, that species of superficial culture which while being the other extreme of vacant sentimentality, only tickles the fancy by such a mechanical absorption of the beautiful ideals of others as, aping the inborn refinement of which these are the external evidence, enables us to shine, as does the moon, in the virtue of a reflected light. What I would like to see is less trafficking in extraneous opinion and borrowed wisdom, and an improved growth of unsophisticated common sense and native originality.

To bring this about we need not necessarily go to college to be hampered with garbled versions of ancient lore; nor need we give up projects and employments, the furtherance of which are necessary for our subsistence; but spend less money on the body and more time on the mind. Do not dissipate the vital forces in false excitement, but husband and develop nature's wealth in tranquil meditation. This of itself will lead on to that most important desideratum of our existence, which is the cultivation of a free, healthful range of independent thought and study. Then without stinting the Imagination, give all things pertaining to the ideal as much scope as possible—and this, without let or hindrance on the part of those craunching, blighting mill-stones, business and especially domestic affairs. It alone can establish our claim, not to the paltry possession of lands and tenements, but to the universe; and while it raises us above the vexed repining over mean estate and humble fare, so does it soothe the more saddening consciousness of our shrivelling and ever-ailing flesh. For just inasmuch as they become wedded to the body or the spirit, and make the one or the other of these the chief object of adoration, so are the poor amongst us wealthier than the rich, and the rich poorer than penury itself. Behold the hermit whom we see cloistered and seemingly sequestered from the world! Is it sanctity, "pure and simple" that eradiates his cheerful soul ? No! at least, not as we think; he enjoys in his voluntary incarceration an undisturbed liberty of the fancy free as the unfettered dream of Paradise! Aye, though the body be imprisoned, let the Imagination sail about the air like a hawk.—It sees in the grand ensemble of nature, outspread beneath, the true sublimity of Creation; then, too, the order of greatness amongst the living is reversed, and while the Mastodons of the human race are seen wallowing in the mire, behold, the despised insects weaving their "mansions in the sky," and in all the atoms that people the air, there is a harmony of purpose which makes their instinct diviner than our wisdom.

XVII.

Here we may observe, that to let these Fancies simply "run wild," were to neglect them. I do not mean that. Give them the appropriate means of wholesome and agreeable expression; and, to accomplish this, Imagination can have no more admirable or satisfying an interpreter than music or painting. But as we observed regarding the ways and uses of culture generally, these accomplishments, as such, we treat as gilding or use as hacks; and, without the application necessary to give them the stamp of our individuality, abandon them after a few lessons, leaving their higher attainment to a few whose devotion is esteemed genius, and whose performances are made, to us, the hired luxury of bodily, rather than of intellectual entertainmet. As it is, with youthful dabblers and even older performers, the exercise and cultivation of the former and most pleasing of these vehicles of sentiment, is made the dreaded task of a penance, and not, as it ought to be, the soul-inspiring delight of a passion. Indeed, to regard those more exquisite strains of melody, we sometimes hear, as mere acquisitions to the duller forms of conviviality, is to debase, (as most of our pursuits incline us to do,) the noblest gifts of man or brute. If, however, we may take a hint from the more soothing and exalting effects we know these produce, may we not presume, as claimed herein, that in the cultivation of the idealistic generally, we bring into grateful play the most refining influences of the mind; and while its exercise, in the many ways conducive to enjoyment, is not confined to music alone, nevertheless to give it tongue its language is song.

All proper minded people now-a-days say take away your novels, take away your romances and give us what is real. I do not intend to discuss the merit or utility of works of fiction. They might be, though rarely are, beautiful products of the imagination, and like pictured landscapes, are, or ought to be, true to nature, and hence no fiction. But now, I admit, they are prostituted and pander, only too often, to those cravings which revel in the portrayal of other and more exciting scenes in the downward stage of life. But then, even the worst of these are only poultices, highly seasoned, with which we swathe our diseased minds and bring to the surface the more corrupt humors of the body. They deserve an item of credit too, and sometimes serve a little good; for like swine, they root about, as many another more pretentious radical, pointing their noses at holes in our fences. And so viewed in an unprejudiced light may be regarded as no worse a visitation, perhaps, than the old time curse of frogs and locusts.

XVIII.

Apropos of realities, however, it is but just to admit that some of them are as pleasant as could be wished, and would be delightful, for that matter, did not our schemes of enjoyment overshoot their mark and leave us unconscious of the goal, which, by the way, we may be in the midst of, but in our haste and ignorance think it far away. The fact is, there is no royal standard to designate that particular hallowed spot, and the truth of its proximity, dawns upon us, if at all, insensibly—most invariably, too, after we have passed it, and when, alas, it is too late to go back.

In this connection I am reminded of one place in our racing, steaming career where our train slacks sometimes, and even offers, now and again, the luxury of a full stop. It is the most genial halt on the line. Then it is we are partially aroused from our listless indifferent state by the shock produced in a sudden cessation of the infernal vibration and rumble attendant on our tremendous speed—and are brought full out of our drowsy lethargy by the porter shouting in stentorian tones, " Nunda! Nunda! twenty minutes for refreshments!" Nunda, we exclaim almost involuntarily, why Nunda is *home!* And there is a tremulousness in the voice in which is breathed the music of that magic word home. Not home-in-law but in-nature; not the teasing invention of a later fancy, but the original and indisputable heritage of immaculate mother love. The old, old home,—that one embalmed in sweetest memories of bygone days,—hallowed and saddened as time goes on with the imperilled wealth of all its early associations, but treasured still as the dear old moss-grown reminiscence of " lang syne."

In boyhood we have romped and revelled there—and in the dust and turmoil of later years, have cleaved to the grateful shade. In distant lands, amongst strangers and alone we have sighed to think of that fair abode so far away, and weary of the fascinations that beguiled us hence, have closed our eyes on grander sights to welcome back again the dear old vision. Is it, indeed, the old, old home? Yes; the old, old home. With some, perchance, this temple of boyhood's idolatry has passed forever away; but even then it is seen in imagination, where it remains up to the very last—pictured in the mind. Old Age, propped upon the elbow of declining years—watching his sun set— sees it in the direction in which the sunbeams slant, bathed in a flood of golden light, and in the puzzled delight of childish rapture, mistaking it for the other Paradise, thinks it the ineffable goal of life's troubled prayer!

Alas, how little does this sentiment affect many of us in reality; and on this occasion, it is appalling how coolly and indifferently we take in the situation. "Ah, Nunda; —let me see, the old people live here now I believe. Twenty minutes! let's see, I'll just have time to drop in and say how-d'ye do. Home right on the way—what a happy coincidence—won't lose any time and I would like very well to see the old folks." So we hurry away with this good object in view. But as we pick our way in vexed bewilderment through the labyrinth that environs home, we are just the least bit irritated by an unpleasant feeling that we are somewhat a stranger in that once familiar maze whose puzzling ways it was amongst our earliest impulses to explore; and we recall, with a certain gravity and even qualm of conscience, the long time that has elapsed since last with tearful pang we dropped the silken thread of its magic tracery.

Clambering up the grass-grown steps leading to those once cherished portals we seem to cast a shadow on the porch. Ah, it is the phantom of "Love's Young Dream," hovering over the sheltered screen of its early slumber. Then, too, that old door-bell, we think, sounds strangely like Vespers, and there are other shades gathering about the place as of the twilight of waning years. Well, it may not be so bright as memory has so often pictured it, and yet it is the dear old home still. And there is about it all a mellow haze, like unto the autumn summer, betokening a welcome assurance of the unquenched source within of all our boyhood love, and sunshine.

There is but little time for meditation, however; we soon find ourselves in the eager embrace of "first love;" and anxious inquiries and tearful eyes greet us in the warm impulse of genuine solicitude and affection. Then it is we feel a slight touch of childishness, and for a moment hesitate about throwing aside our coat and the other paraphernalia of our toilsome pilgrimage. A thought creeps in, and seems more than usually persistent in its appeal, to let our journey end here—at least for a time. But nay; our route shows this to be only a "flag station" where one pulls up when he gets a special signal, it may be, of distress.—"This our goal! No,—it is only the place we started from and here we're back again." Then we think, ruefully, we must have made a mistake in our calculation to have stopped at all, and are nearly vexed at the idea of being in such a profitless place as home. No, we must push on and make up for what seems lost time. But there is MOTHER—Heaven bless her

—she who knew our likings once so well; and at the first glimpse of a face so quickly remembered as ours, notwithstanding the disguise of beard, she is divided in the sweet perplexity of joy at our return and the pleasure she will have in the design of "something good." Then, straightway she conjures up some tempting dish that with her boys never failed to win their suffrage and their praise. It is not necessary they should come home loaded with presents, and followed by the plaudits of admiring multitudes; but hunted to earth—battered and broken, penniless and hungry as they may be, and too often are, still there is the greater wealth of gladness in getting home, and, the son's feast is the mother's banquet.

Ten minutes have passed and we are almost getting to dread we must so soon say "good-bye." Besides, the old folks have so much to tell us and there is such a treasured fund of unanswered query they would glean from our lips. Aye, they brought us into being, and crave, with wistful eyes and longing hearts the welcome boon of a fragment of our, to them, dear life's precious story. 'Tis vain—the bell rings—time is up.—We bid the stunned and bewildered old couple a hasty adieu—it may be their last glimpse of us on earth—and are gone before their enfeebled minds could well have found fit expression for their full hearts. But we have not missed the train.—The cry "all aboard" breaks the spell of home—and again we are rushing on with a frantic, tireless eagerness to realize other and more lucrative stages in the progress to our goal.

XIX.

The florist knows the name and nature of every one of the little wilderness of plants under his care, though we commonly blend them all under the general appellation and aspect of flowers. While the examination of each family specimen of this blooming progeny reveals a corresponding resemblance to the human plant, it is but one of the many sublime objects offered the conscientious idealist in the anatomy of the human mind. Indeed, the analysis of character, presents the same delightful task as the study of all these different varieties of bud and blossom, with the enhanced charm of human instead of vegetable life. And while the cultivation of the idealistic faculties, together with that vigilant exercise of them as will keep them from becoming blurred, tend the more strongly to define and individualize each distinctive feature and phase of our nature, we thus acquire an appreciation of our mental powers and resources, and therein, also, a knowledge of self.

Ideas susceptible of being realized in this life constitute the immediate and most pleasing incentive to action. They incline us in the performance of nearly everything that is said or done, and only tend, in their higher adulterations, to that restless distemper we call ambition. These ideas are identical with that most prolific element in the mind we know as imagination—their conception being that sensation of delight we esteem happiness. The nobler and purer these are the less exciting, perhaps, but the more exquisite the pleasure, and the more prolonged the enjoyment; and just insomuch as our aspirations glory in hopes and expectations which can only be realized in another world, do we revel in those exalted realms of thought to which we may consistently apply the sacred appellation of Religion. Again, that revelation in the mind enabling some to realize the full fruition of things generally found impossible of attainment, and overleaping in their demonstration the commonly accepted bounds of reason, is a conception bordering on the supernatural:— we call it, in some cases, madness; in others, genius; and this phenomenon in religion is either spurned as fanaticism or glorified as Inspiration.

There are many things we know to be not only actual facts but sources of useful knowledge, and as such I have no desire to undervalue them; at any rate, we cannot change them at will. While in many respects facts partake very much of the caprice of things in general, nevertheless they possess this peculiarity for constancy, viz: they won't "budge" just when we want them to; they are part of the heterogeneous estate of man, and many times, alas, standing directly in our path incommode us sorely. Indeed, how often they obtrude themselves, as grim, mouldy walls, built in the exercise of proprietorial greed, right up in front of our window!—aye, reared in the legal right of man to monopolize the air, but cutting off for ever a most charming view of some pet-landscape.

Anticipation finds in Reality the arch enemy by whom she is beguiled and betrayed; he sucks her life-blood, nor is he sated till she becomes a corpse—then, that the sweet ideal no longer lives becomes a Fact. Illusion may be regarded as the dream of Anticipation—when she wakes her smile is gone, and when she dies she gives birth to Experience:—this latter progeny assumes to be resigned and virtuous, but is really all the time plotting to revenge the mother, and for this purpose employs a spy, which we know by the name of Doubt.

Neither *fact* nor *reality* may be considered incontrovertible; talk of either and you confront us with the uncertainty of all things, temporal as well as spiritual. True, we see and know, in one sense, many things that actually exist or transpire, but even then, in our relations and intercourse with each other, comes in the inevitable adjunct of which I speak, to taint the purity and to disturb the tranquillity of our most confident assurances. While this seems engendered in the inexplicable mystery of our separate individualities, we find Friendship, Love, Divinity, sublimest Trinity, conspiring with their subtle affinities and meanest opposites, in unkindly confederacy to nurse Suspicion.—Aye, and thus, pampered and puffed till abnormally plump, does that sinister trait over-lap, while yet a cherub, the rosy bed of the world's sweetest nuptials! Later, old and lean, and gaunt and hungry Doubt is the vulture that sweeps down upon poor Fidelity, and, with a rapacity worse than that which feeds on carrion, laps up the bloom that glistens on the fresh, dewy leaves of Truth!

XX.

There is a feature about the ideal which it may be no more than fair to rival claims to mention. I refer to that discrepancy in the imagination known as Apprehension. This latter quality was intended, we might naturally presume, to be a provision in our nature to insure a judicious amount of caution; but, in the case of many, bad habits and teaching, and still worse consciences, have given it a painfully ludicrous form and growth, and then it becomes a jungle of phantom animals,— many of the magnitude and ferocity of the species termed "extinct," and as grotesque and unreal as those of the " antediluvian period." Indeed nothing was ever seen except in apprehension so absurd, so unreasonable, and withal so terrible, except, perhaps, those regal phantasms incorporated in armorial monstrosities which modern history keeps resuscitated,—aye, and which some aristocratic Democracies still retain, in palatial museums of princely pedigree, as mementos of the less enlightened reign of Griffins, Dragons, and Unicorns!

Assuming for the nonce the smallest animal in all the mimic menagerie of Apprehension to be that grunting pigmy which distinguishes Guinea; then, let this inoffensive quadruped fancy itself a Colossus in whose presence all the other and greater monsters become tame and subservient and virtually lose their identity,' and we shall see typified in the most diminutive of hogs the meaner sort of characteristic called "Conceit." Again, were I a magician I might change all these animals into one, and, giving it the instincts of all the others, call it Chameleon. Then, with the craft of the fox, would be blended the confiding grace of the gazelle;—with the strength and arrogance of the lion, the gravity and wisdom of the baboon;—with the radical impulses of the porcupine, the conservatism of the owl;—and with all repellant attributes of the skunk would be mixed the redeeming characteristics of the musk-rat, together with the peculiar fascination of the anaconda! I would call it Chameleon, because of the presumption that this mongrel would be able to change itself into any or all the other characters to suit the occasion; but in the phraseology we use to make ourselves understood, you will probably comprehend better what this monster would be like when I tell you in plain English it would be MAN!—and the female, WOMAN! and their corresponding affinities in this aspect of human traits would be Egotism and Vanity.

XXI.

In the higher ideal of life we may conceive poor Mortality proceeding along his journey, surrounded by a queenly retinue of sympathizing spirits and goodly influences: each of these is known by a certain name, and the absence of any one of them may be regarded as a moral deficiency. They are incorporeal, but incorruptible, and while they may not control, they point the way. Working against these, however, are all the brute instincts of the body, and the ups and downs of life are but the outward signs of the material triumphs and defeats that distinguish these opposing elements.

In the onward rush to realize—in the turmoil and strife of this great traffic of life, or say in the venture of some pet scheme—as we are about to plunge forward, and are gathering our energies for the spring, we sometimes feel conscious of something nudging our elbow; there is magic in the thrill of that touch, and a voice so soft and sweet, that it seems to blend in the harmony of the air whispers,—"pause, reflect!" It is Prudence!—one of the fostering band above noted—and her duty is to watch and restrain. She may generally be found in company with Patience, whose mission is tranquillity and contentment: and here we may observe to think of Patience as "on a monument, smiling at grief," is an atrocious caricature, and it is such erroneous, but graceful phrases, that give us wrong impressions of these traits of character. She is not a goddess of lethargy, and does not and could not live in apathy. Prudence leaves her to keep us company while we wait, and were we not blind to her winning ways, we should find her maybe, even a pleasanter companion than the doubtful charmer that keeps us in suspense; but we cannot bear to tarry, we even mistrust the agents by which we are delayed, so we regard Patience as a decoy, and suspect and dislike her exceedingly. Sometimes we do manage to tolerate her after a fashion; she is, we think, a necessary restraint; but then we blame Prudence for it all, and she, we find simply insufferable. When we go about the enjoyment of any thing—we may be only going to call on some particularly agreeable and genial companions, or to some entertainment of especial attraction;—or, it may be in the more sober course of business, to look after a speculation or project that appeals with more than the usual force and attractiveness to the weaker points in our nature; but just in the flush of animal impulse, we must needs meet Prudence brushing past us in a contrary direction. And then it is she turns, and motioning us aside from the exciting throng, tries to persuade us to take some other course,—which, by the way, is generally opposed to that we would most willingly have taken, and very often at sharp and galling angles to our inclinations.

No; she doesn't bid us godspeed on all our expeditions, and still she sticks to us like a jealous spouse. She is an imperious beauty, however, and we are afraid to tell her to be gone; nevertheless, we don't like her—dread her, in fact, because she knows all the wrong we ever did, and being about, as usual, in good time, advised us against it. Often have we tried, but not quite succeeded, in deceiving her, or even in prevailing on her to take a nap. Now and then she seems as if she would like to have us make love to her, but she is not our peculiar style, and we can't "warm up" to her.—Nay, there is about the phlegm of that passionless face the cheerless complexion of polished marble!—her air is cold,—and her breath upon our little floral world's a frost! She would freeze us, we say, and we turn away to conjure up some genial and more glowing picture where untrammelled Desire cuddles in the drowsy luxury of heart's-content that less prudish dame, Indulgence.

So much do our ideas partake of the venal, we are scarcely able to comprehend a blessing, and are too prone in our ignorance and selfishness to mistake good, for ill; blame, when we should commend; and lament when we ought to rejoice.

As with Prudence, so with all the other ways of Providence: they may, and often do, seem harsh, and cold, and unsympathetic; nevertheless, they are ministering, nourishing agents of a Love, compared with which the noblest of our own is but a peevish fancy—a base *amour*. With all the sublime consistency, then, of a great, overruling affection, do these messengers perform their silent, thankless part, as attributes of that Higher Compassion that, in the effort to dissuade us from wrong-doing, would, through these means, admonish,—but failing that, the task is yielded to a Divinity who never fails,—and that is—MERCY!

Brutalized as we are, however, we can not discriminate, and our habits and perceptions are not refined enough to enable us to see in the moist eye of Providence a diamond sparkling in pity there, whose radiance is a reflex of the celestial fount. Even while we sleep it falls, and what seems so like a frost to us, is the tears of an all-prevailing Commiseration descending, in a gentle ineffable balm of mist, through the slumberous twilight earthward.—To relapsed but restless, yearning nature, it is the harbinger of renewed vitality.—It is repast to the homeless and shelterless of all dumb creation, and they return thanks in the song of the night-bird, in the purling stream, and in the plashing waterfall.—It reinvigorates the tenderest plants, and gives to the Violets their sweetest attributes of loveliness.—It is the magic elixir that revives the drooping Lily, and touching the ruby lips of Roses, its kiss is their bloom.—It settles upon the twig and it leaves—It is breathed upon the bud and it blossoms—and in the first ardent sunbeam of early morn, blends and expands into the perfect Flower!!

XXII.

Apropos of those phantom spirits to which I have referred, there is one amongst them we may not forget to notice here; and I may say, in its behalf, if there be anything that is able to make the worship of mortals especially acceptable to the Reader of Hearts, it is that one quality to which I desire in this connection to call particular attention.

Imagination may take us to the "Pearly Gates," but to pass the Heavenly Wicket into Paradise, it is most essential to possess the "open sesame" of a spirit whose true virtue is known only to the Custodian of purest love:—I mean, Sincerity. Of all the good traits that commend us to approbation, this one is the strongest element in our propitiation, and however defective our title to favor, it is our highest claim to forgiveness. While Sincerity alone can make intangible thought and intention prevail over adverse deeds, its absence is a mortal defect in the most graceful service, and while needing no adornment to make it beautiful, the want of it is not atoned by the gorgeous trumpery that embellishes its counterfeit. And here let us observe, of that fashionably attired modern Serapis, whose worship exalts Hypocrisy : its glory is the ostentatious profession of a splendid creed !—its prerogative, the pious assumption of an organized power ! and its praise, forsooth, such a "*Deum Laudamus*," as makes the chanting of the most imposing hymnal a chorus of melodized antagonisms, whose sweetest strains are but too apt to be the blending of false tongues, and the mockery of discordant hearts. Then, indeed, the sublimest *Te Deum* is only such a skilful manipulation of sound waves as conspires with the resonant qualities of the atmosphere to make a musical tempest in the air.—The vocal accompaniment, meanwhile, combining in such a disturbance of Nature's tranquillity, as turns silence into uproar, and above the grinding of the modern Juggernaut,* as we listen to the mimic "weeping and wailing and gnashing of teeth," we seem to hear the shrieks of agonized spirits aping immolation through the dulcet medium of a sound-mill. God does not hear it—Christ does not hear it—it has none of that hallowed volatility that can make it rise—it is propelled, and does not reach beyond the compass of our own bodily diversion.

But if there be a voice that awakens a responsive echo in the other world, it is that of Sincerity ; and while

---

* The organ.

her symmetry reflected in us is the nearest likeness we bear to the Supreme, so it is, I venture so confidently to affirm, that the best efficacy in prayer is that mute eloquence of ideal praise conceived by Sincerity in the isolation of secret, silent tears:—it rises heavenwards on the incense of an unburdened spirit, and blossoms at the foot of the "Throne!"—there it is breathed upon by angels, and perfumes all Paradise!

One reason for sincerity being so precious, perhaps, is because it is so rare. We do not possess it as a common gift—it is lent to us—'tis a borrowed attribute, or may be a part of our better nature, that has undergone translation, and giving the hand back to the viler, wins it over to confidence, love, and friendship.—Aye, 'tis that wealth of the most admirable which, by some kind magic, is redeemed from "Treasure Trove,"—and out from beneath the surface of what seems a bleak and barren soil, is revealed the diamond,—the opal,—or that other mellow grateful flame we see kindled from the juices of the cold and clammy rock.

XXIII.

No; there is no exercise so exalting as a systematic, cheerful cultivation of the ideal. While people, too, who have made the noblest use of it have been a class who would rank in a fashionable and financial estimate as both poor and common, we may presume that it does not thrive only in cases of leisure and affluence; and, therefore, within the reach of some whose meagre allowance in other things conveys the impression they are not gifted, and that their little store of treasure, even in a hopeful view, is going through this world *in bond*.

The development of our corporeal inheritance may be all very well in the attainment of muscular superirity or wealth; but then let it become, as it most generally does, the one absorbing object of existence, and where shall we find in the whole range of fateful sequence a more pitiable sight than the bankrupt creature of commerce; unless, indeed, it be that even more saddening spectacle—the broken athlete. The former was always dreading losses and ever haunted by the gaunt spectre of ultimate poverty; while in the case of the latter, the slightest ailment is to him the dreaded admonisher of that greatest of all calamities, which is the inevitable loss of his comeliness and strength. This applies to all who set their store by property or physique. I do not advise letting the body subserve the mind simply, but open the flood gates of the imagination, or at any rate, do not batten them down; and then basking in the refulgent summer light that irradiates all ideal creation, forget the body altogether.

Music, Painting, Writing, may be mentioned as a few of the many pleasant hobbies offered the imagination to dwell upon; and we may, by these means, acquire healthful resources of pure enjoyment which, while they may not be dissipated are infinitely more profitable to our moral being and peace-of-mind than the most successful money-making. Indeed there is no subject viewed in this light that does not offer an always increasing fund of wholesome attraction to counteract the too engrossing cares of business, besides combining therewith, such retrieving graces as assuage those other more grievous bereavements incident to life.

We may note, however, that to humanize the Imagination we must give it *heart*, and to individualize it we must give it *thought*. While it is commendable to emulate, we must admit, it is far nobler to originate, and better even by hard thinking to bring into the world an indifferent pattern, than by sheer force of copying to equal the finer standard. Persevering in this spirit the reward of our exertion comes rather in the effort than in the result, and hours, days, months, years glide smoothly and happily by. We may be carrying forward other work, but then we should not be so impatient to realize, as otherwise we would be and are, in concentrating all our faculties on the mere dice by which money is lost or won.

XXIV.

The counsel herein contained may seem visionary and impracticable; I believe, nevertheless, it is not, and that my view of the case is sustained by actual experience, as illustrated by innumerable examples in the careers of our noblest and greatest men. There is no doubt the relaxation of spirit Disraeli enjoyed in his writings and ideal creations, was, and is still in retrospect, his greatest source of pleasure and consolation, and not only the true secret of his prolonged existence, but at the same time such an important auxiliary to his power and usefulness, as has conduced, in no small measure, to his other successes. Besides, too, is it not one of the finest traits in this man's character, that beset, as he has always been, by so many perplexing cares, he could so far to dismiss them all as to be enabled in the midst of Hubbub to invoke Serenity, and using his pen as the visible emblem of his ideal witchery, to disclose the hidden and abundant riches of his harassed mind (but exhaustless imagination), in a flow of sentiment so graceful and satisfying as that which percolates through "Vivian Grey," "Coningsby," or "Lothair!"—Again, how little did Milton think about or care for his blindness in that resplendent vision and gorgeous revelation of "Paradise Lost!"—Ah, and how oblivious was Byron to the soreness of his love or lameness, in the sweeter amour and symmetry of the "Corsair!"—as far from native land,—on the crest of passion's billow, he smites the pent up pinnacle with an ideal wand, and the breath of the tempest, gathering up the disgorged wealth of "deep blue ocean," scatters broadcast that lustrous shower, whence in poetic sorcery is reclaimed only the glinting splendor of the spray! In the prodigality of imagination, those grosser jewels that will not float in air are left to sink to earth, and naught is treasured but those supernal tints that give to the magic mirror of the Mist the peerless image of its Rainbow.

Again, what mattered it to Tom Moore, that the niggardly estimate of his market value drove him well nigh to beggary—that in the midst of plenty he hungered—

with a sumptuous banquet, like his "melodies," set for the world!

So, too, of poor Bobbie Burns; with his neighbors and (only since his death, his *idolatrous*) countrymen heaping slanders on his head, he could be so blissfully indifferent to it all and so happy in introducing dear old " Tam," that while all Scotland scolded, he, the outlawed Burns, could retort upon them and their children, only with such kindliness and good fellowship as—

> " Care, mad to see a man sa happy,
> E'een drowned himsel amang the nappy,
> As bees flee hame with lades o' treasure,
> The minutes winged their way wi' pleasure;
> Kings may be blessed, but Tam was glorious
> O'er a' the ills of life victorious."

Or take Goldsmith,—England's great hearted vagrant and the world's "prince of poets!"—he who, amid the sneers and contempt of the more industrious devotees of pious jobbery, could record sentiments so beautiful, so sublime as blend in the harmonious song of the "Deserted Village." Aye, how much nobler was his "shiftless" preparation for the final end, meandering down into the "vale" with such thoughts thrilling through his soul, tingling in his heart, and vibrating on his lips, as come to us like the distant chime of monastery bells, in a strain so sweet as that which tells of that once fair Auburn:—

> " When oft at evening's close,
> Up yonder hill the village murmur rose;
> There, as I pass'd with careless steps and slow,
> The mingling notes came soften'd from below;

"The swain responsive as the milkmaid sung,
The sober herd that low'd to meet their young;
The noisy geese that gabbled o'er the pool,
The playful children just let loose from school;
The watch dog's voice that bay'd the whispering wind,
And the loud laugh that spoke the vacant mind;
These all in sweet confusion sought the shade,
And fill'd each pause the nightingale had made."

And then, too, in lapse of time, of its desolation, in that exquisite lament, which bespeaks at once the illusion and disenchantment of youth and old age. Alas! it was only the dream of a vanished abode and the exile returning to realize the vision that solaced long years of banishment, finds his goal a solitude, and pillowing his head upon a stone, thus repines:

" In all my wanderings round this world of care,
In all my griefs—and God has given my share—
I still had hopes my latest hours to crown,
Amidst these humble bowers to lay me down;
To husband out life's taper at the close,
And keep the flame from wasting by repose:
I still had hopes, for pride attends us still,
Amidst the swains to show my book-learn'd skill;
Around my fire an evening group to draw,
And tell of all I felt and all I saw:
And, as a hare whom hounds and horns pursue,
Pants to the place from whence at first he flew,
I still had hopes, my long vexations past,
Here to return—*and die at home at last.*"

XXV.

Here we may observe, apropos of the cases instanced above, that it is erroneous to consider all mere bodily discomfort or pain, suffering,—at least in that crude sense in which we commonly regard and pity it—and however opposed our circumstances may be to the hackneyed notion of enjoyment, there is, or may be through the medium of that higher intellect pertaining to my theme, a source of delight that can make us indifferent and oblivious to mere physical drawbacks. Many fallacies of brute creation, tending to a wrong impression of what is happiness, obtains from such appetizing propensities as have pictured a land "flowing with milk and honey," and a paradise peopled with amorous maids. To corroborate the truth of this, we have only to invoke the shades of that carnivorous tribe who was kept wandering an indefinite period in order that the people thereof, while being admonished of their error concerning an earthly "Eldorado," might disabuse their minds of the monstrous assumption then obtaining, that the higher Kingdom of God should be prostituted to gratify the lowest propensities in man. Then, allowing their conception of the blessed goal, chastened and elevated by long and severe ordeal, to have attained the nobler perfection of the true ideal, it is in accord with the policy herein advocated, that the realization should have been deferred, and by making their "promised land" an ever receding mirage, the so called "Children" had been saved the more pitiable catastrophe of disenchantment. So, Moses, whom we all commiserate for not having reached the delectable region which his imagination and eloquence had so often depicted, was more blessed in the exile of his mountain retreat than all the rest of Israel. Nay, it is pleasing, as well to the instincts of humanity as to the purposes of illustration, to assume that the misguided good man in question, experienced in his denial and banishment, not the wrath of the Master as we are led to believe, but a prolongation of that ideal felicity that made the whereabouts of the body a secondary consideration,—aye, and his spiritual destiny a gladsome perspective far exceeding anything in the exuberant fancy of the flesh!

I have referred to Bunyan in another place; but apropos of Imagination, I would for the sake of illustration once more recall the spirit of the venerable Evangelist, as it shone in the night of its greatest apparent travail. Let us go back to the time when Bunyan lived, and take a peep at him in his incarceration. This picture has been drawn so many times it is in the minds of all, and I will not reproduce it here; but it strikes me we need not sympathize with him in his lonely cell, when we consider how his mind was employed. Is it possible he could have been unhappy with such ideas teeming in his brain as inspired Pilgrim's Progress? Nay, we may sympathize with him, but pity him—never! There was a feast in the creation of that Work of his, which made bread and water, and the hard desert of a donjon, a treat that the gourmands of Louis Fourteenth might be teased with the dreamy inkling of but never realize!—aye, that the gluttons, who basked in the glowing zenith of Imperial Rome, might envy but never attain! Indeed, their pleasure, in comparison with his inspiration, had made the most delightsome rapture of the flesh, simply pining in *ennui* and its swetest thrills condensed all into one exquisite pang a —*Yawn!*

Or, to bring my illustration nearer home, to mark the difference between the material and the ideal, what a poor famished product must be the grand work above contemplated when contrasted with that prolific luxury of thought of which it is, comparatively speaking, the barren, puny offspring! At the same time, how admirable, how infinite, how God-like does the Imagination appear when in the most brilliant efforts of man to materialize he seeks to clothe it in the mean garb of language! It is throwing a dirty veil of cloud over the "starry litter of the moon!" Then, too, while the interval between each of these celestial gems is spanned by millions of miles of hidden splendor, nevertheless, as here and there, twinkling through the vapory bank, we discern one solitary baby smile, it is in rapture we exclaim, —" how beautiful are the Heavens!"

There is an elasticity about the mind—a volatility about thought—that bids defiance to language; and the effort to catch the glowing rays of transient visions that pass in regal bewildering pageantry before us, offers to the most skilful adept and to the most nimble play of words, only the poor, barren recompense that comes of the child's grip on the brittle mirror of some giant bubble. Aye, it is the condensed puddle of a dispelled rainbow! Applying such an estimate as this, then, to an imagination whose puddle is a

Pilgrim's Progress, and it gives us a broader, better conception of a mind and an attribute, which it may have seemed we were praising over floridly.

XXVI.

In conclusion, we may notice that one of the most seductive of all the brilliant progeny of Imagination is, that sweet etherial creature we call Illusion. She is all the more dear, too, strange to say, because she is deceitful; one trait in her angelic nature being that what in the meaner characteristics of our poor mortality had been a fault, with her is a virtue. She is nearly allied to Charity, and her mission is as the sun-beam from the mother-orb, and her smile to brighten and to soothe.

What was HOPE in youth, later, is saved from DESPAIR by becoming ILLUSION, and in age, still vain of what we no longer possess we cleave to the grateful cheat: Thus many charming features which in Reality have vanished forever away, are reclaimed in Imagination, and we cherish the phantom till it almost seems a FACT. The allusions of healthy people are almost always pleasant, and even in the case of those who are ill, the most consoling of all comforters; insomuch that, even in the last stages of "Consumption," we playfully dickey with Destiny for a new lease of life, and to the end enjoy the unctious balm of thinking all is well. Blessed are these illusions; they are the holidays of the soul, and, amid all the threatening ordeals that frown upon us, lend sunshine to hearts that would laugh and be gay.—Aye, and from this ideal realm of bliss to earth and reality, we drop into a purgatory of flesh and pain.

XXVII.

EPILOGUE.

Do you see that poor old mendicant woman there, lying prostrate just off the high-way? See! she with the bleached locks and tattered raiment, with her bare head pillowed on that mean old bundle. I saw her not long since as I passed; she was sitting up then and looked so worn and miserable and sad. I noticed, too, she had taken something from her pack and was regarding it so intently she did not see me although I was quite near. No doubt it was a keep-sake, or something of that kind; because I was certain I saw tears in the poor old thing's eyes—but then, what a luxury there must have been, even in the briny flood, it seemed bring of mellowing, dissolving recollections! Those precious tears!—Crystal drops of nature's balsam, that follow the cold iron and jagged gash wrought in the hard knocks of the world! But behold her now,—prone and tranquil,—and see too, what a placid almost happy look! Ah, what potent pacific could have breathed its drowsy incense over that perturbed spirit,—what soothing spell,—that with all the gladsome obliviousness of sleep, there should be mingled such a rejoicing sense of perfect wakefulness. She seems not to know she is cold, and the chill autumn air of friendlessness and poverty has veered around. The trance may have lasted but a minute, but in that time what a grateful metamorphosis! The keen November blast tugging at those white hairs, is to her, now, only the soft aroma of June—and see how those seared and battered lineaments relax!—that had been a smile on any other face, on hers, it's more a look of pain—a strange anomalous look, as of an aching heart struggling to smile at the pleasures of others who repine. Time and trouble have long since placed their dreaded seal upon that shrivelled cheek; and now, we see only the wintery aspect where once the roses bloomed. That look—that sort of smile—may once have been a mirthful ringing laugh!— that form, elastic and comely,—and she, have coquetted in all the playful tyranny of conscious beauty. But what is she thinking of now, I wonder—what vagary of "bitter sweet" in that absent mind—what tender thoughts of loved and lost make that expression so pathetically divided twixt smiles and tears.—What rummaged leaves were those she turned?—what impress of sweet memories saw she there?— revealed in the light of long ago,—but pictured on that broken tablet and retained in life gloaming,—as autumn foliage, in decay, takes and holds the fairer tints of summer skies! Ah, I have it now!—The magic of an invisible hand has beckoned her back, and now she is with that little prattling one, seen again through a long vista of troubled wanderings.—And how she beams upon and fondles it as of old—that fair, laughing, dimpled cherub! And how completely forgotten are all those tearful years he has been laid away in that cradle rocked by angels! Nay, how beautiful is the mercy shed upon her now—how grateful the respite of that dream, in which her old eyes behold, in the full glory of her blushing pride, that tender blossom which, in the hey-day of her girlish joy, she pressed to her lips and inhaled in its sweet, fresh fragrance, the first dawning consciousness of mother-love!! Is it only a dream? Yes; a mere ILLUSION;—*but do not wake her, let her sleep!*

Chiselhurst

CHISELHURST.*

I.

FOR some time previously I had been looking forward with considerable eagerness to the 16th of March, on which day at Chiselhurst a grand fête was to take place in celebration of the coming of age of Prince Louis Napoleon, heir in exile to the throne of France. It had been made for some time before coming off the subject of editorials in the newspapers, besides being commented on a good deal in a quiet way, and really it might be looked forward to, it seemed to me, as one of the great political events of the day. Under the circumstances, I was bound nothing should prevent my being there.

On the morning of the sixteenth I got away early, as had some distance to walk to reach the station of the South-Eastern Railway, but made a miss nearly at the outset, and lost the train at Sydenham Hill. Having over an hour to wait, I put in the time in an easy stroll to Penge, the next place *en route*, after which, taking the down express at 10.20, had a quick, pleasant run to Bickley. Getting off at the very pretty station which dots the line at

---

* Written some time before the death of the Prince Imperial.

this point, my further destination was indicated by a church spire, glinting in the sunlight, away to the left a couple of miles. This offered another enjoyable opportunity for a "constitutional," and after half-an-hour's brisk exercise I came in sight of Camden Place, where the Bonapartes reside. On nearing the town many signs of a fête-day attracted my notice: there was that hurrying to and fro which denotes in these rural solitudes something unusual, and that enquiring look on the faces of many that evinces both the presence of strangers, and the expectation of something especially interesting about to transpire.

What struck me, also, as a somewhat novel sight was the French "Tricolor," which was flying in a number of places,—there being quite a little colony of Imperialists living at this time at Chiselhurst. It was the first time, I think, I had ever seen this banner, except perhaps in some fantastic display; but now it was hoisted by the devoted followers of that identical party, and unfurled in honor of the nearest living representative of that extraordinary genius, whose pride and prowess, whose ambition and triumph, have made it the most famous and popular emblem in French history. I was not long in ascending the gentle acclivity leading to the picturesque, gorse-covered plateau above: this forms an attractive common, at the west corner of which is Camden Place.

My first glimpse of this now famous dwelling, impressed me with its being an extremely fine old homestead; and although the building itself may lack some of the more superfluous attributes of grandeur, these are all the more substantially compensated for in the general surroundings. The grounds to the rear are sloping, and sink gradually down to a valley beyond, in a magnificent sweep of rich, undulating meadow and timber-land; in the interval of which is unfolded to our refreshed and gladdened vision, a pleasing variety of rural scenery, framed, as it were, in a continuous wealth of superb, English landscape. Not the least, too, of the worthy living features in the prospect, and grazing and feasting on the royal spread of tender herbage, are the flocks of fine sheep and blooded cattle, the like of which one sees nowhere except in this favored land of merry England. The house itself is surrounded by, and almost hidden away behind, a deep, sombre rampart of rich, dark foliage,—the splendid product of a grand array of prolific elms and oaks, that stand guard over and hedge it round; constituting a fitting symbol of that benignant hospitality, that makes this place a safe and princely asylum as it is of royalty and exile.

On my arrival, I found a great crowd of people gathered about—some on horseback, many in carriages, but mostly on foot, and the road through the common to St. Mary's Chapel was well lined on both sides all along the way for half-a-mile. In this little chapel, which is a perfect gem in its way, are deposited the remains of Napoleon III. I had been there before and seen within the alcove to the left of the aisle, the place where the Emperor lies entombed; but on this occasion the church was so crowded I made no attempt to squeeze in, though much desired to have a glimpse of the services being performed there. As it was, made haste to return to Camden Place, and straightway found myself beset by a new obstacle. I had heard somewhere before this late hour, that admission was to be regulated by ticket, but I always avoid bothering myself with that sort of thing when I can help it, so the matter of looking after this little technicality went by default. I afterwards ascertained, however, that these permits were only granted through favor to those who intended making the pilgrimage from France to the Napoleonic shrine, and who being no doubt interested in the restoration, were, as a matter of course, people of more or less political and social importance. So possessing none of these qualifications my petition as an outsider, on the ground of mere idle curiosity, might not after all have been entertained.

Now, however, I began to labor under the disagreeable consciousness that my not having a ticket would be likely to interfere somewhat, and that considerable might be depending on this little flaw in my arrangements. I confess my apprehensions were far from being soothed, when on approaching the main gates I saw the great crowd facing those frowning and inhospitable portals; there, too, as a reinforcement to these towering barriers of iron, was an even tougher-looking line of policemen, standing guard, and turning rudely and peremptorily away, all but the lucky ones who could flourish what was now become a very interesting novelty in cards. I had never before been in such a hot-bed of French men and women and *garçons* as I now found myself. Not a word of English could be heard; I spoke to several, but they only shook their heads.

Boys were selling French papers, badges, bunches of violets and photographs—all in French, and it was for all the world as if I had plumped right down into the midst of the excited populace of Paris, and a mob at that. There was a motley crowd of, comparatively speaking, longshore riff raff, who had like myself, made the mistake of thinking their physiognomy would pass them ; but the mid-current, winding in sluggish uninterrupted progress through this outer fringe, all, without exception, had tickets. I observed this with a sinking heart and it made my chances seem more as they had been from the first,— that is to say, the slimmest and bluest. At the same time it was aggravating to see how carelessly and indifferently these other people handled their cards, and to note the magic fluence those bits of pasteboard had on the iron visage and stony heart of the police officials who received them : ah, how precious they seemed to us, those cherished passports to the inner shrine of imperial exile.

II.

I did not try actually to force my way, because I saw others try it, and become suddenly and effectually disappointed ; found too, that coaxing, and a modest "tip" generally so fertile in the opening up of ways and means, were here of no avail, and then I began to feel very despondent indeed, but all the more anxious to get in. In short, I found the order in regard to tickets imperative, and rigidly and cruelly enforced, and as a natural consequence

I was bitterly chagrined, and disappointed. They say "misery likes company," and according to that I ought to have been happy, from the number similarly situated to myself; at least there was consolation in knowing I was not alone. There was a host of people I now discovered of various nationalities, who had come in from London, probably as I had, to this feast—some with two or three ladies apiece, and all looking dismayed and crushed.

A bright idea struck me; and suddenly and secretly exultant, I sank my hand deep into my pants' pocket, and drew forth a talisman in the shape of a card case. Ah! what a great thing it is to be thoughtful and wise—and after all "what's in a name!" I simply put in addition to mine, United States of America, and naturally thought it would take like hot cakes; but I reckoned, alas, without mine host. All intent on the success of my little enterprise I had not noticed a great number of others employed in the same way. By dint of most praiseworthy perseverance, and all sorts of dumb-show, managed to beckon towards me, an old fellow who was looking on from within, and no doubt watching with self gratulation the chagrin, and wretchedness of those outside in the cold. Got him pretty well in reach of my fond embrace, and stuck my card under his nose with the modest request that he would take it to—not the Empress but somebody—anybody—was not particular whom; even insinuated he might keep it himself if—well, I had got quite as far as that, when a tremendous rush was made for my place, and my man; and such a flourish of cards, and such a clamor of tongues, in a score of different languages I never heard before.

I gently reproved and expostulated, and lost no time in trying to reinforce my claim to precedence under the unpopular rule of one at a time, but only overawed two or three deep of the foremost files; those behind were beyond the power of persuasion, and on they came like mad. The would-be bearer of my compliments made a rush back for dear life; and I made a frantic effort to rescue my hat, which I caught a glimpse of drifting away over a sea of heads. When I got all together again—still outside, but gazing wistfully inside—I riveted my eye on the same old chap in whom I thought I had detected a glimmer of interest in my affairs; but it was no use to beckon him any more; he no doubt felt he had had a narrow escape from being mobbed, and not unlikely did me the injustice to think I had wantonly abused his confidence. Well, I retired a short distance and sought solace in glowering upon my competitors in the crowd, which by this time had meekly subsided. Noticed a few who were so fortunate as to be chaperons, taking the advice of their female comforters, but I was not blessed in that way; and the first thing I did after recovering my presence of mind, was to put away my little card, which by this time, I need not add, I was somewhat ashamed of. Held it with becoming modesty under my coat-tail—a course which I innocently adopted as most effectually to conceal it from observation, and to enable me to produce it at a moment's notice. It was about this time I discovered additional proof that I had not been a pioneer in this new dodge pertaining to the card business, and it was not long before I detected several of those around holding cards in like manner. The spectacle disgusted me too much to persevere longer in so mean an expedient; it was ludicrous enough, though, that it might have been amusing, but for the thought of my hard fate; meanwhile we all looked demure enough, and a band of music striking up about this time set us all off again.

It was not till I had decided upon the sensible plan of going home, and thus avoiding any further aggravation in the matter, that I bethought me of a lane which led away round one side of the estate—I had been through it once before on the way to Shortlands—why not make a flank movement, I asked myself, and come up in the rear? No sooner said than done—I slipped quietly away. Feared the place would be guarded, but luckily for me it was not; so, passing through to the right-rear of the grounds, I completed the detour by crossing over to the other side, through a ravine, to the cover of a clump of trees, which I now had between me and the rabble. So far I had met with no opposition: in crossing the fields, it is true, I startled half a dozen lazy looking cows out of a pleasant trance—they flirted their tails and stared at me languidly, but relapsed very soon into their accustomed tranquillity, and I left them in the drowsy luxury of a stand-up dream.

Seeing my way fairly clear now, and my game well in hand, my anxiety abated somewhat, and I decided to have a bit of something to eat, in case there might not be another so good a chance. I had taken the precaution to bring along a good supply of provender, and turning my attention for a short time exclusively to my sandwiches, made short work of them and started on again. My plan, of course, was to gain an entrance by the garden in the rear. Luckily I hit fairly upon the wicket leading to my goal, and hedge and shrub disguising my movements, I threw back the bolt—walked very deliberately in, and then, " Richard was himself again !"

III.

It was not without a thrill of pleasant emotion that I now found myself within the private grounds of her Imperial Majesty. I did not stop to apostrophize, but proceeded along slowly, taking a close and leisurely survey of everything that fell within the range of my much favored vision. At first it was a sort of tiny forest, a miniature Bois de Boulogne, after which came the evidences of a less sturdy but even more beautiful growth. Indeed the grounds were much more extensive and finer, than I had anticipated. Splendid trees, rare shrubs spring flowers, greeted the eye on all sides, and turn which way you would, you saw, here a rustic arbor, ingeniously modelled, tempting one to linger and rest— or there, a charming grotto, all arched over with blossoming vines and thick, dark foliage, where the dazzling rays of a noonday-sun were tempered to the soft, grateful twilight of eventide! All fascinated the eye and beguiled the senses with a delicious feeling of enjoyment, which I felt to a great degree was owing to the spell cast over everything that comes within the influence of two magic words—Napoleon—Eugénie.

I saw a good many devotees plucking flowers and leaves to carry back to France as souvenirs; managed, myself, to get a few violets, and then, after a short time most pleasantly spent, passed along to the lawn, and mixed with the throng assembled there. Many were promenading, others sitting or standing around in groups, and all in animated conversation, of which I was not at a loss to guess the purport. I was, indeed, in the very midst of the Bonapartist camp, and looking about me felt, not without a tingling somewhere, and a slightly quickening pulse, I was among the children of the "Old Guard," and cheek-by-jole with the family of the "Little Corporal!" Aye, there was I, literally hemmed in by a host of battle-tried heroes, who, with their domestic retinue, composed probably the most influential and devoted of all the faithful defenders of the Imperial cause.

Amongst these were men and soldiers, distinguished in politics and in war. The former, representing in the highest degree the *personnel* of what was a short time before, the most accomplished and brilliant civic establishment in Europe, or the world; the latter, the dismembered fugitive elements of the most splendid martial array of ancient or modern times. Nor was I unmindful of the fact that there were titles walking about there, which, with their princely accessories and noble estates, had been gleaned from the classic soils of Italy, and Syria, and

Egypt, fruits of the gory fields of Marengo, and Acre, and the Pyramids. There, too, were the latest scions of distinguished families, who could have joined hands in legitimate consort, and hobnobbed in kindred succession, and recognised each other back to the dim age when chivalry only began to dawn, and France to learn that art in war which has won her, as mistress, imperishable renown. All who were not present in person were represented, we may be assured, by worthy substitutes, who if I did not know, the Prince and Empress (I noticed later) did, and received most cordially. The reading of an address to the Prince and his reply came off in a large tent provided for the purpose; but I was too late for that, and missed the aggravation it would otherwise have been to me, not to have had a front seat, where I could have devoured, with greedy eyes, the whole Bonaparte family. As it was, by dint of a little effectual elbowing, inflicted with an appropriate air of absent-mindedness, I succeeded in securing a glimpse of the distinguished personages as they crossed the lawn on the way back into the drawing-room. After this the Prince and Empress were to receive deputations from the different departments of France, all of which were represented; a number of others, also, were to receive the honor of presentation. Many of these were influential politicians and gallant officers, who had stood together in high places under the Emperor. They formed in procession and went in by sections. Many wore decorations—the " Legion," especially, being well represented; and all bore with becoming decorum the somewhat-trying scrutiny of the tremendous crowd looking on from outside a line which had been stretched round two sides of the house, to keep the way clear leading to the entrance.

IV.

I, too, watched these once pampered favorites of fortune, now temporarily discarded, and regarded each countenance with an interest and sympathy most reverential and profound. Some bore the marks of hard-fighting and rough-service; all were in plain clothes, although many still belonged to the army, and had come over incognito on account of an order of the French War-Department, forbidding their officers to be in England between the twelfth and twentieth of March. A great many carried bouquets,—some, wreaths, with here and there a banner; all looked unutterable devotion and determination and seemed regardless of everything but the one precious thought that they were about to pay their "devoirs" to their beloved Empress, and offer anew their unaltered allegiance to the Prince and sovereign hope of all. My attention was divided between this spectacle and the doors and windows of the house, through which I tried in vain to catch a glimpse of what was going on within; but we were too far off to distinguish anything, and I now began to feel a mortal craving curiosity to see the interior or even to obtain a glance into the hall. The thought had suggested itself, whether I might not wedge into some part of the procession and get a look in that way; I wondered what might be the result of such an undertaking, but dismissed the idea as being too hazardous. It seemed altogether too pokerish—was afraid that for a novice like me to join the "Legion of Honour," without the appalling initiation of powder and shot and imperial compliment, might involve the asking of a few embarrassing questions, which would make things uncomfortably hot, and the upshot of which would most likely be, I should have to walk precipitately back, with the countless eyes of a gaping multitude fixed in derision upon me.

It was too distressing to think of; still, good Dame Fortune had been very accommodating thus far, and I was rashly tempted to task her indulgence a little further; besides, now that I thought of it, I really had some claim in the award of privilege to martial honors. Had I not had my "baptism of fire?" jewelled decorations might rank first, but barring these, ugly scars, won in honorable conflict, might pass, under a clean shirt, among old soldiers; and if hard pressed I could bare my bosom and point to a symbol there well known in the masonry of warriors—aye, one which speaks in a language the tongue may not utter, a tribute welcome with the brave, and means, though the words be not expressed, "gagné au champ d'honneur!" Yes! that is all very fine to think of, but at the same time it appeared pleasanter in reverie than in practice. In the meantime I observed they did not all seem acquainted with each other,—at least, each, for the most part, kept silent and to himself; besides there was more or less confusion till they got near the entrance, all of which seemed in favour of my passing in amongst them without being challenged. In fact, it was naturally taken for granted no one would venture to intrude without some special claim to imperial welcome.

I reconnoitred about sometime for a favorable chance to get through inside the rope; my curiosity meanwhile getting stronger, I was beginning to feel impatient and fool-hardy enough for any thing. About this time I noticed there was a narrow opening where the different deputations went in, and an imposing-looking genius stood there with pencil and paper passing them through and keeping tally; but sometimes four or five would push on by in their impatience, without paying much if any attention to the excited functionary who guarded the breach. I was not long in perceiving that this was the particular style and example I must endeavor to emulate; and led on by a cold-blooded audacity I never knew before I was capable of, edged up close, got a good ready, and when the next rush in that way was made, was borne inside; a Frenchman on my right and left and one before and behind. In this order we all moved forward half-way to the entrance door, under the admiring gaze of the folks outside; whose homage I now enjoyed, or rather was compelled to submit to, on a par with the rest.

V.

Our progress was anything but lively; the head of our column would advance from time to time as the way cleared, and we in the rear would close up smartly as chance offered. It was literally a "stern chase," and even worse than the proverbially " slow one ;" intensified perhaps in my case, by that unusual strain on the nervous system, incident to one in my pecular situation, and this was far from soothed in perceiving or fancying a certain amount of polite inquisitiveness about me.

Up to this time, I had had very little hope of getting through. Was in constant dread, and all along watching with a restless eye and troubled spirit each shifting movement of the crowd ahead; expecting each moment to see the writhing monster resolve itself into the grim spectre of outraged propriety, and to behold the glimmering, beguiling prospect before me transformed into a scroll, whereon I should read in blighting characters, the dreadful warrant for my expulsion. After turning the first corner of the house to the left, it came my turn to pause before a window there; and looking into the drawing-room, where the reception was going on, was enabled to see everything nearly as well as if I had been inside. I thought this very fortunate, as at the start, only aspired to get a peep into the hall, which I proposed to pass into, and out by the other door; but after watching the proceedings for a short time, I became so interested that all prudent resolves were forgotten. I was seized with the mad desire to get in and indifferent to all considerations of propriety, I determined, let come what would, to follow the tide, and go wherever the rest did.

Well, we came at last to the entrance where stood a pompous-looking servant in formidable livery; I began to fear I should have to produce my card again, but some one a little in advance gave the "open sesame"—the different deputations had a sort of chief at their head to attend to this sort of thing, which was an arrangement I felt like applauding —as it was, maintained a demure silence, and passed through with the rest. The hall in which we now found ourselves was a fine one,—broad, lofty, and with the doors of adjoining rooms thrown wide open, presented the appearance of a spacious lobby. I noticed here, besides the people assembled, many attractive decorations and objects of vertu; some fine bronzes and trophies, many of them, no doubt, of personal, I mean Napoleonic, interest—also paintings which I only glanced at, but would have liked a whole afternoon to study and admire. Aye, relics were they all of the Empire, and sad, (I could have wished touching) reminders of imperial, and we may presume, happy days "lang syne." Here, too, were old battle-flags, dilapidated and torn, and these especially struck me as being far from the least interesting among many distinguished features of the locality and occasion. Appropriately draped, they seemed to me to bear a peculiar significance; they were not—like so many other things that simply awaken tender remembrances—mementos over which to mourn, but symbols as well, through whose rents of shot and shell one sees the "silver lining to the cloud"—and even out of those dreadful battle scars there seemed to gleam quenchless rays of glorious hope!

VI.

Beyond, towards the other end of the hall were gathered a distinguished company of ladies and gentlemen. They were in groups, sitting or standing about, conversing, something after the fashion of an "at home," only there was, I noticed at once, a marked absence of gaiety. It is impossible to overcome French vivacity, but there was a gentle, subdued air about them all here now, as if the shadow of a great trouble had fallen over them; as, indeed, it had. What a contrast to former occasions, it must have seemed to them; and what a contrast to the noisy set outside, it seemed to me. No crowding, no jostling, but an easy, wellbred decorum prevailed, that made every thing that was said or done seem a refined and earnest expression of deferential esteem and homage.

It would have been a grateful relief to me after the excitement and confusion from which I had emerged, had I not been all the more oppressed with the dreadful impropriety I was committing. A little way down the hall, we turned to the left through a doorway, and entered a medium-sized and very plain room, in which I noticed more souvenirs and more interesting things. Over the mantelpiece was a fine mirror, with a curiously wrought frame of silver filagree, and among the articles of furniture two or three camp-chairs attracted my eye, one of which looked as if it might have seen service under the first Napoleon. I have no doubt there were many things that would have been interesting objects to contemplate if I had had time and could have known all about them; but there was no chance to get out a "Murray," or a "Bradshaw," and I was left simply to look and wonder and imagine.

I was a little dashed at this period of our progress to see my companions of the "Legion" doffing top-coats, and coming out in full dress. I had on my best frock and tried to look the enticing picture of juvenile innocence; but was far from feeling the swaggering assurance of a spoiled toddler, until presently I perceived one or two others with morning coats, which relieved my mind a good deal, and I at once became very much attached to them. Adjoining this room was the drawing-room, where the presentations were going on, and my eyes were already turned in that direction; I could see, there, the Empress and Prince, and forgot all thought of embarrassment in the rare and devoutly wished for spectacle. Then we all resumed our places in column again, and prepared to move forward; but some who had been in before us were now coming out, and we paused. I had proceeded thus far without being asked one question, or having to utter a single word; it was the silence of discretion, persisted in with commendable self-control, and endured with the nonchalance of outward calm and inward perturbation. I had ample reason to dread an exposé, which, at any moment seemed inevitable; indeed, I was compassed round in jeopardy, and expected nothing less than to be collared as an interloper,—scooped up, as it were, and shovelled out; and smilingly, placidly, I waited to be pounced upon,—exterminated—blown to atoms by a dreaded interrogatory, shot out of the mouth of some officious cannon. Thus did I scrutinize each successive phase of my progress, with a tranquil heroism surprising in one of my timid, retiring nature; and to this day I marvel I should have presumed so far, and persevered so boldly. I was not unconscious of my danger, and though I saw my peril, it found me by this time seemingly indifferent to my fate, and all the more infatuated with "Destiny." Then it was, I yielded to the sweet intoxication of an all absorbing interest; with now and again a thrill, at the thought that I was not only meandering in the " course of Empire," but in close proximity to that imperial magnet, whose power now drew all in common, and about whose brilliance there was that eccehomic isolation which blent all minor shades in obscurity; and already we felt reflected on our dazzled vision the dawning splendor of our destination.

VII.

This language may seem exaggerated, and it would be, under any other circumstances; but I am endeavoring faithfully to describe my impressions on this occasion, and though I may be peculiarly susceptible to sentimental influences, still, I found myself on this eventful day under what may be explained as that mesmeric power under whose subtle sway, not simply individuals and potentates, but communities and nations, have yielded all their prerogatives of self-government, and acknowledged, if not vassalage, at least subordination. The fact is, from the inception of my hazardous undertaking, I had been drawn within the current of that inexplicable magnetism, whose manifestation and power had electrified a preceding generation; and which had not simply drawn out, but at the bidding of its imperial will had impelled blindly, devotedly forward, the victims of one, whom, forty centuries will look back upon as the God of war! I felt what drew me on was the same power that had led them across the narrow span that separated glory from perdition at Lodi, and through smoke and flame down into the death gaps of Jena and Wagram—the same whose magnetic destiny others followed smilingly, willingly, sublimely, through the midst of winter, over barrier of ice, and craig, and mountain chain,—brushing aside the avalanche, or threading serenely the dreadful gorges of the Alps! Aye, and posterity to this late day catches an undying glimpse of that terrific power and its heroic following, enveloped in the storm-cloud of the St. Bernard, disguised like fabled genii in a tempest, " stealing a march on Fate!"

Under the influence of that same marvellous agency, I should not, any more than these other men, have shrunk from numbering my humble self in the honored category of the sacrificed; indeed, I was ready and willing to march right into the very "jaws of death," but the jaws, on this occasion, fortunately, were the open portals that led to no harder fate than into the presence of the WIFE and SON of France. The Prince, who now caught sight of our party, was standing about the middle of the room with the Empress a little way behind, and to the right of him. As we approached, he advanced a pace or two, and our spokesman, or some one in front, said something, I think, to let him know who we were, and thus presented, all commenced bowing, the principal ones in the front-rank shaking hands with the Prince. Several of these he seemed to know and spoke to in a pleasant, graceful way, that I have no hesitation in saying, won my heart at once. The Empress came forward also, and addressed one or two with that peculiar grace and dignity which have won the esteem and admiration of all who have been fortunate enough to behold her. After a few brief moments, which passed so quickly as almost to seem an aggravation, we commenced our retreat, and were soon back again in the first room. Here I saw another squad preparing to enter as we had, and I quickly sidled over, and joined them with a view to going in again.

It may seem absurd, but I was so absorbed with the desire to get back into the reception room once more, and if possible to stay there a little while, that I really cared for nothing else; and owing to the confusion generally I was not interfered with, and so entered with my new companions a second time. However, instead, of going up all the way got off to one side, which was discreet; as this time they nearly all grappled with the imperial party, and seemed entitled to personal recognition. I thought I might have reason to be satisfied if I did not come in actual contact, so got a little out of range, and took a calm, quiet survey of all that was going on. I wanted to see how the Empress looked, and talked and acted on this occasion, and was gratified beyond my most sanguine expectations. I watched her for fully twenty minutes, feeling tolerably free from observation myself, as there were so many coming and going, and all eyes were on the Empress and the Prince. The former stood facing in our direction, and to her right, and a little behind her, was a very stout but fine, pleasant-looking dame (the Comtesse Poëze), who was the only lady besides the Empress in the room.

The prince was attired in plain clothes, but wore over his left breast the broad ribbon and star denoting, I believe, a high grade in the Legion of Honor. He had his mother's look about the eyes, but in general features resembled his father very strongly, without, however, the slightest trace of a likeness to the first Napoleon. He had a robust frame, a frank, manly bearing, and it seemed to me, performed the task of receiving the deputations in a very happy manner, and with admirable ease and self-possession, for so young a courtier. The Empress, when not engaged in conversation, watched her son with a mother's pride and solicitude plainly depicted on her noble but worn and troubled features; at the same time seeming to hear, see everything that was going on, and to feel, as no doubt she was warranted in doing, that it was a trying and important time for both. Attired as usual in deep mourning, it was, indeed, difficult to recognize the once reigning Queen of Fashion; but although the blighting grief she has had to bear has told upon her sadly, nevertheless she is still a beautiful woman, and all her ways superbly graceful and winsome. In brief, then, supreme without being ostentatious, and affable without seeming to patronize, this widowed mother and that fatherless son acquitted themselves in a manner to reflect dignity on their cause, and merit on their pretensions.

Lucien Bonaparte was in the room at one time, but disappeared without my getting a very good sight at him. Standing in the front rank a little to one side was the Duc de Padua, and near him the Duc de Bassano. I had seen them before on the way from the marquée, and it was in their rear, and screened by their benign and imposing presence, I had planted my humble standard, and took all my observations. Was so much interested in the spectacle I did not mind much about myself, until a plain appearing individual came up and stood nearly in front of me, and while there the Empress stepped up and shook hands with him. I could not understand what she said, but the movement admonished me I was in too close quarters to retain my spectatorship much longer, and I sidled off by degrees. Passing through the adjoining room into the hall, I very nearly upset on the way a stifly-starched genius in livery who said to me quite civily, *à gauche!* It startled me for a moment, as what he uttered sounded very like the English for "a ghost," but I regained my self-possession and turned, as directed, to the left.

At one part of the hall another cuts it crosswise, and at the intersection of these I made a stand for a few minutes. It was a large open space furnished, Moorish fashion, like a room, with the sweet addition of an almost tropical profusion of flowers in the form of bouquets and wreaths and offerings of that sort which had been brought over from France. Here were gathered a goodly share of the *créme de la créme* of all that multitude who had come over to do honor to the occasion, and whose homage and fealty, in the opinion of many, bid fair to bring about a restoration. Among these were a goodly number of ladies, finely dressed and fashionable looking, but somewhat on the dowager order, and nearly all, I thought, extremely plain-looking. Several of the gentlemen I observed wore that decoration of the Legion of Honor, which consists of a crimson ribbon with a star attached, worn like a lady's locket round the neck. I cannot say how far up in the scale of distinction it is, but as those only wore it whose province it seemed to be to do the honors of the Imperial household, and submit to be lionized, and to be treated with immense deference, it struck me it denoted something of a very high order. Whilst standing here two ladies passed close by me, one of whom said "*Pardon, Monsieur!*" and I made way for them. They stopped within nudging distance of my right elbow, and spoke to an old gentleman who had just come up; he was of slim stature, but courtly looking, with a large, square head, fine features, and pleasing aspect. One of the ladies was the wife of a Marshal of France (Canrobert); the old gentleman who wore the grand *cordon* of the Legion was Prince Jerome Bonaparte.

But I must bring my narrative to a close. Much as I have written, I have but briefly, and inadequately described all I saw and felt; have exaggerated nothing; in fact have done no sort of justice to the theme, and simply give these jottings as a truthful remembrance of what really occurred. Suffice it then that as I moved slowly and reluctantly away and took my departure, it was with a profound sense of gratification at all I had seen. I marvelled a little at my extraordinary good fortune, in getting through without a mishap; and whilst being thankful for this, was not a little proud to think, I was probably the only representative of America in that historic picture, to which in thought, at least, the eyes of all Europe were turned that day, with even more interest in its political importance, than I, through mere curiosity, could appreciate; though as far as I was concerned it was altogether the most intensely interesting event in my recollection, and the most novel and gratifying of all my adventures. There was nothing farcical about it, although it is quite possible my description may make it seem so; and the earnestness and enthusiasm evinced on all sides by so many respectable people, and noted men, impressed me strongly with a belief, that the cause of the Imperial party is by no means a forlorn hope. Both from the demonstration made at Chiselhurst on this occasion, and a corresponding one in Paris, there is good reason to believe a great reaction has taken place in the minds of the French people in this respect. The courts of inquiry, too, that have been held recently, have in every instance reflected credit on the patriotism and fidelity of Napoleon and the Empress, who were no doubt basely betrayed and sacrificed. Meanwhile the remnants and scattered debris of monuments and symbols levelled and defaced in madness and ingratitude are being garnered up in kindliness and regret, and preserved as mementos. With the masses, especially the lower classes, these are treasured as precious souvenirs, and despite the effort of government a secret sympathy not unmingled with pride and reverence is fast gaining ground in the public mind. This sentiment is silent generally and in many instances where expostulation is loudest, denunciation is all assumed to palliate a consciousness of self-shame. Not a few may seek by carrying the blame to another's door to shirk the opprobrium of their own perfidy and crime; rival claimants, party men, and blustering politicians may still cry " vengeance on the man of Sedan," but the victim of their dastardly meanness lies beyond the pale of further outrage, and a rival nation and a great people are proud to receive his dust, and to honor his memory. They pulled their Emperor down from the high place which his virtues and abilities had won, but they may not long depose Justice; both were dragged to shame, and buried under a mountain of obloquy, but phœnix-like both have risen— the one to assume the crown of the incorruptible—the other to mount upward like the morning sun over the hill-tops, its beaming rays dispelling the mists of prejudice, and rolling back those dark threatening clouds that seemed for a time to threaten the glorious memory of one whom all must esteem as having been a wise man, an indefatigable benefactor, and, by all odds, the greatest sovereign of his time. Say what they may France glories in the name of Bonaparte, and that "star" which shone so brilliantly on the victorious legions of Austerlitz and Marengo, is looming in the horizon a grand refulgent orb, in a constellation of solar magnates—blazing with a lustre that the destiny of Waterloo could not eclipse, and that the defeat of Sedan is powerless to tarnish! *Vive l'Empereur!*

Amnesty.

AMNESTY.

I.

THERE are other ideas suggested by the preceding essays, and having a sympathetic bearing on the general train of thought which we have adopted in these reveries, and though jotting them down as they crowd in pell-mell on the mind, may make them seem irrelevant and such a digression that each may appear the introduction of an entirely new subject, nevertheless, they are only branches of one broad theme,—tributaries which, diverging at certain points, to embrace a wider field of observation, converge latterly, as is natural with many things in life, and clasp hands finally over that narrow chasm where all differences blend in fraternal accord.

We find two things in the affairs of people, exercising vital influence over their lives and destiny: I refer to the opposite vicissitudes of, on the one hand, a great *triumph* —on the other, a great *reverse*. There is no question which is the more popular.—The former is greeted on every hand with applause,—it is presumptive and undisputed evidence of merit; while the latter, it follows naturally, we despise, condemn, and try to shun. But strange as it may seem at first, when we ask which of these exercises the best influence, the question is more difficult to answer than may be supposed: The one, no doubt, kindles our aspirations and elevates our aims,—its motto is, "Excelsior!" —But the other operates as a restraining power, and rising like a Banquo on the ice, points to the thin and dangerous places and cries "Beware! Beware!"

Crime is not unfrequently the offspring of the first, while a nobler, purer conception of living many times springs from the last; but to give these two exemplary conditions in life, the larger scope and detail exhibited in ordinary careers, they may be designated under the more comprehensive and familiar heads of *Success*, and *Failure*. It is not my purpose here to investigate all the fateful bearings of these two prolific words; it would take volumes to compass even the smallest part of their full significance. We only point them out in passing, as we would striking features in a landscape; comprehending as they do in our social status all those varied irregularities of hill and dale,—of mountain and valley,—which, running at right angles to the more common ways of our humdrum existence, indicate the *crosscuts* of life—those rugged tortuous paths, side by side with graded, luxurious avenues, beneath whose tinselled foliage and beguiling shades, ambition and enterprise lure the eager, restless votaries of discontent and avarice.

All our impulses, if acted upon, may be said to involve to a greater or less extent, success and failure; but regarded in the conventional phase most characteristic of our times, these two flexible words may be defined as the attainment, on the one hand, of positions or the control of means, whereby we may command whatever luxuries and comforts our appetites may crave or money procure; on the other, not only the reverse from this but such an unprofitable issue in all we undertake, as to debar us from making more than a precarious livelihood, if indeed so much. These conditions, we may add, are presumed to represent happiness and abundance, misery and want.

II.

Taking the people who represent these two writhing struggling divisions, we find iniquity inherent in both, and neither exempt; but how much the greater burden of blame are the unfortunates made to carry, and, as things are, how much more largely do they share, not in the good things of life, but in the ordeal of exclusion, expiation and trial. When both are implicated, which of these must suffer most to vindicate the righteous rigor of our laws? Or turning away the darker side of the grimy picture and glancing at that which is generally, if not hidden at least ignored, let us inquire who does all the hard and really dirty work of the world? We may take pride in our factories, our industries—who work them? We may be proud of our army, our navy—who comprise the army—who are the navy? Who do all the fighting in time of war, and gain the victories that overthrow and confound the disturbers of our national peace? Who suffer on the battle field—in the hospital—in the prison hulk— and later, drag through a miserable, thankless, crippled existence? We answer, they belong to that degraded set who some way manage to eke out a meagre subsistence and to live, but who, regardless of their claims to the contrary, are regarded by society, and mayhap by themselves, as—failures.

Notwithstanding the contempt that may be felt for them individually, we are altogether too prone to forget that collectively they have performed such service as to enable us all so proudly to maintain, not simply our families in opulence and security, but, better still, to achieve and retain our individuality and credit as a nation and our prestige as a great military and naval power. They, indeed, are the true "sinews of war;" and on a morning that ushers in a "Waterloo," or a "Balaklava," it is their *valor*, not our *money*, that wins us the day;—their *heroism*, not our *munificence*, that glorifies defeat. Aye, and when, in the midst of our exultation, we give a thought to the cost, well may we turn with contempt from the treasure contributed by the higher class of successful stay-at-homes, and regard reverentially the long death-roll which tells the sad fate of the absent, the heroic,—for the names we read there, are, with rare exceptions, the very humblest in the land; but they are the names, forsooth, that with mute eloquence and speechless pathos, betoken what a hard struggle it all must have been for our country, our home, and our fireside!

Hence it is, when we ask ourselves whence comes the sorrowing tears that through long years have drenched our battle-fields, we have only to trace the bitter stream to its source to find it issuing from the miserable refuge of the poor, the despised, the failure! In time of war, it is true, we bind up the jagged gash whence wells the life-blood; and yet in peace we leave all unattended and unhonored, wounds, that though they cease to bleed, have not healed, and hearts, which though broken, may not die

The living reap their harvest from the battle-field; the dead, theirs: It is well for the poor fellows who comprise the latter that, as we may rationally presume, the price of glory and of redemption being the same, debarred from the enjoyment of the one they may have entered into the felicity of the other. Thus, as we muse in imagination over the scene of former conflict, it is difficult, notwithstanding all our pious egotism, to shut our eyes to the impression that there is something better than our humanity brooding over it all;—a spirit more sympathetic and nobler even than our Christianity—with its long train of disputed right—its holocaust of bloody sacrifice. The strife for these poor fellows is past, with us it is only hushed; the roar of broadsides and batteries, the crash of volleys have ceased, but to all that murderous din there seems still a commingling of faint and mournful echoes—they lead far away—they are shivered and scattered like birds fleeing before the wintry blast;—scattered, they are not parted, but only divided, and meet later in a chorus of angelic song.—Ah, they are the death-sighs of the fallen, wending their piteous way to the spirit land; they leave the reeking trophy of war behind, but carry with them the passport to higher distinction:—It is that grace and forgiveness *wrought in a stifled sob of pain.*

In the last sentence of the foregoing was struck what is claimed herein to be the key-note of final and universal amnesty, and up to the word "pain," we have given an inkling of the drift of thought (I will not say argument) which is to follow.

III

As what we have written thus far would indicate, we find the subject of amnesty bristling with antagonism; indeed, so far as this life is concerned, it is really less a matter of amity than of enmity, and, confining the issue to class, the inquiry resolves itself into one of strife.

As regards the two great divisions of society we have in view, it is not so much my intention to go into an elaborate analysis of them as they stand in relation to success and failure, although in this connection they could be picked to pieces to advantage; but my design in bringing them together is to strike a level in the apparently uneven surface thus presented, not simply in business affairs and social position, but in human nature. In doing this, it may not be irrational to assume, on the principle of the husk, the possibility of clearing away, not by argument, but by a more potent and diviner influence, the enormous superstructure of good, bad, and indifferent that has accumulated above such level. Then, however strongly these opposing elements may seemingly incline to a disseverance of ties, and to a division of race, it might be shown to be so only in the temporal affairs of men; and that pertaining to the conventionalities of life merely, they have no more to do with our hereafter, than have the habits and crotchets of good society or the petty decrees of social ostracism. Thus, while being superficial, the irregularities of life are neither profound nor eternal, and, while obstructing, do not bar nature's evidence of common destiny.

IV.

In my estimate of those comprehended under the term success, I may fail to justify such apparent abasement as shall bring them in the manner proposed down to a level with the rest of mankind; and judging from that standpoint, which I confess to be the general sea-level of failure,—contemplating success it may be in bias,—I would seek to measure the lofty heights before me not in the light of their crowning radiance, but grovelling in the mire below and taking their altitude by the shadow they cast upon the plain. I make no stint of confessing, furthermore, that my sympathies are most heartily enlisted on the side of those who, as in the case of poverty and failure,—seem to have the greatest difficulty in establishing their claims; not that I love them best, but because they are condemned the worst; not that I think them blameless, but that I would not have them bear the whole burden of culpability.

Contrasting the respective qualities of the two classes we have in mind—the high and the low, the trained and the illiterate,—it must be admitted the latter exhibit the most marked natural characteristics whether of good or bad; and notwithstanding the many blots, we read human nature (as it is) among them, better, and feel when we put the volume down it deserves the title not of polished duplicity, but of plain unvarnished truth. In some respects, these two classes stand in the relation of *heads* to *hearts;* indeed, one of the secrets, and a vital one, in the achievements of that success which in the world's idea is the accumulation of property and power, is to be all head and no heart. Success, too, always couples with it the affectation of refinement, and now-a-days one marked feature in our vulgar appreciation of that, if not its special function, is to enable heads to banish or dissemble all sentiment pertaining to the rival sect of hearts.

It requires very little experience of the world, however to teach us with which of these the vantage lies; and when we consider our state offices, our seats of learning, our temples of precept are all monopolized by men whose pretensions, at least, marshal them under the banner of "brains," we need not feel surprised to find authority yoked up with arrogance,—and the rules and regulations, the *dicta* emanating therefrom, if not to the prejudice of the lower class, are not, we may be assured, at variance with that consciousness of high-toned desert which we may expect to find in such an exclusive appropriation of all the superior virtues.

It may be urged that the learning and enlightenment of the higher and cultured class are a blessing and a guidance to the set who are groping (as represented) in intellectual darkness and moral obscurity. Education, it will not be denied, is a useful qualification, especially to him who possesses it; but how far we may ask, is such exclusive eligibility influenced by motives of personal aggrandizement and individual and selfish monopoly? Wherein has all this polish and erudition evinced in any degree, much less demonstrated, an exemption from the venal instincts and petty spites that stigmatize the duller and less refined capacity of our unsophisticated and sturdy yeomanry. Moreover, so far as the blessing of their guidance is concerned, I must admit, I for one have lost much of my schoolboy admiration for that high-cultured benevolence and patriotism as exhibited in our public men, who, while professing to cater exclusively to the welfare of the needy and distressed, never fail to make the wants of a people of personal advantage to themselves.

Of course, for me to impugn the integrity and disinterestedness of these men and the learned professions, would be a shocking presumption; however that may be, we may instance, by way of general application, the fact that experience has shown the necessity of representation, and that our highest judicial authorities needed, and still need from time to time, that regulating themselves which we do not always see emanate from the spontaneous exercise of their own wise volition.

V.

Not being one of those commendable exceptions who boast of being dispassionate, I may be biassed when I say it is not surprising the lower classes—I mean those who figure in the comparative obscurity and dread proscription of failure—should sometimes feel a consciousness of desert which, it must be admitted, except in rare instances, is not recognised, and far less substantially appreciated by the class above them, who, having achieved a little success, feel the overshadowing importance of their own superiority, and use the privileges in which they profess a generous pride as the medium of an ill-disguised contempt and as the means of an equally unjust and cruel oppression.

While this tendency, of course, is most strongly to widen the breach of social relationship and mutual goodwill, it follows naturally these two classes should become, what they really are, adverse, discordant and opposing elements. Under circumstances so favorable to provocation complaints arise and combine in a baleful nucleus of ill will. Round these are clustered—in the pacific guise of societies or benefactors—organized legions of sympathizers, agitators, and adherents, who raise a mere partisan grudge, or local irritation, to the dignity of a class grievance—and this, under various pretexts, breaks out, from time to time, in those savage irruptions that go so far to make history a mere partisan recital of bloody atrocities.

This state of things, it is only common sense to predict, will obtain through all time, nor is it paradoxical to aver, that the danger is most imminent when peace seems to have accumulated the most abundant and gratifying evidences to the contrary. Thus it is, when all things assume an air the most pacific and admirable, there is revealed underneath the outer scale of our opulence and splendor, the Scourge of War who, in the glitter of a more polished barbarity, has burnished his weapons, and only awaits the signal to begin the fray.

Unlike the spark that ignited the great fires of London and Chicago, in the case of social combustion the flame is spontaneous, like that which precedes a storm in the clouds. There may be no appearance of fire, but from the impact of two or more sensitive and highly wrought up elements, there issues in this case not an electric flash, but a steady, deadly flame; not the crash of thunder, but the roar of cannon; not the rush of the tempest, but the rumble of revolution! We see in the half frolicksome tussle of "Town and Gown," a glimmering of the conflagration; but increase these combatants by the hosts pertaining to the ups and downs of society—the rich and the poor, the patrician and the plebeian, as they severally belong—and we have marshalled under our observation not two local factions merely, but the colossal armies of two great rival classes, between whom have been and is being engendered, in the nature of things, an ever smouldering and irruptive hostility. It has been most providentially neutralized by the ceaseless fluctuations of success and failure, and the ever drifting sands of party lines; besides, in the dire extremity which seems must usher in that dreadful and most needless arbitrament of the sword, a soothing calm has been breathed over the turbulent passions of angry men, and elements that loomed in the horizon and threatened to inundate the country in a great ensanguined wave, have subsided into safer channels and a kindlier, more pacific feeling has prevailed.

VI.

Again, too, in the case of threatened collision, extremes must yield, and compromise, which has done so much for both sides and sided with neither, has been as "oil upon the troubled waters." It has won illustrious patronage too, in high places; and by way of example we may notice that the innovation of new titles in the British Peerage, is but the ostentatious display of a prudent foresight, as well as a conspicuous evidence of what the great world of failure loses by success. In other words, what prejudice may not abjure, it is policy to conciliate; and in our inability to exterminate the next best resource is to patronize. As invective sobers, so flattery intoxicates; and thus an element that may not be conquered by force, is vanquished through the graceful medium of an impotent prerogative. So it comes about, that a ceremony which in a mediæval age had been deemed a sacrilege, in this is looked upon as the ordination of a more enlightened policy. Hence the world in our generation is treated to the significant pantomime of royalty invoking the spirit of amnesty, in the sprinkling of plebeian blood over the hallowed dust of pedigree!

Notwithstanding all this the ire of class is not appeased. It is baffled in the loss of a chief perhaps, but the monster grievance of real or fancied wrong is fostered and suffered by the lower orders. It recuperates from every blow aimed by the opposing set at its subjugation or extinction; aye, and when deemed no more, is only like many another evil, taking new shape and ground, and not only existing but gaining increased strength. Thus when it seems after a terrible wrenching to be eradicated, it is only masked under some new aspect and after a severe blow kept hidden and resuscitated. This incubus can never be driven away; it cannot even be induced to migrate; and to banish it, forsooth, would require not only the extermination of the cause of feud, but the utter annihilation of the race of man, and a repeopling of the earth, under the devoutly wished for *régime* not of strife but of amnesty.

As things are, however, the mischief I speak of as conspiring against amity and peace, not only lives but while being the rankest, so it is the most flourishing attribute of our nature. In its frenzy it would riot in anarchy; and barring the helplessness of all human authority to keep it in subjection, there is brought to bear at this critical juncture a means for its control the happy adaptability of which might have been suggested by that subtle instinct we call tact, but the successful working of which—saving the dispensation of an all-wise Providence—would seem more like the artifice of an astute governor:—That is, it is kept *diverted;* and a current too strong to be resisted is simply turned aside.

VII.

Here, we may remark, (and it will sound like a favouring of the "all-is-for-the-best" principle) that the more numerous the divisions of public opinion, the smaller and less formidable the innate mischief we are considering; for then these diminutive factions not being strong enough to undertake each other's destruction, find vent for their ill humor through a species of harmless irritation; the general effect being comparative harmony and to some extent co-operation. Thus, through a complex system of petty storms, are we enabled to approach nearest to a perfect calm.

There is no doubt that much of the dissension amongst us may seem all wrong and out of place in our time; but while we may regard it—as we do so many other things—with distrust, as threatening our welfare and security, this is only another one of innumerable reminders that we do not always know when or for what to be most grateful. In fact, we are constantly admonished how erroneous and unkind are many of the estimates on which we borrow trouble; and it is not too much to assume that those very differences which appear so dreadfully agitating and even leading, as they often do, to worse contention, are not simply beneficial to our moral health, but indispensable in acting as the waste-wears of inevitable spleen, and as the safety-valves of irrepressible ferment. Hence in the wear and tear which is so much deprecated, and in the sadder destruction at times of life, as well as of property, the tendency is most mercifully to soothe and assuage that tiger in our nature which we see, not alone in the darker epochs of history, as in the "reign of terror" in France, but also in a small, but no less vindictive way, snapping and snarling individually, throughout every class and sphere of society.

In this view, then, much of that strife which is regarded as so deplorable, may come in the divine order of appropriate concomitants and be admirably suited to regulate those human animosities which must be appeased and, as is often found necessary, fought down. Here we may note, more particularly, that the people inheriting these dangerous traits of character are not, as so many are inclined to think, that much despised species of ghouls which they assume are to be found only in the lowest stratum of society, and inhabiting those dens of corruption which are thought to distinguish the dwelling places of the poor.

There is no doubt that in the eyes of some, Poverty and Opprobium seem always to walk together and to be inseparable from vice; indeed, it is characteristic of our benevolence to yoke these two up together; nevertheless, I believe it is a grievous mistake, as well as a very common error to imagine the worst kind of wickedness may not be found most prevalent in those places which are surrounded by the most seductive of all excuses that embellish our highest refinement. Of course an evil propensity is or seems to be a very general descrepancy in our organism; but in none is it more deeply rooted, if not so contemptibly conspicuous, as in him who piques himself he is exempt. There is no exemption! No, not even alienation; and, in the case of the best of us, no amount of "moral suasion" ever did or ever will coax it away. It may be diverted and pacified in many ways that are pleasant and legal as well as highly respectable, nevertheless, however palliated it exists all the same. We may recognise it readily in a criminal or a mob—we sometimes detect it amongst friends, but in self, never.—It is a distemper that none of the nostrums known to our shrewdest adepts can purge away, and, like some other ills so hard to wrestle with, we rarely recognise its true character till too late.

VIII.

According to the popular idea, wickedness is not only moral *disease* but moral *deformity*. It may wear this aspect sometimes in the case of others, but in self, never; and generally speaking it is a wrong conception. Personally, it has none of the sickly symptoms of a baleful malady —none of the alarming concomitants of a wasting pestilence; it comes, on the contrary, commended to us by our conceit, and, not unfrequently, by all the rosy witchery of robust health and lustful good nature;—then, childlike and irresistible, it pillows its head upon our bosom and we cuddle it!

The qualities, also, by which some of our worst propensities are generally known, may be the very ones by which in self the evil is harbored, screened, and beautified. They are closely allied to self-love, and though we give them the most endearing names in all our tender heart's sweet vocabulary, yet the cruel, unfeeling world calls them by such harsh, opprobrious epithets as "Envy"—"Jealousy" —"Hatred." Traits like these—with which we are all amply endowed—nourished, not maliciously, we will say unconsciously, grow into a species of gaunt, ever-hungering carnivora that, out of their refuge in the trackless fastnesses of our darker passions, issue forth to grub on the tender blossom and to poison the more healthful juices of the better fruit.

With individuals the evil is localized, and may not in the case of some seem more obnoxious than may be indulgently dubbed spiteful; at any rate it is short lived, as the span of existence; but under the fostering influence of congenial "associations" that never die—commingling with kindred flocks and nursed by confreres in the hot-bed of secret conclave, these traits of which I speak are no longer the piecemeal of ill-will, but with the homogeneousness of all unkindliness, become the gigantic embodiment of sectional enmity. Then it is, we see exhibited in private, the voracious beast we read of in holy metaphor,—only that it is erroneous to think it is always "roaring;" indeed, between the periods of its savage irruption, it is the inert monster of smiling duplicity,—and then, in the saintly guise of certain "societies," solicits and obtains patronage with an air of urbane and even pious benevolence. Although ever on the trail of its prey, it appears on such occasions impelled by a more sympathetic impulse,—as if in tender curiosity it was seeking out the erring and wandering ways of poor troubled spirits; and thus transformed, without even the "cloven foot" to indicate the brute, it meanders forth the personification of zealous philanthropy. To strip these animals of their disguise—to harmonize them—to reconcile differences and obliterate feuds—all constitute the professed object that has engaged the attention of the Moralist, the Demagogue, and the Evangelist, in every phase of human existence,—through struggling generations as far back as we have known those seething, warring elements, Politics and Religion.

IX.

Meanwhile the tendency of all this laudable intercession has been and is, (whether fortunately or otherwise), to inculcate and foster new ideas, envolving our fathers in the past (and in the entail, our children in the future) in a heritage of unseemly controversy which, under the pretext of glorifying causes, has been pushed to extremities. Thus strife is engendered,—war precipitated,—and the result,—failure—or, at best, such a patched up compromise as leads to further contention and later to a resumption of hostilities. The charge of failure, in this connection would no doubt be denied, as both sides generally claim a triumph; but, notwithstanding the great bulwark of authorities and opinions to the contrary, it does seem to my humble perceptive faculties most conclusively evident that, the upshot of each of the innumerable crusades attempted in the virtue of the one side against the so-called iniquity of the other, following the rule of circumambulation, has been and will be simply to bring us back to somewhere in the hazy past where all our opinions seem to have diverged, and whence we started. Thus the end of one conflict has been, and is to be, the beginning of another.

This I believe may be said with only too much truth of very many of our best works, and a great deal of our boasted enterprise; indeed, it is no idle hallucination to assume, as I do herein, that we have been for hundreds and thousands of years circling round a magic pivot termed the "Millennium," and calling the rotary exercise "progress;" at the same time looking back with contempt on the foot prints of past generations, we call the last step in our own "civilization." Occasionally we discover along the line of march, signs of having been over the route before; that is, we see directly confronting us or remotely looming up ahead, virtually the same obstacles that presented themselves, and that we understood were overcome, may be centuries ago; and this application may be carried as far back as that remote age when necessity first conspired with expedient, and locomotion first suggested obstacle. So it is, that nearer our own time we see old wounds that were inflicted in the wars of the Huguenot and Puritan, the Catholic and Jacobin, breaking out and bleeding afresh and witness all about us, and menacing our future, atrocities perpetrated in the names of reform and religion, that bear a striking resemblance to the barbarity of St. Bartholemew, and the fanaticism of that human grill of Smithfield.

But what does all this show? It shows that the great work of reconciliation, notwithstanding our splendid and flourishing system of philanthropic and evangelical enterprise, has not been accomplished; and taking the amount of dissension as a criterion, it is not even commenced. It would seem unfair to allege that the stint has been altogether neglected, and may be a great deal has been done; but we have been so much absorbed in doctrinal controversy and in sectarian triumph, as to overlook the main object underlying all our exertion.

In one sense it is true, we have kept the good work of amnesty before us, but such a long way ahead that, so far as our little world is concerned, the worthy object may have, and very likely has, lost its centripetal force, and been attracted to some other planet; at all events, it seems to have left our sphere. Maybe it is temporarily absent in search of the millenium, or wandering about somewhere on this terrestrial home of ours in some inexplicable disguise—circling round, as it were, resurrecting and beautifying some dusty landmark whose term of purgatorial probation is ended. Thus, instead of coming down like a beaconlight and commencing with us and our generation, it is groping its sluggish way along behind, and will reach us at a later day when, in the pride of our humiliation, the dust of our monuments shall have mingled with the ashes of our ancestors!! But where, let us inquire, are those good shepherds in whose care was entrusted that most volatile of all properties, amnesty? Well, there are those amongst us whose duty and calling it has been to go out as did the dove of old, and reclaim the lost spirit of brotherly love; but, alas, they leave us on their errand of grace, and, like the raven, never return. They perish by the way; or, making a luxury of the "olive branch," they stay and roost there—

awaiting with the cunning of the possum and the supine idiocy of the owl, the twilight that shall usher in the vesper-call of Gabriel!

X.

In the above connection we may remark, that while the breach occasioned in the conflict of rival sects is not unfrequently made the bloodless arena of clerical heroism, it is rather in the trivial affairs of social intercourse are planted the germs of universal love and of universal pacification; and out of the tropical beams of the fireside spring a fruitful vegetation and golden harvest that may not sprout and grow in the dim light and frosty air of cloister and pulpit. We may not address masses of men as we would individuals, and those dry, didactic utterances discharged in the stiff order of professional routine, while they may not lack in many of the requirements necessary in the elucidation of doctrine, are too frequently, even in their highest erudition, only a fine species of prosodical mosaic, manipulated with all the cold, polished asceticism of faultless art. They may appeal to the ear as gracefully chiselled marble to the eye, and some of these models, amongst connoisseurs, seem indeed more highly esteemed than flesh and blood.

My "bump" of reverence may be abnormally small, but I have to admit, it is absolutely wanting in appreciation for the sort of pious automaton to whom this description applies. They are the bloodless incarnation of a phlegm— their voice, the aimless barking of a rheum! This may seem like extravagant language as applied even in exceptional cases; and yet I claim theirs as applied to us, is not that of a sympathetic spirit, conscious of other's pain and peril—with voice vibrating in the trembling yearning solicitude of that great ordeal of suffering which we are all standing by and contemplating! Nay, 'tis rather the monotonous, hastily-despatched jargon pronounced, in the official discharge of an unpleasant duty, over the odoriferous clay of spent humanity. Besides, their apathetic pantomime ever so gracefully "entoned" to masses, falls as far short of individual application as the spasmodic zeal of the partisan overshoots the mark; and the blank cartridges of the one, and the random discharges of whole broadsides of invective by the other, are blended in the smoke and brimstone of a species of sham warfare, that has for its prototype the early battles of the church. All, too, so far at variance with the good work of pacification —let alone evangelization—that Christian brothers and "societies," professing a fraternal "grip" with all mankind, gather in those once gory fields—that would and ought to be smiling, fruitful meadow-lands—and with insufficient provocation to commend even their prejudice, unearth the skeleton of defunct antagonism, and in the spell of an abominable incantation, rake with bony hands the ashes of an ancient grudge!

XI.

In my own behalf, however, I may say if called upon to choose between the *drone* and the *rhapsodist*, I should be disposed to favour the latter; not that he is my ideal of what he should be, but all mingled as we are with the failing, and dying, and dead, I cleave to whatever exhibits the most unmistakeable signs of life, and vigor, and animation. Indeed, I have no fellowship for that ghastly caution which says of silence, it is " golden,"—no more than for that other dreadful inertia where nothing moves and all is still.

Of the above preceptors one preaches by rote, the other dilates upon the record; one entones a dead ritual, the other vocalizes a living thought; one rivets his opinions to set forms, the other emancipates ideas, and fosters liberty of expression.—Both take their text from Holy Writ, but while one gives it the strict interpretion of his "school," and is stifled in the narrow crevice of his " creed," the other leavens it with the promptings of impulse, and sprinkles it over with the fertile gleanings of miscellaneous reading. One is fixed in a system of dogmas changeless as the solar constellation, the other enjoys in the free use of his faculties a perceptive and responsive power as wise and as necessary as the cause he advocates.—The first is correct according to his "standard," and the last as near right as the conscience from which he speaks; the former at best is the obedient servant, all zeal for the master, the latter, the loving brother, all sympathy for the slave. Finally, both are wrong in proportion as they adhere to our corrupt version of old time impression and resist that gentle opponent of rusty prejudice which, coming in the persuasive guise of some tempting need, advocates that modification of ideas which is as much a necessity, and as natural a growth as the improved vegetation of the earth.

Apropos of advancement, it may be seen that I do not mean that which is striving for the van—aye, crowding forward to arrive and complete everything in a day, a year or a generation; and in this respect it appears to me this age of enterprise is surpassing not only others but itself. The fact is 'there is a subtle element of progress inherent in all things based upon latent qualities of good that lie dormant or covered up until the veil shall be drawn, or which, crumbling away piece-meal, like husks, disclose the fruit so wisely fostered but concealed till the sublime hour of perfect fruition. And herein lies an essential evidence of equality in man, and the germs of universal amnesty. Some of these husks are smooth and beautiful, some rough and repulsive; but beneath the outward aspect is nourished a kernel whose perfection indicates the all perfect foresight and impartiality of the Creator.

That some of these should be sweet, and some sour, and many bitter and disagreeable, is only a matter of taste and not a defect in the thing itself; a peculiarity rather, of the palate that should not be taken as a common standard of good and bad—of our likes and dislikes perhaps, but not of our wholesale approbation and condemnation. While, however, we find some of these husks natural, many are artificial; and here we may note particularly, that in the clearing away of much of this outer garbage, and, in the truthful development of fact, there is a wholesome tendency to wear off, if not entirely to obliterate, many of the glaring differences that characterize individuals and classes and sects. Then, while there comes out of the downhill side of life many redeeming traits, we have only to glance upward along the higher incline, to see revealed in that pampered realm a downward slide and a lamentable drooping and dwindling away of splendidly adorned mediocrities.

XIII.

We find artificial husks everywhere. Indeed, many of the acquirements with which the "cultured" classes plume themselves, and set up in contempt against the humble and illiterate, are no more than the thin-skinned ornament of mere outer embellishment; and much, too, that is attributed to our boasted "higher enlightenment," we find, in truth, founded upon a substrata of information, ingenious and entertaining, no doubt, but to a great extent artificial and false. This is not true simply of the fashionable novice, but also of the erudite professor, and applies as well to the teacher as the pupil.

In that literature and learning which form such a goodly share of our industriously garnered wealth, how little, strictly speaking, is the quantity of grain to the enormous bulk of chaff,—and yet we may justly add, how large the kernel of precept imbedded in an almost impenetrable outer growth of husk. This husk, in some cases, may be likened to a sort of fungus obtruding itself in a most unhealthy form; not unfrequently, too, springing up in sacred soil, it seems after a time to have inherited the reverential attributes of hallowed birth; but while inspiring, as it may often do, the pious conservatism of a denomination or sect, and appealing to the kindest, purest instincts of a people, it is none the less a scabby excrescence. Then it is, that the incursion of an alien power or other ruthless element, to do what in love and tenderness we may not have the nerve or heart to do, is a healthful God-send to a nation, if not a general blessing to mankind.

There is one feature about our historical literature, too, the importance of which may not be overlooked here.—I mean its sanctimonious glorification of such brutal atrocities as happen to be on the right side. And to this we in no small degree owe the fact, that to-day we stand by the "fire eaters" of the 16th century, and with all their fanaticism, with all their hostility—with none of their provocation, with none of their sincerity,—we, their posterity, in this remote land of mutual hope, and fear, and trust, congregate in our temples, and there, ignoring the death harvest of three hundred years of oblivion and reform, and the pathetic appeal of six generations of prayer and suffering for amnesty, bridge over the "bloody chasm" that separates us from, and brings us into closer communion with, that damning epoch of historical and religious feud,—and shoulder to shoulder, heart to heart, and hand in hand,—marshalled under our respective banners, fight over and over again, in abominable mimicry, the squabbles and battles of Church and Creed, and exult in the gory triumphs of their conflicts and their victories!

We are admonished that "sufficient unto the day is the evil thereof," but that applies only to those who can neither read nor write; it is reserved, rather for cultured soil, and that harrowing medium, the professional demagogue, the enlightened mission of transplanting the seeds of partisan record, and through them perpetuating the ills of other days. Nay, not even the poor and the illiterate are spared the baleful heritage; they and all are made,—in the never-ending obsequies of the past—to reanimate the grievances of the Huguenot,—to re-echo the war-cry of the Covenanter,—and to sanctify the "cant" of the Puritan. It is not that we admire them so much, or that we feel so especially grateful for or unanimous about their doctrines; nay, it is imperative that we maintain the *rôle*, not simply of "Christians," but of "Protestants." The fact is, we are just sufficiently at variance with the old reformers to be haunted with an uneasy apprehension of relapsing; and the situation is thus made to appear a good deal like that of a timid man clinging to the steep incline of a slippery roof. But while there is no more sense in it than in whistling because we are afraid or to keep awake, we keep alive prejudice without having the confidence to confess, or the manliness to disown it.

XIII.

In this emergency we turn again and again to a select few in our midst who may be called the good shepherds of "Peace on earth and good-will toward men." If there be one blessing more than another, for which the lower classes are indebted to the upper stratum, it is the preaching which, with all the professed simplicity of our orthodoxy, can only emanate in its purity and highest essence from those who make the study of truth a profession. I would not detract from the efforts of earnest workers in this vineyard; but what are the peculiar traits or acquirements possessed by these particular individuals, so much out of common with man's natural endowments as to make them not only profess to be, but really seem preternaturally divine and immaculate beyond question? In other words, wherein lies the virtue of their especial and exclusive eligibility to holy office?

Take the young fledgling of to-day—not only aspiring to, but initiated into the business of saving souls—let us examine him practically, as we would an applicant for a certificate to sail a great ocean-steamship freighted with human life, and what do we find. Why, an ordinary individual whose education consists mainly in his having acquired an aptitude in reciting a stereotyped solution of certain abstruse problems pertaining to his profession—problems which outline, like a system of bulwarks, the dogmatical stronghold of his creed. As the soundness of his theology, however, does not admit of mathematical demonstration he falls back on the convenient and hackneyed expedient of faith; and believing, may be conscientiously, it is his duty to feel as strongly as possible, he has set to work and read up till he is crammed and saturated with the malignant prejudice and antagonism that distinguished the early Reformer. Then, when charged and soaked to repletion, if he be an energetic talker, he straightway becomes the indefatigable mouth-piece and bell-wether of a whole congregation of bigotry and hypocrisy.—Aye, and with a volubility erroneously dubbed eloquence, opening up the flood-gates of invective, in the same breath that he preaches paradise for his own flock he invokes perdition on rival sects. Meanwhile, what is the most forcible truth to be deduced from all this man's exertion? Why, he has shown, incontestably, that the venom, narrowmindedness and meanness that obtained in times past, and from which we claim exemption, have not simply had their warping influence on the present, but that with the constantly reanimated impulse of clerical and political partisanship, they flourish to-day in all their pristine strength; they may take upon themselves more acceptable forms, and they do; but these and other like monstrosities, we identify with our household gods, and have come to regard them only as lap-dogs, hobbies and pet-weaknesses. Nay, these very qualities, so characteristic of the brute, are neither annihilated nor even decimated; on the contrary, they have not only multiplied with the increased population of the earth, but with the rapacity of their instincts, have fattened in the luxury of greater indulgence,—till the major part of them have become, through very obesity, so unwieldy and inert, that they seem good-natured and may be harmless; but poke them up a bit, as it happens sometimes they are, and we see only too significant signs of those barbarous propensities which were once drowned, as Scripture assures us (like

T

rats), in a flood, and which only need a little starving and goading to make them the lean and hungry monsters we claim extinct. Now when we reflect that the poor, the destitute and the oppressed, are undergoing this goading, excoriating process, if anything would disprove my assumption of unmitigated barbarism, it is that this class should bear the ordeal so well.

XIV.

In one sense, this big world of ours is a great railway-station where people are arriving constantly and are waiting with their little packs in hand to take passage to foreign parts. The walls are plastered all over with placards, some with red and diverse-colored letters, setting forth the peculiar advantages of the different ways of reaching the particular "Eldorado" which all seem to have in view. There are three classes provided for: saloon, intermediate, and steerage.—The first is luxurious and expensive; the second not so stylish but comfortable; the third peculiarly adapted to the lower class to whom the sort of accommodation is no object so they reach their destination in safety. Here as we look about us somewhat bewildered, we are pounced upon by some dozens of liveried officials representing the different companies. These latter individuals vary, nautically speaking, all the way from the evangelical "crimp" to the ecclesiastical iceberg; some are vociferating and gesticulating in a violent and excited manner; others hang back and are more dignified, as if assured of the superior inducements of their line; and, notwithstanding the former are so anxious and solicitous, the latter seem calm and indifferent. All are regularly licensed forwarders, but it is very easy to distinguish those among them who enjoy a monopoly as old firms, and especially those dispensing government patronage. One of the most forward says authoritatively,— "come with me!" and, as in the impulse of a thing habitual, makes as if to relieve us of our little pack; but we cling to it lovingly and beg him not to be so hasty. While their manners, particularly among themselves, do not always seem to commend their offices, their demeanor generally is that of professionals; being not unlike what we have observed in matter of fact, business-like dentists, surgeons, and undertakers who are very much sought after and greatly pressed for time; indeed, they even carry about them the sepulchral odors of their craft.

Added to this, too, the way some of them have of going at one seems horribly suggestive of the work in hand, and they make no stint of parading before our dazed and terrified vision all the appalling preliminaries of the dreadful ordeal that awaits us. So it is we shrink away with a renewed relish for the good things of life, and say to these liveried gentry—who would take possession of us and our little bundle, and put the brand of their dreadful monogram on our quivering heart, its loves and pleasures—I prithee wait a while. But then, as if our dilemma encouraged the others, they all make towards us as by one impulse and hedge us round; and a dreadful controversy as to which shall have us, is opened up and waxes warm.

Their abuse of each other, meanwhile, is alternated by sundry direct appeals to us: one says,—don't go by such and such a line—" they only carry cattle "—"they are not decked over," and are wanting in " modern conveniences;" they are not " Clyde built," or they are not " classed at Lloyds." We are advised that the course taken by some is too " high,"—that we shall get frozen in ; then, the opposition retort against this by enumerating all the dreadful contingencies of the more tropical route; and we are almost persuaded at the mention of perplexing currents, treacherous gulf-storms, and devastating typhoons. Ah, if we take the opinion that each of these entertains against the other, we must perforce condemn them all; and we reflect that there may be more truth than scepticism in saying to ourselves :—Alas, not our poor heathen, but the impeccable shepherds, how may they be saved !

XV.

Am I depreciating an excellent class of men whose sublime mission I envy ? If so, I am perpetrating an atrocious libel in this criticism, but then, in warning the poor man against them, only rendering the more conspicuous those opposite qualities that prove it false.

However that may be, I confess I cannot listen to the majority of these men and drink in all they have to say, as the thirsty wanderers of the desert quaff the crystal liquid of their own precious oasis; aye, and feel at the same time that delightful quenching of a thirst that naught but immortality can slake. The fact is, we see the average preacher of to-day ascend the tapering temple of his creed, and from the summit of that narrow pinnacle expound a conception of God's love and mercy as cramped as the little scope in which he is railed. Socially he is the amiable friend and patron of all he periodically preaches against and condemns ; but here, amid the hushed awe of the living, surrounded by the mute but expressive symbols of a faith professing only peace and good-will, not unfrequently he loses his individuality as man in the saintly character of vicar. Then it is we see before us the living, modern representative of the old time apostle; which, according to our modern church interpretation, as demonstrated by this example, is a very ordinary compound of such a reputable trinity as bigot, partisan, ranter. He mounts his pulpit, clad in the neutral garb of an evangelical order—his countenance congealing in the passionless chill of the cloister—and presto ! the transformation begins. " 'Tis then he sniffs the battle from afar," and shines down upon his congregation " in the full panoply of war." Contention is to him a luxury—the Sabbath the anniversary of pious warfare. True, he may not fight the battles in whose triumphs he glories, but bravely, heroically, he throws himself into the bloody breach of ensanguined history and bravery, heroically, entones the war-cry of a passed generation.

On this gladsome day of rest the Lord of Light is smiling down upon his people in such a wealth of sunshine as would draw bird-songs from snow-banks; but the effect on this divine proxy is only to thaw away a greater torrent of ill-humor and he overshadows all about him in the portentous cloud of his little storm. It is then we hear the snivelling refrain of the Puritan—the battle cry of the Covenanter—the wail of the Huguenot; and while the groan of the Martyr is blended with the menace of the Protestant, the screams of "Smithfield" mingle with the moanings of the Inquisition. But who is this hostile interpreter of a faith not his own,—this pious burlesque of a cause sublime? Whence issues that torrent of coarse invective that follows to this day the discarded fugitive, King James, and heaps obloquy on harassed "bloody" Queen Mary? Who is it, do we ask? Why his "name is legion;" and condensed all into one, I can dispose of them in no truer or more appropriate language than to say,—it is the bleached skeleton of the sixteenth century, grinning through the gloomy lapse of three hundred years,—and denouncing as victims those in our midst, who may bear the name and have none of the faults attributed to those who were condemned in that early age. Aye, it is even worse now than it was then—it is farcical and does not rise to the dignity of real tragedy.

No; we cannot leave the work of Amnesty to our good shepherds; they are working like our demagogues and others against that harmony of opinion and simplification of doctrine that would wipe out differences and obliterate professions. Nay; they are no exception to our lawyers and doctors who would mystify their business in order to enhance the importance of their services. This state of things does not simply retard the promised reign of "Peace on earth," but it conflicts with our professed exercise of an enlightened policy; so that, what may and is found from time to time to be unwise and absurd or false and pernicious, very often and for a long time is persistently maintained, and the new light ignored, to keep an institution intact wherein signs of crumbling might shake human faith and disturb the sacred infallibility of records. This too, when obduracy does not passively obtrude itself in the way of common sense, but actively sets itself up in opposition to the most pathetic appeals of justice and humanity.

XVI.

Here we may observe that notwithstanding the effort made to maintain intact, as above stated, all forms, customs, and ceremonies—together with their extended retinues of privilege and perquisite, of prerogative and emolument,—there is a power stronger than the wisdom of our councillors or legislators, whether they pertain to Church or State, and truer in its native intuition than all the learned acumen of our professors and ministers and judges.—It is resisting encroachments in high places and modifying excesses and the instruments by which its good offices are performed, are found, as in the case of universal suffrage, in the lowest, the commonest and the humblest in the land.—Those, in fact, whose very poverty and abandonment is, in one sense, a distinctive feature of their fraternity; and the similarity of whose wants and grievances is not alone the chief element of unanimity, but a guarantee of that mutual sympathy which underlies the public weal.

In close alliance with these, there is another mighty leveller of aristocratic bastiles, which, while it seems like the other a ruthless destroyer, is the kindest, the most faithful and effective of all retrievers. Empires, dynasties, and systems bow before its potent sway; and probably not the easiest nor first to budge is that opprobrious element in which spite and prejudice have embalmed names, characters, and events, and thus handed them down to posterity and to us as a heritage of hate entailed by the father on the innocent credulity of the child. Unlike the barb we not unfrequently find corroding in the flesh it brought to dust, the spirit of feudal vengeance is not quiescent; but as the arm that wielded it becomes paralyzed, it is picked up in turn by younger successors and with increased venom made to rankle, again and again, in the quivering hearts of subsequent generations.

The only power that would seem to cope at all successfully with this atrocious madness is—Time. Time is the great tireless ameliorator of ill-will. It may often seem, and really be dreadfully slow and could the one most especially concerned, live in the hope of justification one or two or three centuries, he would see them drag their weary length past to the end, and while he still waited and watched, hear the clock strike the hour which completed that long probation and be admonished he must still be patient; aye, and that he must die unvindicated. It is not that Time is waiting for our dragging system of evangelism to catch up with and direct the good work of Amnesty, nor that its virtues may only be developed through the slow progress made by our pioneers in their efforts to civilize. Indeed, it works in one sense, independently of them, and frequently the two are so much at variance that what the one completes in reverence the other topples over with indifference. And yet, notwithstanding our difficulty in reconciling our actions to Time's decrees while living, insensibly it is working in many ways for our good, and long after we have been deprived of other means to justify our deeds, it garners up and cherishes these redeeming traits by which they are vindicated and that we are held in kindly remembrance.

XVII.

There are many evidences that go far to place Time not only in the first rank of pacificators, but to entitle it as we have said to the rare distinction of being the greatest and most effectual ameliorator of ill-will. It is a common saying that "second thoughts are always best"—they are certainly kindest—and if the fraction of a second is sufficient to change the harsh retort into a gentle response, then what may be expected of months, years, centuries? Even great qualities may not be fully appreciated, in fact they rarely are till time has sanctified them and then they stand out pure and noble and are beloved and emulated. So it is with deeds of the past; and much of that evil that stigmatized a former age and rendered its people despicable, has grown obsolete as the flesh that inspired it mouldered away into dust. Then, the better spirit which retrieves is alone remembered, and disembarrassed of the baser material, comes to be regarded as the most perfect of all virtue, the most exemplary of all goodness.

Thus it is that all true greatness is retrospective, as also the little of good-nature inherent in all and even the worst actions; and, in this way, the very atrocities of a remote age have sought and found absolution in lapse of time. Then, as the strongholds of mediæval vice and arrogance crumble away, the outlines that still remain are treasured up and pointed to in this age as trophies won by the higher order of enlightenment, from the older period of so-called darkness and tyranny; and even in the association of two such opposing elements, time has eked out a better comprehension of truth, and—we might at least hope—a kindlier spirit of forgiveness.

We point to the Tower of London, or to the Dungeons of the Inquisition, and those grimy tableaux overshadowed as they are with historic deeds of darkness, betoken all that was once most cruel and barbarous. Cries long hushed in anguish seem re-animated and to call for vengeance; but we enter and see the hand-writing on the walls,—there too are the "rack," the "block," the "axe," all worn and hacked and nicked in a use the most dreadful and appalling,—and we weep and turn from the bloody reminiscences only with a softened feeling of pity. So it is, also, that the "cross," the "spikes," the "crown of thorns," once the instruments of a diabolical assassination, are come to be regarded, not as the ghastly souvenirs of "man's inhumanity to man," but as the most precious symbols of that new and happier destiny wherein the "end justifies the means. We do not regard the deed as the crime of the few only, but as a reproach to the whole human race; we do not even condemn the perpetrators—we cannot; they were only the meaner instruments in the partial execution of a great design and "they knew not what they did."

What I have said, by way of tribute, of redeeming features in what seems a dreadful scourge, I have said and believe to be true; but while this view obtains in a certain retrieving sense as regards the faults of a people, and as such I apply it gladly, nevertheless, the thought of Time as the ravager which it is so natural to feel it to be, intrudes itself like a black pall even in the effort to speak kindly of it, and hence, I yield my guerdon of praise grudgingly, joylessly.—It is, indeed, an eulogy in which pathos deepens into pain; insomuch that notwithstanding the blessedness of Time's redemption one feels in the impulse of the flesh a yearning tenderness to get back again that precious boon,—the price it costs! It is inexpressibly sad that Time, which robs us of our youth, our beauty, our love, our life,— may alone come to the rescue of our good name.—Nay, but then, as if remorseful for the havoc it has made, it comes back, a dove to tell us, "wrath has been appeased," and that "the elements have subsided." Time! thou dreaded chastener, art indeed our friend?—it is a long sleep we have cuddled in thy lap, but there is a consolation in knowing that when we wake, the voracious monster that would devour all kindly remembrance shall have vanished, and in its place there flit, fanning our face with its perfumed wing, only the harmless butterfly. Go back to earth thou tiny thing and bid those who love us rejoice!—for time is oblivion, and spite losing its venom in forgetfulness, turns from the chrysalis of a crawling worm—takes wings and flies away!!

XVIII.

At this juncture, in what I trust may not have been altogether an unpardonable digression, and bearing in mind whatever lessons may be gleaned from the foregoing, we now turn our attention to a portion of that class whom we introduced in another part under the head of failure. There is a tier of failure amongst failures, as much under that we have referred to as it, in its turn, is lower than the comparatively successful stage above. And here let me say, whoever may be disposed to favor those in this, the lowest grade, need not despair if he looks only to his clients and himself for encouragement; for, notwithstanding the obstacles cast in their way by those who may seek to disparage their cause, he will find no greater difficulties than that shabby pair Truth and Merit, themselves, often have in proving and establishing their claims to consideration and patronage.

It is observable that. Benevolence, in the broad field and abundant variety outspread before it, generally, and I may say naturally, sheds the light of its benignant countenance not on the darkest but brightest spots; selecting, invariably, such cases as seem most entitled to "charitable" distinction. These latter constitute the oases in the broad desert; the fortunate ones amongst the unfortunate, and represent, of course, the most exemplary distress. In my humble efforts in behalf of the unfortunate generally, it is not my purpose, however agreeable the task might be, to advocate that virtuous sympathy which culls out those particularly whose qualifications render them especially eligible to succor, and who manage, under the most critical inspection, to come up to the high-toned, exclusive standard which it is thought proper in these cases to bring to bear. I desire it to be understood, however, it is not that I bear the set last referred to any malice, that I don't go in all for them as others do; nay, it is because these favored ones are so abundantly able to maintain their own character without any help, that I curtail my good offices. In fact, I could say nothing to improve their condition in this respect, and any attempt on my part might result in my making myself disagreeable; besides, novice as I am, I might blunder and injure a cause in which many of them are a professional, not to say, beggarly sort of success. Mind, I do not exclude them, but those others in whose behalf I would seek to raise the most pathetic notes in my weak voice, and touch most gently and lovingly the tenderest chords in human sympathy, include those who are so low and degraded that I, at least, am encouraged to feel any effort on my part may not, nay, cannot result in their further disparagement or abasement.

Many of these are not only pronounced by our most respectable authorities, but feel themselves, hopelessly depraved and irrevocably lost, and by all but those similarly situated are utterly and severely abandoned. In the case of many of these, buffeted and kicked from pillar to post, it is impossible for us to realize or it may be to ease their condition. They are so badly off they feel they have forfeited all claim to help of any sort, and much less do they look for any degree of reform or prosperity; besides, they are too brutalized to be able to look down, as most people can, and be comforted in the reflection there are others worse off than themselves. As all about is scorn and repulsion, they can feel in that quarter no particle of hope, and their little, rapidly-contracting world, on all its four walls, looks black, and grim, and drear. A fashionable exhibit of so-called "charity," may now and then put its gloved hand through the chinks, or, with its embroidered and perfumed handkerchief to its sensitive nose, makes its appearance bodily; then, indeed, like a bit of canvas to the castaway, even that is no doubt a welcome speck looming in the visible horizon; but there it dwindles away to the infinitesimal, leaving only such an impression on the mind as is produced by the latest novelty in the genus nebula.

XIX.

None probably will deny that these poor creatures suffer, and I only wish I may be exaggerating when I say one sober, conscious moment is to them hours of intolerable anguish. Is it surprising or unnatural then, they should seek a "Lethe" in whatever may assuage pain, and offer them ever so brief a respite? So they drain the deadening draught with a gladsome sigh, as those in the luxury of high-toned moral living would tooth-ache drops; their only enjoyment being the to them ineffable bliss that flavors the dregs, and the abatement, it may be ever so little, of a dreadful, hopeless remorse.

This is the class whose enormities and sufferings our moral-agony painters attempt to portray in the luxury of their leisure hours, and it is to them that we are indebted for those dreadful scenes of privation and atrocity depicted, not so much for the benefit of the poor and miserable, as in a warning way to admonish the rich and the gay. That is, I mean, not so much to mitigate the distress of the former as to season the pleasures of the latter. They are the vile and incorrigible, whom our moral doctors have long since given over, or rather ignored altogether, and from whom the better community shrink from in disgust, or point to in triumph and self-satisfaction, as offering the best reason for their own want of "charity." They are a crouching, shivering, tattered band, with minds all debased, and their every thought and action seemingly under the baleful dominion of the most abominable brutality and wickedness.

Can there be anything about this grade of misfortune to invite sympathy? I may be committing a grievous error by not joining my voice in the chorus of pious condemnation which consigns these poor creatures to the devil; I sadly,

I fear, too, I am wanting in respect for that virtuous indignation which points to them only as illustrating the dreadful and inevitable judgment visited on all departures from those rules and regulations by which people, aspiring to a very high reward and a superabundant felicity, feel it worth while to be guided.

Here it occurs to me as being a nice question, how far one can befriend these hopeless ones without giving offence. If a kind word in their behalf, for instance, would seem, as it might to some, an eulogy, what will be thought of such a shocking misplacement of philanthropic eloquence as shall seek in them to embellish even so mean a virtue as, like a lost diamond, may be found glistening in the filth of such degradation. If one sees it, recognises it, and knows it to be genuine, how shall he know exactly what estimate to put upon it? Aye, what shall be the measure of praise to be awarded in our admiration of a jewel so rare, even amongst the best of us, so that while we may not be so shabby as to underrate its real worth, we may not, at the same time, commit the unpardonable blunder of adding a cypher too much!

In other words, if one happen to be so imprudent as to give the reins to his feelings, how may he know when to stop in time so he may not exaggerate their redeeming traits, and thereby make them appear too deserving? To err in this respect would be to commit a most shocking, I may say, an unprecedented impropriety, and yet I think Justice would be the least angry, and the great Judge-in-Equity, Himself, less offended and scandalized than those who seek in condemning to forestall his wrath.

While I would not abjure the staler fact that doles out to them a modicum of credit, I would try and discover in the more generous and ever fresh abundance of imagination the means to polish it up. This is doubtless a poor seasoning for a crust—a kind word only—and offers nothing, in one sense, either to eat or to drink or to wear, but it were a poor tribute, indeed, that did not knead into it a little of the spice of better cheer,—a little of the mellowing, expanding luxury of hope,—and after all a crumb of that is worth a whole loaf of despair. Far be it from my purpose to screen their faults; for in misfortune, and even infamy, these are, in one sense, what the wounds of Roman generals were in glory, only not to exult in, but to mourn over.—Nay, so far am I from covering them up, that I would handle them tenderly as hurts all sensitive and palpitating with pain.

This set is to the more moderate tier of failure, what it in its turn is to the well-to-do class, whom we have designated by the term success. Between these strata the lines of demarcation are marked as by the rough edges of drifting, grating ice, moved by counter currents in opposite directions, but all pertaining to one great element, whose general tendency is down stream toward a common destiny. Each one of these grades, to speak in a critical sort of way, may be regarded as a deformity to the one above it, in all of which, however, exclusion or exception would simply result in general expulsion.

Having to take the good, bad and indifferent together in the composition of individuals, then why not apply this principle to the grades that go to make up the great body

U

of mankind? and regarding humanity as intact, we must then, as in contracts, take all parts to get at the proper interpretation and estimate of the whole. In this view, our triumphs and defeats, our successes and failures, are interlaced in the warp and woof of existence; and while the worst may claim a common identity with the best, the latter may no more shake off the disabilities of the former than a cripple can repudiate his deformity or a blind man his blindness.

XX.

In looking over the great army of unfortunates, and having regard for that sympathy which may propitiate Amnesty both in this and in the other world, we need not stop to discuss the question who is to blame; suffice to say all are to blame; and whether the prolific family of Failure brought suffering on themselves or were born to it, it is sufficient for our purpose to know they are in trouble. Indeed, their dream of Paradise is only such an Elysium as that which the higher orders possess, although they may not enjoy. Many of them, as we have observed, are degraded and despicable; whether, however, they seem more so than they really are, is a question turning upon the spirit in which we regard them; but be this as it may, in high toned nostrils they are in bad odour. They are steerage passengers away forward where the sight and smell of them will not give offence to the more dainty occupants of the grand saloon. They are not named in the list the world sees, but are lumped as fifty or a hundred, more or less,

"Steerage." Each of these has a soul, doubtless, and in a greater or less degree all the various attributes that distinguished their worthy progenitor, Adam; but then, they are so numerous, besides, their names are of no account, anyway, (except they are lost), so they are designated in herds.

As our orthodoxy would class them, I believe over nine-tenths fall outside the pale of the Christian catalogue; and so they are located, as are the barbarous non-descript tribes of interior Africa—there, we know is a great extent of territory, which is populated, and that is all. We leave it a place in the geography (of the mind) and to discriminate between it and its surroundings, kindly and knowingly give it a dash of pink or yellow.

Would-be philanthropists whose sympathies are influenced very much by pocket-editions of other people's troubles, and humanitarians who suffer many demands on their compassion, like this sort of map very much. They are not troublesome and give all demands on their "charity," the enchantment of distance and the superior attractiveness of a "foreign mission." If, fortunately, the the distressful locality be surrounded by a cool strip of water two or three thousand miles wide, so much the better, as the boundaries are more easily given and maintained.

It may be said this is hardly a fair comparison even for the great Arab family amongst us—giving them so much blank space. Well, it must be admitted they do have some characteristics peculiar to civilization. I think, indeed, it is possible they have degrees of merit, in their way, and "caste," too. Yes, they have their grades; they have their proud and their humble men and women,—to some of whom it is the last ditch of quondam snobbery and of Beau Brummel-ism.—They have their chiefs and moguls; their great leaders in social and political economy; their oracles and men of renown. All these and myriads more, and still so far as the upper class of our noble country's good inhabitants are concerned, if they or the thought of them happen to intrude at all, they are dismissed with feelings of contempt and aversion. In the eyes of aristocratical evangelism, and with a great many zealous advocates of "foreign missions," their homes are only haunts of wickedness, and the occupants wallowing in the filth and mire of moral corruption. Generally speaking, however, they are simply ignored; or, when forced upon our notice, present about as barren a field for polite observation and cultured study, as the map of Africa or the desert of Sahara.

It is wonderful to reflect how these people keep pace with "Civilization;" but they do, that is, as the tag-rag and bob-tail one sees on gala-days hanging on to the outskirts of military bands and Lord Mayor's shows. They are swept by the coat-tails of more important humanity, like dirt, into the cracks and crevices opened up by meandering street pageants; and constitute for the most part, what the parent of Hamlet calls "The blunt monster with countless heads." They wait upon Czars, welcome Shahs, and gape at royalty, and pull and haul. They vegetate like mushrooms, in the damp and gloom of the fetid nightshade, and on a given signal rise right up, seemingly from the very pores of the earth, as did the warriors of Clan-Alpine, and disappear as quickly; but whence they come and whither they go we know naught nor take the trouble to enquire. At the same time, we have a creeping consciousness that all that is most corrupt and diabolical on earth is crowded somewhere within the confines of their murky sphere.

Were these people not so numerous and so common, we should look upon them as monsters, that it would be something to say we had seen; as it is we feel it dangerous to get too near. They are to be seen in that most wretched thoroughfare, Radcliffe-Highway, in London; in the dirty dens of Wapping, and in the higher-toned penury and vice that flit in the classic shades of Drury-Lane. They have been known to venture as far away from these genial haunts as St. James' Park,—especially on "Drawing-room" days—and have been caught alive staring with blank amazement in at the carriage windows, feasting their eyes on the gauzy clouds of silks, and satins, and feathers that go to make up the dazzling and bewildering paraphernalia of titled dames and peerless beauties. Aye, and by such as these, are regarded, if seen at all, as people sailing down the back rivers of Florida, look upon the alligators basking in the sun on the banks.

I wonder if these great people ever think that that miserable human herd is recruited from some of the best families in the land; that many amongst them, indeed, could trace their genealogical descent down from a period coeval with the Norman Conquest. Only a slight irregularity in the birth of some, that is all; but no more than great people in the past were liable to, even to the extent of making the legitimate succession to the "Crown" a matter of high-toned competition. Others of these have only fallen from wealth and mere social greatness; but of all the class of whom we speak these probably constitute the worst ingredients. That is to say, in their obduracy not to become reconciled, they plunge into deeper depravity and take on and disgrace those others whose birthright for the most part is poverty, and whose ways being faithful to their antecedents, are in accord with privation and misery.

In this connection we may add,—can any one who has not experienced it, measure the depth of bitterness that must be felt by this set; I mean those let down from wealth, reduced from affluence, and whose misfortunes have brought them and their children to this low ebb' What grave treason have they committed against the moral sovereignty of the world, to be thus ostracised ? What mysterious law of expiation are they fulfilling, to be thus cast down and humbled in the dust. Talk of trouble, what must these discarded favorites of fortune suffer, ejected, as it is no exaggeration to presume some have been, from manorial homesteads, where pride and affection may have nourished and venerated the kindred growths of generations; many, too, dragged down from positions in a society whose social attractions, education, habit and intercourse had not only rendered pleasing diversions but vital and necessary ties. And to be thrust, like Daniel, all naked, into a den where to them the beasts, though human, seem even less congenial than lions and not less repulsive than reptiles! It is kennelling in the vestibule of hell, to be tantalized by all the cherished memories of the other Paradise!—aye, and in comparison the fate of Robinson Crusoe—the worst disaster the most exquisite imagination could devise—were a peaceful and grateful solace,—and that of the "Iron Mask," or the living tomb of the "Chateau d'If," a luxury!

XXI.

These select ones probably realize, more acutely than their more brutalized associates, that the miserable sphere into which fate has driven them is, after all, the veritable Pandemonium whose terrors, in a way, inspire our zeal to obtain Earth's immunity, and to merit Heaven's eternal exemption. Now, while this Pandemonium amongst us is no classic myth, nevertheless, we may observe in this connection, that many of its most obnoxious features come of false and absurd impressions; and in this case, as in many others, we have obtained our notions of this more miserable part of our existence through a medium of gross exaggeration; all so far, however, sanctified by expediency as that it strengthens our incentive to work and to pray.

Indeed, a great deal of our zeal to get a larger share of enjoyment, both in this and the next world, is animated by placing in contradistinction two extremes,—one good, the other bad—and we increase the charms of the one by simply adding to the horrors of the other; but as we are better fitted by nature to appreciate what is bad, that extreme is dilated upon with a view to favoring the contrast of good.

To such an excess, however, is this process carried, that parts of our future estate, as well as of our present beautiful world, are made to appear to our modern intelligent and naturally liberal mind, as veritable bug-a-boos; and, as in the days of paganism, the imps of Satan were made to appear in festive intercourse with certain dwellers of the earth, so now, portions of the human family are thought to have become merged in a species of ghouls, into which the rest of us, if we do so and so, shall also be changed. They say this is the result of not doing as we ought to have done, and to attempt to propitiate or to excuse the aspect of this dreadful antipodes of virtue and rectitude, is about as unorthodox and thankless a task as to endeavor, by any means, to abate, by even so much as one jot or tittle, that eternity of misery which our theological doctors and churchmen have piously prescribed for the souls of the wicked in another world. From this dreadful scare-crow of poverty, brutality, and ignorance, we are made to see our refuge in those agreeable attributes pertaining to an opposite goal of wealth and refinement.

Now then, to say our highest acquirements and advancement in this direction leave us virtually no better than those we stigmatize, would be to degrade and to disenchant all incentive to improve. Nevertheless, saving and excepting the wisdom of such views as may be dictated by policy, I venture to affirm that those superior social attractions pertaining to the condition of the one, are greatly over estimated in their moral effects, and that our average devotee of fashion is no whit better than his ragged brother in penury and reprobation. In other words, that the great discrepancy we seek so strenuously to establish and maintain between individuals and classes, are artificial and altogether abnormal, and much of the superiority arrogated by the upper set, no better than comforting delusions, partaking rather of pride than virtue, and indicating actually only such extraneous merit as pertains to appearances. Hence it is, too, our sense of superiority as a class should find its most appropriate expression, not in sympathy, but aversion—not in amnesty, but in strife.

XXII.

To become reconciled to this view, it is necessary either to practise a little wholesome humility, or to cultivate a higher esteem for our less fortunate fellow-creatures. And here, we may pertinently remark, that there is no position in life, however lowly, in which a person with an ordinary endowment of reason, and a properly appreciative mind, may not look down still lower and feel a profound sense of gratification at his elevation : and, conversely, there is no position, however high, that with our yearning instincts on the wing, will not make our abasement seem comparatively contemptible. Inasmuch, then, as the standard, not only of "success," but of morality may be raised to infinity, so any position, or any reputation under heaven, is as infinitely mean and low as the other is infinitely high and perfect. Thus in all things are we exalted in looking down, and humbled in looking up, and just in proportion to our ability to see high are we enabled to feel low. It follows that the higher our conception of an all perfect character, the greater our consciousness of personal deformity, and the thinner and more insignificant the degrees of merit we see about us. Down on the earth, people who are an inch or two taller than the average, look like giants, but the higher we rise above them the more do these differences blend, till they are seen to harmonize. Then, too, persons who can conceive no standard other than self, or the favored set about them, are utterly unable to feel any sentiment but the most vain and bigoted towards those beneath, and their impression of God himself is as stinted as their appreciation on earth of His image,—no matter if it be seen in the disguise of the most abject degradation.

Again, while it is commendable in some respects, neverthless there is something faulty in the fact that many people not unfrequently bring to bear in their criticism of each other that standard which is their loftiest conception of splendid qualities; so high, indeed, that it is rather an ideal of moral heroism and the romance of virtue than that disappointing sort we see and call "fogy." With this most perfect model to which, in our conceit, we are ever making love and are jealous of, we compare the homely and scarred visage of others' characters and their every day's hackneyed doings. Ah, but if their appearance, only stained with the sweat and toil of a busy day, disgusts us, what shall we think of their mistakes, and how shall we express our contempt and reprobation for their faults. This ideal as regards ourselves becomes identified, not so much with our being as with our self-esteem, and though at first it may have been only the remote pattern to which we aspired to mould a living copy—later, old and ugly, it is this image in self we contemplate as self, and behold reflected therein all that is most graceful, juvenile, and lovable.

In a social estimate, taking the lowest position as a standpoint, all above are successes, and as any pitch in the scale to which we may attain, simply raises the standard by which we judge, it follows that the higher stations in life need not raise men appreciably one above another, and that why they seem exalted to some, is because they are below and look up. We boast of our refinement, but if it raised the standard by which we judge to anything approximating what is perfect, the result would be that the proudest moral autocrat would not feel in the slightest above the lowest of his subjects—nay, and but little, if indeed any, better than the meanest and most depraved in not his but God's kingdom.

This train of thought disposes one to think that taking all the evidence commonly accepted as showing one class of men to be the greatest and best, and another to be the most depraved and worst, the social scale will indicate opposite spheres of good and bad; but if we take either of these separately, or both together, though it may not be demonstrated, I feel fairly justified in affirming that an impartial inquiry into all the circumstances, and a rigid probing of all the testimony—not simply that IS, but COULD BE adduced,—would so far equalize the apparent discrepancy as to make the two sides balance.

XXIII.

The fact is, good and ill in our natures are not antipodal but merge like the colors of the solar spectrum; and, as in the case of light, so with human virtue, stripped of its illusions one shade predominates,—that is, black! Again, that notch in the moral scale which marks the highest elevation, is only separated by an infinitesimal space from that indistinguishable degree below which crowns the summit of highest corruption; and though that may not be the depth of lowest depravity, it is, none the less, the point of highest culpability.

In this connection, we may glance at what may be termed the *subtle affinity of opposites*. Much of our disposition to glorify superiority in men comes of our regarding "talent" as a virtue, and the fortunate possessor, in our predisposition to idolize, is exalted into such an object of adoration as can be conceived only from an ideal standpoint.

In elaboration of this idea, we may note, it is not always true that a man may be correctly known by his works, for these may convey a sentiment the very opposite of his real character, and be either conceived in apposition to, or evolved in the mysterious providence of, an opposing spirit. In the conflict of opinion concerning men of note, we may call attention to the fact that they have two characters: the one, private and real; the other, public and ideal. The relative merits and demerits of both are disputed and maintained; but, as is generally the case, the better view naturally prevails,—then, while the former dies, the latter, which is furthest from the tell-tale flesh, lives, and is the one by which posterity professes acquaintance and passes judgment.

The exception taken here is, that this impression is not obtained from personal intimacy and contact with the man, but, what is a very different thing, familiarity with his works. These, in the case of literary men, and the majority of others, it requires no argument to show may color our spectacles with ideal fancies; and, in the prospect thus presented of a brighter conception of living, we are only too pleased to ignore or forget the real tableau of a poor miserable mortal like ourselves, weighed down with the ignoble burden of ordinary human failings. The fact is, that just inasmuch as the written record of individuals differs from the living, is the former cherished agent of conservatism made the means, not of their preservation, but extinction. And in rummaging the dark corners and dusty cubby-holes of old-world literature, we find, with rare exceptions, that however opposed to the impression conveyed by their works, the authors of some of the finest productions in the domain, not simply of letters but the adjoining field of politics, were in their private life what, if we hesitate to call profligate, dessolute, vile, it is only because we feel they are deserving of those choicer epithets which, meaning the same thing, have been invented by polite society to be applied in cases where outrage and enormity are palliated by education and refinement.

XXIV.

It may seem invidious to refer to these draw-backs, but the spirits of the great men we honor, are become so thoroughly emancipated from the flesh, that the recollection of even their misdeeds seems to restore to them that humanizing influence which commends them to our sympathies.—In this respect, then, amid so much that is only fancifully God-like, it no longer detracts from our heroes to be assured they were only men. Hence, we feel less delicacy in saying, that many of those whose bright intellects constitute the major part of that brilliant constellation to which I refer, and who have described so cleverly and pathetically the wiles and vicissitudes of man and society, were themselves the sport of the very appetites and propensities they held up, with so much zeal, wisdom, and eloquence, to public reprobation.

It would seem, in the case of some, their very efforts conspiring with the antagonism they sought to overthrow, they fell all the easier victims to those temptations and sins which their vivid imaginations had exaggerated and intensified. With others, however, it is harder to excuse the fact that, inconsistent as it may seem with the fine and salutary precepts evolved in their literary and Public career, in their private life and personal habits they were a living lie to the sincerity of their professions and covertly evinced the most abominable disregard for the simplest dictates of morality and even humanity. The evil one within them, it is true, may have whispered sublime things, but it was only to embellish those hazy lines of demarcation that distinguish the kingdom of Satan, from the Dominion of the Immaculate. And then, indeed, their most virtuous efforts may be likened to the remorse of the drunkard entoning with greatest pathos the lessons of sobriety;—the veriest rogue haunted with fairest image of honesty;—and, the hypocrite enchanted with the most angelic vision of piety!

Thus, too, in a greater degree than is commonly supposed or allowed, must these men have not only needed, but absolutely possessed, all the wickeder promptings of the devil himself to have enabled them so correctly and graphically to interpret the hieroglyphical language of the human heart, and, not only to divine in others but to exemplify in themselves those gorgeous contrasts of opposite qualities. With men of letters, they have managed to maintain the empire which mere fancy has reared in our hearts; having won the title by which we esteem them, by giving to the world a creation of matchless heroes and splendid principles, in whose sublime characters and resistless precepts we have embalmed the memoirs of the authors. For example, we do not think of Dean Swift, as the remorseless iconoclast desolating the beatiful world of woman's love, but as the hero of those inimitable "Travels," whose charming fancies first explored the wondrous land of Lilliputia.—

We do not think of Byron, as the inhuman monster whose crime has given rise to the most atrocious libel on record, but as the boyish "Juan," the maturer "Manfred," and still riper patriot.—We do not think of Abelard, as the betrayer of a sacred trust, but as the pious martyr,—consumed in a flame from whose embers sprang the darling of Héloisa.—Finally, we do not think of Edgar Allan Poe, as the drunken maniac disgracing the little circle of his social orbit, but as the muse whose sweet minstrelsy inspired "The Raven!"

In the case, however, of the compeers of a goodly number of these men in the kindred line of politics, the sequel peculiarly incident to the latter sphere, tells a different tale; also, further illustrating the two character phenomenon before mentioned. The political views of Rienzi were of the most exalted description, and not only those of an astute statesman but such as became, what he really appeared to be, a patriot and true lover of his country. He was withal a poet as well as a politician, and not only a scholar but a genius; and, on the strength of these qualifications, mounted from the lowest to the highest stations in a country where his predecessors were Cæsar, and, Augustus. His latter career, however, as dictator developed a new character so much at variance with the sentimental one professed while a suppliant for public patronage and honors, that, with the freedom of unlimited power, he became a tyrant; unmasking, ere long, and displaying in an intolerable degree, every trait most despicable in man. Thenceforward, from being, as he had been for a considerable time, the benefactor and idol of a grateful and adoring people, on the true and not the assumed and visionary character of the man becoming known, he was degraded and stoned to death by an outraged and indignant populace. This case is cited at random and is only one of the many we read about that go to sustain the view herein taken.

These examples, we may add, finally, are not confined to profane ranks; nay, we find them in the adorable company of the divinely inspired. We have substantial evidences going far to show that Mahomet was the greatest preacher and the most powerful leader of evangelical reform the world has ever seen.—By his personal efforts he founded or least compiled a creed, and converted to his views a goodly share of the population of the globe. But however effectually he may have played the part of prophet and preceptor, as friend and as man, in his social relations (if we may credit the most unbiassed of our authorities), he was a brute whose carnal instincts made him a mammoth animal, whose relaxation from the rigors of penitential office, was spent wallowing in the mire and filth of unbounded lust.

XXV.

As I have said, I do not seek these cases and quote them invidiously;—in favoring the uncouth but robust claims of the masses it must be to some extent in disparagement of that more refined mania, whose delirium is hero-worship. If I decline, then, to shrink from such an ungenial and unpopular task, it is because I feel the tendency in the case of merit, as in that of property, is, and always has been, outrageously in favor of gigantic, isolated monopoly; the effect of which is not only to aggrandize the minority, but to canonize the few at the expense of the many. Exalting to absurd heights spots here and there, and depressing in like ratio the general surface of mankind, is not a fault of modern birth; it obtained in ancient times, and we have only to look back a few thousand years, to behold the hierarchy of those days degrading humankind, and elevating tutelar deities. It was the glorification of individuals that culminated in the "Heroic Age" of Grecian fable! And since then, and up to this day, the system and practice of beatifying and sublimating men, whose business and abilities have made them simply eligible subjects, is illustrated, and will be perpetuated, in the questionable teaching of a Theology which not only endows certain persons with the attributes of an all-mighty superiority, but sets rival bodies and jealous people in conflict as the proxies of contending gods. Indeed, it is commonly inculcated, that the spirit of the supernatural incarnate may be supposed from time to time to spring out of the very bone of contention—to father and champion hostile sects whose chief virtue is in their mutual hatred of each other's crimes and their unbounded faith in the spiritual leadership of a being apart from the Omnipotent.

Nay, the phase of hero-worship obtaining to day, is only another form of the old pagan fallacy, to dispel which, while detracting from the preposterous pretensions of the few, would raise the standard of the many! It would disperse the oligarchy of merit, but distribute its sinecures amongst the people! Temporal kings and peers and sundry lords would go by the board—all the lofty pinnacles reared in false glory would topple and fall like the temples of Isis and Serapis!—but, by the sweeping down of those star-crested domes, toilsome acclivities would be levelled,— great valleys and yawning chasms would be filled—and, without prostrating the high standard of public virtue, we should see, not the exaltation of the few and the corresponding degradation of the many, but a great universal upheaval of the common sea-level of mankind.

XXVI.

Regarding those whose portion in this world is privation and misery combined, and whose prostration hides them from the view of most people, I would reiterate what I said in another place, to wit: that in the two classes popularly known as high and low, the latter exhibits the most marked traits of character.—But how, it may be urged, can there be shown any greater characteristics than those exemplified in the lives of our "great men?" Well, theirs is the greatness of heads and proportionately less a measure of simple character. It is easy, as in the case of Peabody, to be not simply benevolent but munificent, and that to a degree and in a manner that shall make all the world resound in praise; besides, he evinced what is rare with men generally, that is, as much ability in the disposition of his wealth as he did in its acquisition. But you say, show me a case to compare with this one.—Talk of the greatness of character in the haunts and amongst the filth and vermin and depravity of the poor, it is not only scandalous to mention such a thing, but an aspersion on society and civilization and Christianity!

Yes it is, I will admit, and for that reason it makes it all the harder to do the miserable set justice; more especially, without reflecting somewhat on the upper classes and even detracting a little from their superiority. But I have been a little amongst them, and got hold of a few signs, by which I have been able to penetrate the outer vestibule of dirt and degradation. Yes, I have seen a little what was going on where the world neither pities nor applauds; and from what I have observed and know, I confess it seems to me these people have, or seem to have, certain peculiarities characteristic of the higher race of men. There is not, as they appear to me, that ferocity, which the heroism of our police who capture them, would incline us to think; nay, nor that ravenous craving for raw and bloody meat, which is supposed to be inseparable to a condition of relapsed barbarity and brutality. They do not, I have noticed, seem to be wanting in stomachs like our own, and with appetites that bear a striking resemblance to ours; indeed, they sniff the air of better living and seem to relish it, as if they had an instinctive conception of better things. I have seen *atoms* among them (youngsters I mean), even in some of the more frequented streets of New York and

London,—particularly on dark and stormy nights, when they could come out like rabbits and have what we would call a holiday.—Well, I've seen these, actually, peering through shop windows and gazing with wild, famished eyes, chattering teeth and watering mouths, in upon a luscious wealth of aggravating pies and cakes and frosted doughnuts! Aye, and the want of two or three pennies, which looked to them like great blood-red moons, and in a sphere quite as remote and unattainable, walled them out as effectually as are we from the good things of that other planet. Meanwhile the "Dinner" at Delmonico's, and the "Banquet" at the Lord Mayor's, proceed, and are partaken of as mere thankless items, intended only to satisfy the higher toned craving for a change of *menu*, or something, anything, to mitigate the intolerable monotony of dining at home.

But what have you seen of the older ones, you may ask, those who have run the full length of crime and debauchery; if you can show me one or two that are worthy then there is hope. Well, I have seen amongst the castaways of society, women whose degradation would shame brutes, but who displayed a heroism and devotion that despite all the disfigurement of vice, while it honored and sustained some of my best conceptions of true womanhood, threw even the charm of sanctity over the ruin of a lost character! I have seen, too, the debased scion of broken royalty among them, with raiment like the "tattered banner of a lost cause," and with the withering pinch of hunger stamped all over him, relax his grip on a treasure more precious to him than the wealth of a Crœsus or a Peabody,—his last penny—and bartering this, his only claim to kingdom, for a crust, *give that away.*

XXVII.

Heroism like the above may not be known,—I know it is not honored and numbered with the "Legion"—nevertheless it deserves all the homage, and more, that we involuntarily yield to the glorious remnant of the gallant "Six Hundred." I bow to a banquet like that;—aye, it is the crumbs that fall from such a feast that exalt the spirit and fatten the soul! And how do examples like these compare with the benevolence of our Millionaires or the munificence of our Billionaires? They do not shine on the page of history;—they are not commemorated amongst the treasured mementos of our national archives; —they are not recorded in the "annals of our times," nor do we find the name and date blazoned on the granite walls of palatial "charities;"—nevertheless, they do not escape that restless Vigilance that watches the "fall of the sparrow," and caters to the wants of the tiniest insect.

Now that we come to think of it, how the blank, inhospitable expanse of sand,—the Sahara of scurfdom,—does change and become peopled with forms and faces whose uncouth outlines and grim lineaments seem worthy, even though they do not invite, a second glance. And approaching a little nearer the arid waste we see—can it be possible? yes, it is no deceptive mirage for those are indeed grass-spots,—clover-fields,—flower-beds,—fresh and blooming as any that embellish the richest of our own fertile landscapes! They are small, very small; indeed, to discover them we must be looking especially for them, and not only that, but with eyes that see out of the heart. Then, through the dank and fetid atmosphere that hangs over them like a malarious mist, are revealed those redeeming tokens of that ubiquitous humanity that shines out of the clouds—crops up from the soil—and blossoms in the fissures of the rock!—And here, amongst the most despicable of heathendom, it is presented to our own more cultured and delicate sensibilities, in its poverty of refinement, it is true, but with all its wealth of untutored amenities symbolized in the typical sweetness of blooming, fragrant flowers.

Many people there are who have never seen these particular garden-spots and discredit their existence. They are difficult and disagreeable, perhaps, to find—they are hidden away behind the bleak walls that meet the eye as we hurry along the street; but why should the Elysée of our own fancies monopolize all our thoughts? We go in-inside, sometimes; it is true, we do not always hurry by, but then it is only to wonder at destitution and to catechise distress. Why do we not visit them now and then,—ask to see their little garden-spot and find out where it is? they have one somewhere in their nature, and what a chord you touch when you have discovered the Rose or the Lily in their hearts!—It may be all they have that is pure and undefiled, and the tear-drop on its petals sparkles like the diamond whose lustre may not be dimmed. It is a decoration bestowed for some good deed which in this great battle of life none is so mean as never to have performed; and though the other qualities may be all adverse, and the wearer maimed and mutilated, still this alone may claim recognition—claim recognition! aye, it may claim *Camaraderie* with a marshal of the Empire!

XXVIII.

I am reminded in this connection of an incident that came under my observation, during one of the many delightful excursions it has been my good fortune to have made to points of interest in England. It was to the home of the Guelphs,—that grand old castle of Windsor. On this occasion I found myself in a crowd not far from the great gates leading out on the "Long Walk." The Queen, who had been out for a drive was momentarily expected to return that way, and I was waiting to have a good look at her; a privilege which up to that time I had not had the good fortune to obtain. I had not long to wait before there came in view a very plain equipage, which I was informed was the royal carriage, and in which was seated Her Majesty, also, if I remember rightly, the Princess Beatrice.

As they were going on past, for some reason or other there was a slight delay near the entrance; in that instant I was horrified to perceive a dirty ragged little urchin, a girl it seemed, and a mere child, but with its hands full of flowers, break away from the crowd on our side and run, all impulsively, right up to where the Queen was. I say

I was horrified, because I looked upon the matter at first as a terrible breach of decorum,—involving confiscation of estates and exile or "The Tower," and it made me nervous. The little wretch, with a half-frightened, half-gladsome look of baby pride and timidity, put up both its chubby, brown hands full of violets, and with an appeal on its rosy, English face that I shall never forget, offered this simple and touching tribute to one whose high station naturally conveys the impression of her being the most austere, if not the proudest dame in England.

My heart stood still, and it seemed to me as if every breath in that motley group was suspended. The "Empress of India," who took in the situation at a glance, lowered her stately head just the slightest; but the smile that lighted up her benign features was not the Queen's—it was the regal urbanity of a great-hearted English matron, and in a low voice which I thought touchingly soft and sweet, and which I may only have imagined was just a little sad, she said, "Thank you, my child!" I felt a choking sensation in my throat—my eyes grew moist and dim—I could have blubbered like a school-boy. Those were flowers from the little garden-spot of the poor, the despised, the outcast;—and this was the child of democracy, unlocking with those tiny hands the rusty portals that lead to the most invulnerable, if not the most formidable, stronghold of monarchy in Christendom.

XXIX.

Those whose misfortunes we take as an evidence of moral perversity and deservelessness, those we give over and feel are lost, must their lives have been all a blank desert? Take the worst of them, those whom Society ignores and all sober folk repudiate, and everybody feels a distant dread about—houseless wanderers whose homeless abodes fringe the outskirts of civilization—all sand and sky,—may there be no hope for them sometime? Shall it always be burning dust, in this world and the next? No tree, no shrub, no leaf? Our "creeds" say they are irredeemably lost; or at best the conditions on which they would take them in, are such that it is simply impossible for these poor wretches either to understand or conform; besides they have no sufficient inducements by way of appearances, even if they had the dissimulation necessary, to make them take up with a hollow pretence. But if they do not conform, must they be lost for ever? The brutality of Bartholomew says YES! But the heart of Gethsemane says NO!! Then leaving out the harsher interpretation of a monkish creed, let us ask, in the name of the only good Samaritan through whom we claim exemption, is it possible these people may not be endowed with some great redeeming virtue. I claim they are—disguised, perverted as it may seem.

It is said that one of Murillo's finest paintings lay virtually unknown and abandoned for years, and, changing hands many times, was bartered and sold for paltry sums; when one day, the effort of some kindly hand, or it may have been a sorry purchaser, to restore a battered old bacchanalian scene, led to the discovery of the concealed treasure; and underneath the outer coating which was then carefully removed, there stood revealed to wondering generations the priceless chef d'œuvre of one of the greatest masters the World of Art has ever known.

We cannot all expect to find gems like this, hidden away in every old picture; but I claim each one of all of us has stowed away in the lumber-room of his heart, a treasure in some good quality even more precious, which, as the heir-loom of the poorest and meanest, only seems worthless because it is not exhibited, and cannot be exchanged, nor pawned, nor negotiated; but while it may leave its possessor shabby, famishing, and in debt, nevertheless, I believe, in his greatest need, the shrine shall disgorge,—even as the earth, which yields in its mineral wealth of "treasure trove," the most abundant compensation for its greatest seeming barrenness.

XXX.

Taking the apparent caprices of nature and the altered conditions of life into account, I fail to see and to appreciate the vast difference between the best and the worst of us; so far, at least, as to make it all unction for the one, and to preclude all hope for the other. And it certainly does seem very hard to discover the appropriate parallel in the portion alloted to each, of everlasting felicity and perpetual hell-fire. I would like to think otherwise; I want the "flaming sword" held aloft over my head, to appear as appalling as possible, as it might have a stronger tendency to deter me from evil; but I am so obstinate or opaque as not to be able to distinguish any higher virtue in "brimstone," than what common sense and humanity incline me to feel. Nay, I repudiate utterly that theory of savage coercion, which in the form of an appalling phantom, and obtruding itself on the weakest and most pusillanimous qualities in man, makes him start aghast at that typical "boo-man" which our rural talent sets up in the field to scare the crows away.

Moreover, it seems to me the question of the duration of punishment in another world is of such secondary importance, if indeed, of any at all, that it may be regarded by the humbler classes, as simply one of the many examples of the want of native sense in our learned men; those I mean who have spent their lives in grafting on their minds exotic ideas, and in transcribing volumes of speculation, discussion and dispute on the subject. And, furthermore, considering all the discrepancies incident to life and understanding, with the little time allotted us to make our peace, is it not absurd we should go on arguing over the length of eternity,—whether it be that of joy or pain,—and never cease propounding doctrines, wherein our most erudite and venerable pupils, in their efforts to comprehend and eke out comfort, seem but infants "muling and puking" in the great Master's arms!

XXXI.

As we have already intimated, the prospective reign of Amnesty, at least so far as this life is concerned, is met with such an insuperable obstacle in human nature, as to make the very hazy question of its establishment on earth, a matter of future attainment—based upon that slow theory of progression which, regards man as in a state of gradual improvement.—Nor does the prospect seem to brighten with the assumption that, commencing with the regeneration of the monkey, the human animal had attained, nearly two thousand years ago, the sublime eminence of that perfect specimen, whose precocity won him the imperishable honor of crucifixion.

But, leaving out the ultimate destiny of the race in its temporal pilgrimage to the goal, I deny the right of any man or creed to say, that in the great ordeal of death and dissolution the most dilatory may not overleap, in the untrammelled spirit, the most formidable barriers of either theology or the flesh,—and, catching up with the most forward, take his place hereafter in the front rank of unctuous progress. Here we might refer to advantage to what we have already said about the subtle affinity of opposites, and, pointing to the tableau of the "crown of thorns," institute a comparison with less exalted suffering, showing a closer connection between the best and the worst than is exhibited socially. But suffice it in this instance to call attention to the fact of three crosses, and not simply one; and, twining the everliving vine about them, let it indicate not a mere accidental association, but a kindred tie, uniting in mutual hope the thief and the Christ,—the most corrupt and the most perfect of men.

The broad ground which I have taken herein of universal merit and forgiveness is difficult to maintain, coming up as it does on the trial of very hard and knotty cases, wherein sympathy, we are admonished, so far from ruling, must not even influence the verdict; and though the views which favor the boon of a general amnesty, come in direct conflict with those great formularies known as Creeds, yet it does not so much oppose them, after all, as that they simply differ with the prevailing hallucination which holds them divinely indispensable.

We may observe that while Creeds, as formulated systems, are the work of heads, they had their origin in the commiseration of hearts—conceived in pity, they are all too often maintained in cruelty, and just inasmuch as they favor strife, they oppose amnesty, and defeat the object of their institution. I would not, however, wantonly disparage these great succoring agencies; considering, too, they may be available and even satisfying to those minds wherein understanding is not a prerequisite to faith. Moreover, there are many people who have been nurtured in creed; they have grown up in it, and may not be unsuccessful in the extraordinary mental feat of regarding the Church as a second mother—its womb as their tomb, and the second birth as the devoutly prayed for resurrection. It may be a beautiful illusion, which I have no wish in their case to dispel; but, aside from the question of fact or fancy as concerns them, I am now seeking what remedy there may be for a class who, for whatever cause, creeds abandon; and in these cases where the systems of Heads may not avail, I would appeal to the primitive and innate religion of Hearts.

XXXII.

I make no vain boast of liberality, because I dread fanaticism; indeed, liberality is very apt to be to religion what license is to law; the one not unfrequently degenerating into contempt, the other into what is even worse, indifference. I have always felt dubious about being liberal, and tried hard to be as bigoted as possible, but there is nothing I have failed so completely in as in my efforts to believe that Paradise is a little space—a sort of cosmopolitan reliquary, where it is intended to preserve a few, only, of the finest specimens of the extinct race of man. Then the substance of all these rambling ideas of mine as bearing on this point is, that if Christ died for any individual or class it was for that one in whose nature I have been searching and probing for redeeming, healthful, life-saving veins.

There is no doubt in my mind, too, that the utility of the crucifixion is too exclusive and "high-toned," and altogether erroneously appropriated. I don't know what the sensation would be like, but it must be very peculiar to feel, as some devotees do, that there is but one narrow path to Heaven—that they are on that path.—Am not quite sure, it would seem especially objectionable, to feel there was but one system that could save, and that was mine; and while I understood and could comply with all its requirements, if it would make my faith any stronger to believe all the others would perish, I could even bear that, and feel my own triumph the more marvellous and gratifying.

There are a great many who seem to feel this way, and yet a larger portion profess one thing and believe the very opposite. It is not always dissimulation, however; society and custom regulate these matters as they do the law of weights and measures, or the taking of a wife or an oath. Indeed, conformity is not simply optional, but in most cases necessary; and, generally speaking, people are just indifferent or thoughtless enough to comply without objecting. Some other worthy minds there are, who, dazed and confounded in the apparent need of believeing something, are sore beset by a puzzling diversity of opinions ; indeed, in their honest perplexity, they may bring upon them the opprobrious epithets of "atheist" and "unbeliever;" and yet, are these same people scandalized by that unconscionable set, who, donning the habiliments of pious assurance, invade the sanctuary with a nonchalance that would shame as sceptical the harassed mind of the meekest of the apostles.

It is not quite a paradox to affirm that, with people who do not, or are not able to, think for themselves, the strongest argument in favor of holding a certain conclusion is the great diversity of opinion concerning its correctness; and, as in the case of the trial of a criminal, they give the thing impeached the benefit of the doubt. Again, giving faith a property qualication, it is made hereditary; and, as in the case of the the Chinese women, who are said to stint the growth of their feet by keeping them in the wooden shoes of children, so is the bumptious fledgling our Christian school nurtured in the evangelical groove of the parent; and he follows it with about as much thought and consideration as is given to a road that offers a convenient turnpike in the general direction one desires to travel. While this is a natural tendency, it is suggestive of a query:—Did anybody, however severe regarding other people's "persuasion," ever conscientiously feel that his own dear friends and relatives who differed with him in faith or even without profession, would not be saved? Our very instincts revolt against the idea of kindred exclusion. Show me the son who, though a Protestant, feels his own kind mother, because she is a Catholic, will be damned; and though I should wonder prodigiously at the inhuman monster, yet would he be only the very commonest type of the class of people who stand up and solemnly affirm to believe what they profess. But you tell me no such a man could be found, or excuse the case on the ground of partiality; then, I have only to say that the exception and not the rule is the ground of my hope herein; for filial reverence is a chief ingredient to faith in God, and the simple reciprocation of natural love is one of the special attributes of an all-wise benevolence looking towards universal Amnesty.

XXXIII.

We heap opprobrium, not upon our fathers, but our forefathers, for their bigotry; but, in a mild, pusillanious sort of way, we are more bigotted, in many respects, than they were. In this age of enterprise and reform, for instance, it is taken for granted that everything opposed to Indolence is Industry, and what can there be more praiseworthy than industry? So, too, everything opposed to "Popery" is counted "Protestantism," and what a glorious triumph is Protestantism! Well, both these assumptions may be, and are to a great extent, fallacious. I do not approve of Popery altogether, but then I must demur to Protestantism being regarded as Religion.—I do not approve of indolence altogether, but then I beg to say, I think it a strong argument in its favor, when we look about us and see the great number there are industriously serving the devil!

Our forefathers revolted against the ministers of Rome and, afterwards, against the Church itself. Without questioning here the righteousness of their conduct, it is a pertinent query, do we inherit their pious zeal, and are we right in appropriating, as we do, indiscriminately the virtues of their martyrdom? It is true we do inherit their prejudices—ah, yes, we have Celtic blood enough for that—and these are fostered and applied as leeches by the moral physician of our spiritual health, whose hobby it is to feel that everybody's blood is poisoned; so now we swarm with leeches as Egypt once swarmed with locusts.

Why may not our leaders in the good work of moral reform do more in the privacy of individual intercourse, and not wait for the accumulation of huge congregations. Now we hear their voices only in the solemn isolation of sacred places,—in a dismal drone which, although it is wanting in the healthful vim of a more spontaneous eloquence, does, it is true, warn us like the fog-horn or the bell that moans and ding-dongs over the sunken ledge. That is all well enough in its way, but the voice that would oppose evil must enter the arena where evil is advocated, and then, not unfrequently would it find itself opposed to itself.

Give us the dash, the energy, the courage, that led the invincible squadrons of French Cuirassiers at Aboukir, or the English Guards at Waterloo—not to command battalions, not to war against each other, but to go into the midst of the carnage and succor the wounded, and that irrespective of the side they are found fighting on.—All have received a mortal hurt and are bleeding to death—that is enough. I do not mean mere stretcher carriers and funeral officials, we have too many of them now; but the Napoleons and Wellingtons of Amnesty—vanquishing Enmity and pacifying Strife! Above all, when time and nature have closed a wound, don't let them tear it open afresh; don't, because broken limbs may not be healing quite according to rule, go about breaking and setting them over again! The sublime project of universal amnesty (if it must march as an army), should move on, in all the potent dignity of men who have won peace and are going home,—and not as a panic-stricken herd, whose cry of *Vive L'Empereur* has dwindled to the contemptible wail of *sauve qui peut*.

XXXIV.

If we see a man drowning, what is the first impulse,—to go and inquire how he came there? Yes; our churchmen, in effect, tell us that is the proper thing to do; and would leave him till he passed the ordeal of a searching catechism, before reaching down and pulling him out. They don't favor sudden "conversions,"—not they. We must needs be "born" and suckled over again, and be technically washed of sin,—aye, as in the "Peerage" they are put through the "Bath," to be cleansed of the taint of ignoble birth. And then they haggle over the quantity of water needful to perform the unctuous ablution; all this, too, when we see people not only "sprinkled," but "immersed," in right good earnest, and treading water in an agony of suspense and drowning, and the emergency is treated with all the ecclesiastical dignity and supine deliberation of a hackneyed routine.

In one sense we enjoy all the luxury of perfect security, with the ineffable boon of a green old age, growing and expanding its fostering wealth of branch and leaf and blossom all over and about us,—and it makes our declining years seem a delightful shade, a grateful respite from the blazing rays of youthful passion, and from the bustle and turmoil of the world.—But then, this is an allusion which may be dispelled at any moment, and is seldom realized; nevertheless, so is "conversion," (whatever that may actually mean), held up before us as a convenient mirage, and our authorities say, in condemning sudden changes, it must come, to be lasting, in the gradual progress of events, and be, as it were, the slow growth of that fostering tree.

The mistake lies in regarding death, as the law of England does an interregnum,—that is, the King never dies; so also a congregation never dies, but lives always like a corporation, and is preached to. So, too, the great world of fashion we see promenading down Broadway or Regent street, never dies; and "conversion," preposterous as it may seem, viewed in that light, may go on through an endless series of progressive stages forever and ever. How different is the exhortation to the poor condemned.—And viewed rationally and individually, as we may all feel, who shall guarantee any one the morrow? Let it be assumed we are to lead the forlorn hope at two o'clock to-day, and march over a mile of glacis, covered with abatis and pitfall, and swept by twenty batteries!—Ah, indeed, says the advocate of gradual emancipation, that alters the case materially. Yes, the case appears altered very materially, but, mind you, it is only in his view, and not in fact.

XXXV.

The truth is, we are all shipwrecked mariners.—To say we have our compass and chart, is but a mild illustration of the means of navigating; presupposing, of course, we are in a good ship that is comfortably divided up into sections to suit our convenience. This is the disposition our creeds generally make of us, providing we profess to "believe." Well, then we have adverse winds and storms to contend against, and have not unfrequently, in our greatest emergencies, to fall back on "dead reckoning."—we could manage, nevertheless, to get along, but the fact is, this favorable aspect of the situation is false and deceptive; the impression being conveyed more in the zealous commendation of rival systems than in any actual test of their respective merits; and, according to modern survey, it is not all certain the ship we are in is seaworthy, with, as we are given to understand, a sure prospect of a pleasant voyage and a safe port. Indeed, the impression when this questionable assurance does not obtain, is that we are all really adrift on a wide ocean—buoyed up in the frailest of cockle-shells; and liable as we are to be swamped at any moment, the question of our safety is not one that need alarm a few of the worst of us only, but rather excite the more genuine concern of all for all.

The strong men among us, we have no difficulty in perceiving, are pulling against each other; and the helpless ones, the women and children, are,—well, I was about to say, huddled together in fear and trembling; but that would be carrying the simile too far, as they are simply unconscious and basking in the sunshine of their own adorable loveliness. And yet to get nearer the truth still, we are floundering in the water and drowning; there is but one hand can save—He hears our supplication, it it matters not what way, or where, or when it is uttered, it is sufficient if it be *only a cry of pain*.—Ah, but if a heathen, or a pagan, or an infidel, be rescued by mistake, who then shall be the champion to stand forth and say, throw him back again!

Take any one of our fellow creatures, whose end was most miserable—does he not stand in fraternal contrast with Him whose death was most sublime? and this notwithstanding the repudiation of all our moral orthodoxy to the contrary. Both equally serve the good purpose of example, and yet one gets all the praise, and the other all the opprobrium. Yes, the repulsiveness of the one, it is true, may seem to preclude penitence as the absence of all graceful virtues repels approbation; he may claim no title in the Autocracy of creed, and stands in gloomy, cheerless contrast with its serene and pampered nobility; and yet, who shall say all may not share alike in that other great Democracy of pain and of pleasure? Aye, and despite that orthodoxy, which arrogates to itself the authority to say, thou art "polluted," thou art "sanctified," may we not hope and believe, all are sovereign by the grace of God, in their eligibility to mercy!

It may be objected that reasoning like this brings us into too close fellowship with those who are depraved, and a doubt may be entertained that the pity and countenance of better natures would have a tendency to lend encouragement; but the terrors engendered in the minds of some, on that score, are mitigated in reflecting, that the highest standard he or she can conceive, much less embody, is comparative degradation; and if they judge and condemn by that, how shall they in their turn appear under that scathing criticism whose criterion is the Immaculate.

XXXVI.

In our casual glances into the seemingly opposite, but really commingled spheres of success and failure, we have had regard for two great corresponding divisions of society; but while the socially successful, and those deemed especially fortunate, have been left to take care of themselves, our object has been more especially, to see if there could be thrown, even the smallest rays of hope towards those unfortunate ones, whose manner of living and whose death place them, according to our Creeds and their expositors, outside the pale—and whom the glad, thoughtless, frolicsome world indifferently abandon, — doubtless feeling toward them as they do about disease, that is, the further they remove from it the nearer they approximate to health.

Had my purpose in this essay been simply to dignify the world of failure, I need not have been told how much easier my task had been, to have carefully avoided those who would cast disrepute on the cause; and leaving them underneath their veil of obloquy, have unearthed, in their stead, the memories of that undecorated phalanx, who, falling in an inglorious stage of the conflict, were buried by stealth in the smoke and debris of defeat. I say unearth their memories, because in our hasty glance over the past, and into the careers of men, it is a natural impulse to commence and leave off with success; and thus, in the history of projects, those who are so fortunate as to cap the sheaf get, it may have been only in the routine order of sequence, the crown of glory.

The fact is, Civilization only marks the consummation of great achievements, and the progress from inception to completion is not all through a vista of triumphal arches; but rather through a crucible of fiery ordeals and blighting disappointments; and the sandy, burning desert, in the rare intervals of oases, are strewn with the bones of unwept, unhonored martyrs. Thus it is no idle envy to presume that oftentimes the truest merit gets the least applause, and to find it we need to abandon the grand highways paved with the memorial slabs of biographical lore, and grope in the slums and dank and fœtid gloaming of penury, starvation and failure.

As it is, I have not attempted argument; the subject, indeed, doesn't admit of that sort of measurement and demonstration which learned men, who discuss people's chances, here and hereafter, affect to apply; and who, unravelling fate with the same logical precision they would solve an equation, multiply and subtract the lost and saved with the same equanimity that they forge syllogisms to annihilate adverse opinion. And here let me add, that it seems to me in our pulpit arbitrament of right and wrong, and of all things pertaining to our evangelism, they indulge too much in the *euclid* of religion. I don't object to *chemistry*, but I do think that conversion to spiritual belief is not a simple matter of logical sequence; and I, for one, object to being plumbed by them, and squared and angled off,—geometrized, in fact, and ignoring the little story of our lives, we are told to accept certain conclusions, in which there is about as much heart and sympathy as in a clalk mark on a black board.

XXXVII.

There are two cardinal points in our mental compass corresponding with the north and south of the physical,—I mean the *past* and the *future:* the former is replete with disaster, and inspires us with such a wholesome dread that on the least inkling of danger we take to scanning the latter to see what it has in store ; and, like the mariner at sea, note with more or less anxiety the indications of sky and barometer.

I don't propose to dwell so much on the subject of the future, here, as it comes in better under the head of Imagination ; besides, there is not very much to be gained there, anyway, save pleasant pictures. For the matter of that, it might be called the picture gallery of life, so much are we disposed to turn to the future only with thoughts of enjoyment ; and it being the place where we may fashion things to suit ourselves, it is there we feast our fancies to the full.

While the past may condemn, the future only rarely admonishes, and that so lovingly that it smiles in the very look in which it chides ; but as it has its sunshine, it also has its shadow, and the very element of uncertainty in which we rejoice, is tinctured with phantom shades which it is wonderful only perplex, and do not, as might be expected, dispirit and appal. All our enterprise takes its vim and charm from the future,—and like the youth, going forth into the world, we are looking smilingly forward and tearfully backward. In one sense it is disheartening, in another encouraging that that happiness which is supposed to come in the performance of good deeds, is not adequate to our wants ; and that it is not, is shown in the fact that even our best and greatest men, seem to labor under a constitutional disability to rejoice over past life ; and they, equally disconsolate with the meanest and poorest (I was about to say, the most guilty and remorseful), lament it might not have been better and more fruitful. Thus, together with the ragged and needy rabble, we find them, in obedience to the equable influence of some great law of nature, turning their backs on what seem to them the insignificant triumphs of the past, and with their faces to the future, wishing, hoping, struggling on! No mortal power can diminish the speed, much less stop this great tide of human energy; in fact no effort is made with that intention, although we know when we catch the back-wash it will bring with it a mighty wave under which we shall be overwhelmed as effectually as was the little village of Pompeii, submerged by fifteen feet of burning cinder and molten lava.

Alluring as the future may seem in some respects, any attempt, out of the usual course of nature, to realize or to pry into its mysteries, is promptly met with a most emphatic and discouraging rebuff; we may enjoy the flower, but we must not pick it to pieces, else the charm is lost and we see only the seed whence we came and whither we go. At times, startled as is the hunted stag at the certain doom coming toward him, we, too, turn to the future and scan its veiled aspect closely to see if we may divine the nature of the refuge there; but the knowledge vouchsafed to us is encumbered with still greater perplexities; and, like the harassed Indian who finds civilization a plague, we turn from the fretted, puny realms of fact to that trackless region which imagination pictures,—hidden away in a wilderness of bright colored, sweet smelling foliage, and seek to plunge yet more deeply into its grateful shades and perfumed grottos.

It is consoling no doubt; but, beyond the gratification of our fancy, what do we find?—That in reality the great blank wall of eternity shuts right down before us, or opens out into an illimitable sea of surmise.—What we thought we knew, later we find furthest from the truth, and the great problem of the day takes us into night; the puzzle is tiresome, and twilight and reflection bring no rest—no peace. We really only find the question the more obscure and the ways of providence the more inscrutable; vexed and fevered we know not what to think, and then all fagged we doze away! Ah, it is the tired spirit resting and recuperating in the great maze of mystery that clogs thought and dazes intellect; then, in the magic of a grateful trance, we dream we are awake,—and wake,—to find it all a dream.

XXXVIII.

Turning to the past, the spectacle presented to the mind's eye is that of a more fruitful field, and there are evidences of a more substantial growth; but then again, the fields have a harvested look, and while the signs of fruition may be greater, there is withal the musty smell of dissolution.—The sickle has been there, autumn and winter have intervened, and we detect very little of the lingering perfumes, and none of the fresh, budding look that distinguishes the later months and makes the future seem a perpetual spring. Although, generally speaking, we do not like the past, it often intrudes itself on our notice; turn which way we may events throw us back, however unwillingly upon our past. As I intimated in another place that the world with all its seeming progress was retracing its steps, so with individuals, they must go back and, though it may not all be an ovation to some, recontemplate the marks they have planted.

Regarding the past generally and reflectively, what, let us ask, has become of all the people and fruits grown there. Where are the nations and the granaries and the accumulated wealth of man and of nature for the seven thousand three hundred and eighty-eight years jotted down in our memorandum, and for the indefinite margin of time twixt our earliest dates and the time God said, "Let there be light"? It is impossible to realize the awful devastation comprehended in the reply,—they have vanished! What have New York, London, Paris and all the other capitals of the globe, together with their mighty tributaries and accessories, animate and inanimate, to show for the productions of a hard worked, ingenious, prolific world since the occupation of space and the creation of Adam? We answer, comparatively so many tiny grains of mustard seed!

Of all the countless millions that have passed away, what are the evidences left of our great enterprising humanity? Bring forward all your arguments of chemistry respecting the economy of Nature and the indestructibility of matter, to convince me the leaves that deck the benign brow of our own peerless goddess of plenty, are the same that veiled the nakedness of Eve. Or, to moderate our tone a little and to make our demands more in accordance with the limited ability to answer, let us enquire how much do we know of the great world of extinct life?

Briefly and in round figures, nothing! At most how few are the traces remaining;—a shred, a particle, an atom here and there, but comparatively no more than what is left of Solomon's Temple, or of the tail of Ben. Franklin's kite.

It is appalling to reflect how complete has been the destruction; and making the most of what we have read and think we know, we must confess of times past, our records are most fragmentary, imperfect and unsatisfactory. It may not have been the intention of our scribes to disfigure or to mutilate, but they embellish till they obliterate, and in the effort to preserve, annihilate. We may illustrate this by glancing at that capricious luminary of the past, yclept *tradition* whose dazzling corruscation, eradiating the murky atmosphere of history, enlightens the modern world.

XXXIX.

It is an old saying that "language is given us to hide our thoughts." I would go further and say that writing is bestowed on a people to enable them to pervert the truth, and to deceive posterity. The written form of tradition, is legend; and whatever may be said of the former applies in substance to the latter. What was not written we would not naturally expect had been preserved, hence our contempt for tradition; but this, since the era of writing, we find taking the later guise of legend, which like its counterpart and older kin is only a moral and instructive metamorphosis of truth. Here we may note, too, that many charming narrations found fathered on both legend and tradition, owe their being to an ingenuity and invention almost exclusively modern ; being, for the most part, the offspring of those splendid and prolific imaginations by which they were conceived and adorned.

We do not complain of these fancies, on the contrary we are more than reconciled, we are happy to be humbugged by them. They are to nations what illusions are to individuals,—a precious birthright,—and we dread that scourge of idoldom,—the Iconoclast,—as well we may; for once let that king of midges invade those floral exotics that embellish not only genuine tradition, but that more recent effusion of newfangled coloring falsely ascribed to legend, and soon what will be left ? Nothing,—but the waxen outline of dried up honey-comb from which has been sucked the luscious sweets of fable. *Fetching* nearer the point still, strip Roman or Grecian history, or English or Scotch, of its legendary lore what would be the effect ? We cannot realize the prodigious havoc that would be made, but it is no idle speculation to surmise, the splendid fabric would topple in the first breath of wholesome air; and a structure that seems to gain with age an even greater fund of youth and beauty, would crumble into ruins and, dissolving, like the florid outlines of an exhumed corpse, leave the appalled and contemplative student only such a sparse accumulation of pulverized relics, as might constitute a respectable collection of fossil remains.

If there be any truth in these observations, it goes to sustain the exception I have taken to the infallibility of records; and the position is still further exemplified in the more trivial affairs of our daily intercourse. There, it is a hackneyed fact that "stories" so short lived as not to attain beyond the longevity of mere gossip, bandied from mouth to mouth and from pen to pen, even in the same language, become discolored and distorted. It would seem, with each, as in the case of an organic substance, decomposition had set in from its very inception; but denied quiet extinction, under the recuperative impetus of morbid curiosity, the putrid mass becomes animated; then, giving forth, as in insect life, myriad specimens of which there is not a trace of the original, these, assuming to be true versions, wriggle and crawl till, at last, they flit away into the elysium known as "small talk."

It may be seen, then, in our efforts to preserve the narrative of past events, truth must have gone through a somewhat complicated process, each stage of which is assumed to be historical, and of course perfect; and this, according to the period in which we live, constitutes the commonly accepted standard of our belief and judgment. But would it not be marvellous if, in the multiplicity of representations commended to our credulity as true likenesses, the majority were not absurd caricatures; and in this connection I will venture on a suggestion which occurs to me at the moment as illustrative of my meaning.

Suppose a few of the more noted worthies of antiquity, with whom we profess intimate acquaintance, were brought to life—I trust it may not be irreverent to call them up—then, allowing they could be made sufficiently reconciled with the drama of to-day to be induced to witness a performance—let the play be "historical," and founded on a fair specimen of the so called "facts" recorded of their period and lives. What a prodigious burlesque it would all seem to those old patriarchs, and how they would roar and laugh to split their sides!—never once imbibing even a hint whom the characters and events thus re-enacted were intended for. I may be doing our noble scribes injustice, but the fact is, in my efforts to commit their voluminous productions to memory, I have become meditative and sceptical; till now, I am very much at a loss to know what part or how much of modern history to believe; and only read ancient, as I would "Tales of a Grandfather,"—that is, for amusement and as standard specimens of ingenuity and wit.

XL.

As we sit contemplating the past, these are the thoughts that brood, phantom-like, over the scene; and out from the darkened vale there comes croaking on the night-air the reiterated query, what about the millions upon millions that are gone, and where is the lost Diary of the dead World! History, as we have intimated, records and contradicts some of the triumphs and reverses of nations; and biography has made us, as we think, familiar with the success and failure of comparatively a few of the most noted men, and still fewer women; but what a puny epitome is this of the world's boundless volume of good and ill since creation—wherein, each *letter*, were a long life's troubled career—each *word*, the vicissitudes of a whole generation—and each *sentence*, the story of a nation's rise and growth, its decline and ultimate extinction!

Biography is replete with the renown of emperors and prolific in the exploits of chieftains in war and state; but where is the chronicle of the lives and doings of all the rest of mankind? Those, I mean, who failed to make for themselves a name conspicuous enough in deeds, good or bad, to resound over the earth and to echo through all succeeding generations. Passing by cases in a remoter period which, like that of Hannibal, stand alone in the grandeur of utter isolation, and coming down to times comparatively recent,—it must be admitted we know, or think we know, a little about Napoleon; but what about the heroes that composed the grand army of Napoleon? Here and there, it it true, a beam of reflected light is cast on a few such characters as Ney, and Murat, and redeem from perpetual shade two or three or may be five or ten of the million human physiognomies that frame the portrait of one man. But in this case, we find the glory of one great name exhausting the research and satisfying the ambition of biographers;—the world has no market for any more dead greatness and supply the demand for the living; so what becomes of all the rest,—what becomes of the fathers, brothers, and sons whose devotion and heroism made Napoleon emperor, and France the most renowned in modern chivalry? One word suffices—oblivion!

XLI.

Where, then, is the true diary of the world that is dead? There is none; never was and never will be. The nearest thing we have to it, barring an immense mass of irrelevant garbage is found in the Bibles of nations; and that, not as *narrative* but as *precept*—not simply in the chronicle of events, but in the lessons which they inculcate. All parts of these good books may not be, and certainly are not, inspired—none of them, in fact, in the crude notion of what the word inspiration means; and to maintain that such works, however highly they may be reverenced, should have no particle of alloy, is simply claiming for them an impossibility; indeed, the very effort shows a lamentable want of esteem for those other parts which are evidently sound and incomparably perfect.

Who knows anything that is not made up of a certain amount of "dross;" nay, one of the greatest difficulties in life is the stint of separating the intrinsic from the extrinsic so as to make the proper distinction between good and bad, and to divine what to cherish and what to repudiate. This, however patiently or zealously or devoutly it may have been essayed, has never been accomplished to the complete satisfaction of either individuals nations or posterity; and that, whether as regards private affairs or public works.

While that estimable volume, compiled from the theologies of consecutive civilizations and races of people,— our Bible,—forms no exception in the application of the above, it must be confessed in that great granary, the harvest of fruitful ages, the separating of the grain from the chaff, may seem a stupendous undertaking, and in one sense it is; Nevertheless, while it is a job that may not be let out to be done by others to suit our convenience, yet, to grapple with those facts, the only rational ones, that appeal to our moral nature, need not dismay even the humblest intellect amongst us.

Nay, even in those subtler distinctions to which we have referred, it is encouraging to the less pretentious classes, to bear in mind that the "race" is not always "to the strong," nor victory on the side of "the biggest guns."—The fact may be stale, but it is none the less a fact, that the major part of our grandest discoveries are not, as many think, the result of profound mental penetration,—of prodigious wisdom and indefatigable research,—but, on the contrary, are mainly attributable to mere accident; and, as in the case of the marvellous revelation that gave us the telescope,—to the sportive observation of merry-making children. Aye, and passing by the trophies of occult science,—glancing into the bewildering labyrinths of philosophy and metaphysics,—the novice is astonished that men of greatest learning and astutest minds, dazzled with too much light, grope blindly at noonday and are lost in a maze, wherein the veriest dolt has pickde his way in triumph *at midnight.*

XLII.

I would like to say here, it seems strange to me that that grand monument of evangelical faith, the Bible, should be regarded as a granite shaft, changeless and without the vital qualities of a living growth. On the contrary, I believe it were not too refined a conception of its sublime mission, to regard it in the light of a sentient Being,—with veins ramifying the hearts of men and surging in the living throes of every breath they breathe.—Otherwise, its functions in our spiritual organism, were only such as comes of grafting a dead trunk on a live tree. Then, without looking with supine imbecility to the pompous bickering of antiquated ecumenical councils, successive generations would be its revisors; and, adding the mite which the experience of each had adduced, the "Ark" would be kept moving,—its pedigree in the past would be legitimized, —and for the future, the Bible of a thousand years from now should not be stinted to the forest of dead leaves upon which we look, but have leavened with it the vitalizing properties evolved from twenty generations of precept.

Regarding the distinction of what is genuine in the Bible and what is not, I believe it may be left to conscience, the interpretation to be *bona fide* through that medium, each in a way most applicable to his need; and not left, as the learned professors would have us, to them exclusively. The great force and effect of its teaching depends on ones own particular case, and that no one knows but himself. He need not hesitate to trust to conscience to give those good lessons of life their true bearing and significance. All the details of individual cases may not be known, but we have not only our own Bible, but that of others, and also our own observation, to convince us that the precept at least we find therein contained is infallible. But, while admitting this, I claim that the world, notwithstanding its manifold professions to the contrary, is directly guided and influenced very little by them; being taken up rather with those parts which pertain to doctrine and lead to strife.

Referring to the sad case mentioned in a preceding article, we may quote in this connection one of the many old sayings, "Beware of wine and women." We are disposed to interpret this wrongly; it does not mean bad women any more than it does bad wine; the warning finger points to all alike, and to every species of intoxication. Beware of wine and women! How stupid and ungrateful is the perversity with which we put aside as old shoes or scorn as vulgar this time-honored and friendly advice!—not always viciously nor yet intentionally—it may be thoughtlessly, and frequently with a certain amount of what is called reverence for the sacred source whence it comes; but presuming, almost invariably, it means something or somebody worse than we meet in our everyday life and experience; whereas, it no doubt applies to all mankind and womenkind without exception.

But arrogating to ourselves virtues we do not possess, wanting in the fundamental principle of righteousness which is charity, we seek to find in the too apparent depravity of others immunity for ourselves; hence it is only to admonish the vulgar, it is written, "Beware of wine and women." Alas! what an unwelcome heritage of good counsel; what pathos in that grim injunction, coming down to us as it does from generation to generation of loving hearts and blighted lives! As we look back over the blank, silent solitude of the past, we can only imagine how many have struck on that fatal ledge and gone down right in the offing of the most serene and pleasant of all peaceful havens! Ah, we listen in vain; not a single cry, but such precious old warnings as these, comes up from those placid waters.

XLIII.

We know of the "prodigal" that returned, but what of the one of millions that did not return? Far from friends and all who loved him, who smoothed down his pillow and comforted him in his thoughts of kindred and of home. Well, there is a something prevailing, so far as we will allow it, against all adversity and against all ill—it goes with us and knows our thoughts, when none else in the world would care or understand; and though we may never know whither our brother went or what became of him, yet one lesson of his harassed life we do know,—it is borne on the wings of that brooding angel who is ever on the trail of missing lambs,—and garnered up in the "Good Book," we read, "Honor thy father and thy mother, that thy days may be long in the land."

Or, take the counter part of the "Prodigal"—the sister betrayed—the sport of passion, the companion of infamy, and the most contemptible in the eyes of self and the world.—What would be her last loving words, it may be, to that offspring of her shame vouchsafed to her as the most potent incentive to reform.—In the great agony of close impending dissolution, she sees the only object left her to love or to be loved by—what heritage does she seek, then, to bequeath—what boon more precious than gold would she, if she could, leave behind?—She cannot speak—she is too far gone even to gesture;—but One who knows all hearts,—that ubiquitous spirit of infinite commiseration, is there, and sees, in what seems a great spasm of pain, the last best tribute of a breaking heart;—and, reading, gives it to the weeping child—what! only those hackneyed words that make us all laugh,—"Be virtuous, and you will be happy!" Maxims like these are about the only reliable words that come commended to us through the dim shadow of that hushed past; and while some, though virtually belonging, may not actually be incorporated, in Holy Writ, nevertheless they are just as strong and binding, wherever we find them, as Commandments; and while all our better nature teaches us to obey, they may only appeal to our common sense of right and our instincts of self-preservation.

XLIV.

There is another matter that we may take a look at here—I mean *danger*. You may say what about danger? We all know what that is, surely. Well, there are different kinds of danger:—there is the hazy sort of general idea of danger which is preached and croaked about, but which we think too remote to trouble ourselves with; then, there is glaring danger; and again, a trivial sort where we feel tolerably certain there is none at all. I believe we need not trouble ourselves about glaring danger; there is generally in this case a look-out somewhere to give us the signal.—A flag is waved in the glare of the head-lights, and tells the engineer to put on brakes—a bridge may be down—a culvert washed away—or a train rushing down like an avalanche in an opposite direction —it means stop for your life! And of course we do stop, all trembling with apprehension and fear. The shock to our nervous system is great, and when we have collected our terrified senses, our gratitude for a brief time knows no bounds, and generally takes the form of new and better resolves.

Here, then, the danger was terribly apparent, and we were greatly frightened, but the real danger was proportionably less; besides, we only stood a chance of getting bruised or maimed, and the thing that threatened and the object menaced were material. There is the glaring danger, also, betokening hostility and manifest design; but it need not be dreaded by any one tolerably courageous, and not utterly defenceless. At the same time, this is the form we take the greatest pains to guard against, and on those points most conspicuously exposed, we mass all our forces, and, standing firm on the outer bulwark that shields the Palladium, defy the enemy openly, boldly.

In our general appreciation of danger, this is the system of defence most commonly adopted and relied on; it is commendable, and virtue, armed to the teeth to repel boarders, may find it sufficient in cases of glaring danger or open hostility. But there is another greater danger, where this defence utterly fails; indeed, to the wary invader the very show of so much determination indicates, if not debility, at least vulnerability; and in all this display of defensive armament, there is an evidence of conscious weakness. Most evil finds its greatest triumph where the purest virtue sits enthroned; but, while the most impregnable strongholds may offer the strongest resistance, where, in all history, do we find one that has not yielded to the final assault. We have noticed that because danger is very glaring, it does not follow the actual peril need be very great—it is then only comparatively alarming, and as a rule, proportionately less.

We may illustrate this by referring to a battle-field, and to the only case, perhaps, that might disprove our proposition. To see, for instance, two lines of hostile cavalry —with that most formidable weapon, the sabre, drawn— advancing against one another in a "charge," is a sight well calculated to inspire dread, and it does; almost the complete annihilation of all concerned may be apprehended. But what is the general result? In nine cases out of ten, each horseman in expectation of the cut or thrust of his adversary, remains on the defensive; and the two lines pass completely through and do one another comparatively little or no harm. I don't imagine this, I have seen it, and know it to be true, and a more glaring and apparent danger could not be conceived. Again, let us be on the water when it is rough,—in some tiny craft, floating like a bubble, and nearly as frail.—There comes a great wave rolling in on us,—a perpendicular wall of water,—does it break over and bury us deep down?—No; in almost the same glance of terror the novice casts upon it, he sees his buoyant bark all gracefully and tranquilly riding on its crest.

The same, too, may be instanced of the lower grades of animal life.—They, too, get their warning, but their senses are not blunted with high-living and stupefying indulgences, and they heed, as is proper, the slightest indications of alarm. Do you see that feathery innocent crouched low in the grass? it sees the ponderous boots of the sportsman coming crunching along; and to that little silent beauty nesting there, they do seem veritable monsters and real dangers. Of all things most easily affrighted, its little heart throbs, and it pants with fear,—but instinct, the *hush* of the bird's presiding spirit says, be still. And silent, regardless, immovable, as if transfixed in death, or petrified in stone, it conquers its ruling impulse to fly— it does not move—the danger passes—it is saved, and the little one is left unharmed to its sweet mission of singing and of hatching songs.

XLV.

No, it is not the very glaring danger, but the seemingly trivial or none-at-all sort we have reason to dread, and especially is this the case in our social relations and intercourse with each other. Then, the whole aspect of danger is changed, and its warnings obscure as the doubtful signs of a coming storm. Here, there is no head-light to warn us, no waving flag, no startling tooting of down-brakes. One aspect of this kind of danger is that it may take upon itself the most attractive disguise, and while coming along in our better humors, unawares, its approach is pleasing and seductive as the dulcet wave of some sweet, melodious song.

Thus it is we may lapse into danger insensibly, even when we mean conscientiously to avoid it, and this is the weak place with the most impregnable—Then, indeed, it comes upon us as does sleep in the drowsy vigils of the night; and the weary sentinel, with his musket clutched in his nerveless grasp, dreams he watches and is betrayed! We may be lost in the effort to save; and when we would indignantly disclaim, and sincerely, all sinister intention or thought of guile, the evil has, by some inexplicable cunning, spun its web about us and within its meshes we find, when too late, the mischief lay not in the mighty wave, but in the almost imperceptible mist;—not in the issue of loudly heralded alternatives,—not in the violent rush of rude contending bodies,—but in the fragrant exhalation of kissing rose-leaves, or in the dreamy incense of sleeping lilies!

Thus, we observe, the danger most to be dreaded is masked, and one special peculiarity about this fatal to the victim, is, it seldom if ever appears in exactly the same disguise;—indeed, its wardrobe is so multifarious we may not exaggerate in saying no human eye ever beheld it twice in the same garb.—It is not uniformed like soldiers, and never appears when we are in line of battle, ready to receive it; or if it does, it comes in a deceitful, phantom form and insinuating itself like a pestilence, creeps in through the joints and crevices of the most invulnerable armor. We cannot photograph it,—we cannot point it out and spot it, any more than we can the bee that stung us. No; —it always appears in some novel form, and while it does not answer the hackneyed description of what is bad, neither does it suit the indictment appended to the reward which all mankind has set upon its head. On the contrary, there is too apt to be a plausibility about it, that to properly understand, calls for all our sobriety and vigilance, and even then are we all too frequently misled.

XLVI.

We are reminded in the above connection of the grand old Frigates that lay in such imposing security in Hampton

Roads. They were the last to perceive danger in the absurd little experiment of an "Iron-clad;" and also Troy, that was proof against all assaults of arms, and could defy the prowess of an Agememnon, fell, at last, an easy prey, not to the ordinary engines of war, she could laugh at them, but to a whimsical stratagem—an almost ludicrous contrivance, that stalked boldly in, under the apparently harmless guise of a horse. Affection, even rarely divines the danger of which I speak, and it may, indeed, it often does (by way of temptation), come in the form or in behalf of those most cherished and loved. Nay, we may inhale it in our most innocent admiration,—then it is the poisoned air breathed in the perfume of sweetest flowers,—and finally, it may wear the livery of our most trusted slave, or robe itself in the mantle of our dearest friend! " Aye, there's the rub!"

But you say, what is this danger all so puzzling and so baleful, which you so unkindly attribute to our best beloved and bid us beware? Well, it is a latent mischief inherent in the nature of things, and is propagated in the human organism from the vital essence whose qualities combine in the higher growth of animal life, all the attributes of the universe.—The germ whence it is communicated is at once too infinitesimal and etherial to be seen and too grand and sublime to be comprehended,—though in the highest state of moral sensitiveness it may be felt.—All too intangible for the mind to grasp, its creation is as the dream of the "Immaculate Conception,"—its existence, the impregnation of a glance, and its spawn matures through the progressive growth of ages, aye, even of eternity itself, all in a second,—and that second is the first long drawn sigh of the new born babe!!

Around this helpless epitome of humanity and of sin cluster all that phantom band who claim affinity to virtue:—Pity is there—Hope is there—Charity is there,—and Fidelity, and all the rest.—The Father of all is invisible, but present in these, the pledges of his love,—and it is their kiss upon our lips that first startles us from our long trance and wakes us into life!! As we open our eyes they vanish away—nay, not quite away—they have only taken refuge in our hearts, and thenceforward become as the inspiring spirit we call our "Good Angel," to incline and persuade us to better things. We may prove obdurate, perverse, wicked,—we may go all astray, and friends and society abandon us, but these remain always faithful and kind.—Ashamed of our ingratitude or finding their company irksome and in ill accord with our appetites, we may seek to give them the slip and steal away; but they know all our haunts and find their way straight to our hiding place—like absent members of a convivial band, returning, thread with familiar ease the labyrinth that leads to the social meet of boon companions. Often when the world rejoices they weep and are sad, and when it mourns they smile as if in the triumph of an unrevealed glory.—Do you mind that poor girl, she whose life was one of shame? "Creed" said, "let her die!" and there, in that place all sequestered and shunned they put her away. Ah little do they think that place is above all others "God's acre,"—the seclusion where peace and reconciliation is made with his erring children,—and far away from the stigma of an earthly tribunal there is rejoicing.—It is that band of ministering spirits, attributes to a Love sublime, welcoming to their better home a sister long lost, but now restored.

XLVII.

I may be wrong in my views of the abandoned and condemned; but though I oppose, in this respect, those of a more rigid orthodoxy, still do I claim that none of these people have lived in vain. The book of their justification may be sealed, and the little story of a life's secret die, but it leaves its seed in precept, and their part, even to posterity, is not all a desert of barren dust. For their sake, then, I trust, it may not be the concatenation of an idle chimera to assume that, as in the sterile waste of fallow ocean, there is planted a treasure more precious than gold, so in the slums of the most ignoble career abides a "pearl of infinite price;" and though the wages of sin be "death," may we not hope therein lies the soul's equity of redemption.

While the good and ill of life are the effects of caprice and circumstance, it's only in the last flickering impulse of our vital energies the spirit grapples in a conflict whose quietus is eternal amnesty. Condensed within the narrow scope of a death-pang, there is a boundless measure of expiation—it may not be contrition, but it has the redeeming element of pain,—and therein is ensconced a germ whose electric fruition is eternal joy. We have no assurance that the pang of which I speak may not be prolonged and attain to an intensity of agony we wot not of;—then, mayhap, we can bear it no longer—the flesh must succumb, and a great cry goes out into the gloom. It penetrates into the caverns and crevices of the earth—it reaches up into the Heavens:—"Watchman, what of the night?" It echoes from hill to hill—it reverberates amongst the mountains and rolls down into the valleys:—Watchman, *tell* us of the night! Then all is hushed, and a voice is heard,—the same whose dulcet cadence in ineffable balm descended upon Jacob, and Job, and Abraham:—*Peace, all is well!*—

A gray beam is seen gleaming in the east—it unfolds and expands—it is the shimmering light of an all-prevailing Love, the Aurora of a great pitying Redemption.— The darkness yields,—the dawn breaks, and all hail the perpetual morning of never ending day!

FINIS.

www.ingramcontent.com/pod-product-compliance
Lightning Source LLC
Chambersburg PA
CBHW032018220426
43664CB00006B/287